JACK DANIEL'S
COOKBOOK ®

STORIES *and*
KITCHEN SECRETS
from
MISS MARY BOBO'S
BOARDING HOUSE

LYNNE TOLLEY AND MINDY MERRELL

THOMAS NELSON ®
Since 1798

NASHVILLE   DALLAS   MEXICO CITY   RIO DE JANEIRO

Published in Nashville, Tennessee, by Thomas Nelson. Thomas Nelson is a registered trademark of Thomas Nelson, Inc.

Thomas Nelson, Inc., titles may be purchased in bulk for educational, business, fund-raising, or sales promotional use. For information, please e-mail SpecialMarkets@ThomasNelson.com.

JACK DANIEL'S, OLD NO. 7, TENNESSEE HONEY, GENTLEMAN JACK, LYNCHBURG LEMONADE, JACK, MISS MARY BOBO'S and THE JACK DANIEL'S WORLD CHAMPIONSHIP INVITATIONAL BARBECUE are all registered trademarks of Jack Daniel's. © 2012 All Rights Reserved.

Photo on page 211 is courtesy of Julie Allen.
Food and event photographs on pages viii, 1, 8, 14, 19, 22, 39, 43, 50, 53–54, 56, 59, 69, 72, 76–77, 80, 82, 86, 88, 92, 94, 98, 106, 117–118, 123, 125–126, 131–132, 139–140, 150, 153–154, 162, 166, 169, 174–175, 177, 179–180, 183, 186, 198, 210, 219, 222–223, 227, 231–234, 241, 245, and 256 provided by Richard B. Quinn.
Food and event photographs on pages 13, 18, 68, 82, 96, 112, 120, 127, 152, 156, 204, 208, and 222 provided by Eric England.
Food and event photographs on pages 104, and 250–251 provided by Debbie Baxter.
Photographs on pages 4, 62, and 157 provided by Jack Daniel's Properties, Inc.
Photographs on pages iv, 60, 90, 110, 164, and 238 from Fotolia.com.

Library of Congress Cataloging-in-Publication Data

Tolley, Lynne, 1950–
Jack Daniel's cookbook : southern recipes and secrets from Miss Mary Bobo's Boarding House / Lynne Tolley and Mindy Merrell.
p. cm.
Includes bibliographical references and index.
ISBN 978-1-4016-0490-5 (alk. paper)
1. Cooking, American—Southern style. 2. Cooking—Tennessee z Lynchburg.
3. Cooking (Whiskey) I. Merrell, Mindy. II. Title. III. Title: Southern recipes and secrets from Miss Mary Bobo's Boarding House.
TX715.2.S68T65 2012
641.5975—dc23

2012024007

Printed in the United States of America

16 QG 6

CONTENTS

Introduction | v

We're Tennessee Whiskey | 1

Cocktails | 5

Cocktail Snacks | 33

Breads and Brunch | 61

Salads | 91

Vegetables and Sides | 111

Dinner | 137

Barbecue and Grilling | 165

Sweets | 203

Relishes and Little Extras | 239

We Offer Our Thanks | 257

Index | 258

Introduction

To me, Southern cooking is warm and welcoming, it's family and friends, and being neighborly, it evokes a real sense of "come on in and join us." That's how it is in our little town of Lynchburg, a rural agricultural community tucked in the hollows of Middle Tennessee filled with generations of good country cooks and even better eaters.

Never would I have imagined the relatively recent swell of excitement in home cooking, outdoor grilling and barbecue, growing and cooking with local ingredients, practicing age-old home economics skills like canning and preserving, sewing and quilting, and even raising chickens and pigs out back. What are inspiring new "back to basics" trends for some have been common, everyday activities happening in and around the hollows of Lynchburg since time immemorial. We're still canning late summer tomatoes, putting up a freezer full of corn, cooking cane juice into sorghum molasses, and baking pie after pie.

Does the name "Lynchburg, Tennessee," ring a bell? I'll bet it does. Most folks have heard of Lynchburg because the name is printed on every single bottle of Jack Daniel's Tennessee Whiskey. My Great-Grand Uncle Jack's whiskey is one of the best selling whiskies the world over. Every drop is crafted here in Lynchburg, just as it was in his day.

Whiskey making has been going on a long time around here, even before Uncle Jack's time. Our hills were once dotted with distilleries on account of our pure spring water and the abundance of corn and sugar maple. My daddy's family once owned the nearby Eaton and Tolley Distillery and both my Great Uncles Jess Motlow and my Uncle Lem Tolley were master distillers at Jack Daniel's, two of only seven in the company's history. You could say whiskey truly runs in my blood.

My brother, Lee, and I grew up in my mother's country kitchen, talking, laughing, helping, and mostly getting under foot. Mother has always been a happy, joyful woman, and it comes through in her cooking. Thanks to her, our lives have been filled with fresh homegrown vegetables, locally cured country ham and fresh sausage, and chicks

pecking in the backyard. We picked turnip greens in the back field, poke sallet along the fence row, and blackberries wherever they grew. And no one can top her fried chicken.

Thank goodness Mother has been such a good teacher. Since 1984, I've served as the proprietress of Miss Mary Bobo's Boarding House just off Lynchburg's town square. Every day but Sunday we serve a midday dinner of two meats and six vegetables, homemade biscuits, rolls or cornbread, iced tea, coffee, and dessert in the old boarding house tradition. Our food is simple, delicious Southern country cooking. Our guests dine family-style at big tables spread throughout the beautifully renovated 1820s white clapboard house.

When I was a child, the Bobo Hotel was filled with folks who needed a place to call home. Miss Mary served her boarders and special guests three home-cooked meals a day. My family ate there when I was a kid, but the boarding house wasn't a public restaurant as it is today. I often played around the boarding house while Mother and Miss Mary's daughter, Louise, ran the flower shop down the street. I recall the many times when Miss Mary stopped by the shop for an afternoon break and gossip session while Mother arranged flowers. After Miss Mary passed in 1983, just shy of the age of 102, I had the wonderful opportunity to succeed her as proprietress. We opened Miss Mary's as a boarding house-style restaurant and have been going strong ever since.

Visit on a Monday and we're likely to serve slow-cooked pot roast and skillet fried chicken and gravy, creamy mashed potatoes, speckled butter beans with sweet red pepper relish, a vegetable casserole or two, and homemade biscuits and gravy. We serve fried okra and Lynchburg candied apples every single day because our guests can't get enough of them. For dessert there's fudge pie served with Jack Daniel's whipping cream. And that's just the Monday menu.

Each year Lynchburg welcomes more than 250,000 visitors from around the world. Most everyone tours the distillery, and many join us for dinner. I get such a kick out of introducing folks from Germany, Japan, and even Wisconsin to grits, okra, and black-eyed peas. Many of their stories appear throughout these pages.

This book is the result of a life of good eating, cooking, entertaining, and sharing food with others. My Uncle Jack loved to host

extravagant parties and feasts. He so enjoyed dancing with the ladies that he kept a ballroom in his home. Like Uncle Jack, we Lynchburg folks take our fun and our food seriously. Whether it's an all-night whole hog roast, church supper, tailgate party, or dinner at home with a few neighbors, someone in Lynchburg is preparing a welcoming spread. Of course, Uncle Jack is still the life of the party.

Over the years my longtime friend, collaborator, and coauthor Mindy Merrell and I have cooked up friendships with talented home cooks, fancy chefs, and bartenders across the nation. These creative exchanges have enriched our interpretation and love of Southern country cooking. We're pleased to share these recipes and the stories that inspired them, all of which draw together the time-tested traditions of Lynchburg, Tennessee, and my Uncle Jack. We all agree—a little Jack makes a whole lot of things taste better.

Lynne Tolley, Proprietress
Miss Mary Bobo's Boarding House
Lynchburg, Tennessee

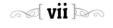

We're Tennessee Whiskey

Contrary to what some folks believe, Jack Daniel's Old No. 7 is a Tennessee whiskey, not a bourbon. Jack Daniel's Tennessee Whiskey is made only in the hills of Middle Tennessee using a blend of the finest corn, rye, and barley malt available, combined with our iron-free water from the limestone cave spring. We do share a connection with bourbon, but we take the crucial extra step called charcoal mellowing. Before barrel aging, our whiskey travels through ten feet of hard sugar maple charcoal to give Jack Daniel's its characteristic smoothness. All our whiskey is aged on the Moore County hillsides surrounding Lynchburg in newly charred white oak barrels.

Empty Oak Barrels Have Many Uses

Because federal regulations allow us to age whiskey in a barrel only once, you're probably wondering what happens to all those used oak barrels. Even empty, our barrels are full of flavor, so many of them are sent to Scotland where our Scotch whisky distillery friends put them to use. Some of our barrels head down to Avery Island in south Louisiana where the Tabasco folks age their world famous pepper sauce. You or someone you know may have one sitting on your patio full of petunias. A half barrel makes a handy planter and grows happy plants. And then a few we just bust up to make our popular Jack Daniel's Tennessee Whiskey Wood Smoking Chips and flavor pellets for outdoor grilling and barbecue.

Jack Daniel's Old No. 7 Black Label Tennessee Whiskey

Our world-famous whiskey has been awarded seven international gold medals, including one for "world's best whiskey" presented to Uncle Jack at the 1904 World's Fair in St. Louis, Missouri. His famous square bottle and handsome black and white label is recognized around the world because of what's inside—charcoal mellowed Tennessee Whiskey, a well-balanced mix of caramel, vanilla, wood notes, and a slightly fruity and distinctively dry finish. It is 80 proof.

Jack Daniel's Single Barrel Tennessee Whiskey

Each barrel of Jack Daniel's has its own personality, a distinct nose, color, and taste. Master Distiller Jeff Arnett and Master Taster Jeff Norman, along with a team of experts, select exceptional barrels to be bottled as Single Barrel Whiskey with no blending of whiskey from any other barrel. These special barrels age on the upper floors of the barrelhouses where the hot, humid Tennessee summers and cold winters create more movement of the whiskey in and out of the wood. The result is a rich, amber, mature, 94 proof whiskey with heightened flavors of toasted oak, vanilla, and caramel. I love to present a bottle of Single Barrel as a present or a hostess gift. Maybe that's why I get so many party invitations!

Buy Your Own Barrel

Whiskey connoisseurs can place an order for an entire single barrel of Jack Daniel's Single Barrel Tennessee Whiskey. Each barrel yields approximately 240 to 250 750ml bottles. The happy purchaser receives the bottled whiskey and the barrel in which it was aged, a customized metal neckband for each bottle, a brass naming plaque, and a framed certificate of ownership. Plus, you get your name on a brass plaque on the wall at the distillery.

Gentleman Jack Rare Tennessee Whiskey

My Uncle Jack experimented with double charcoal mellowing but never did much with it. In 1988, we decided to dig up his notes and give it a try. The result is Gentleman Jack Rare Tennessee Whiskey. Gentleman Jack is made using a slightly different recipe and is the only whiskey in the world that is charcoal mellowed twice, once before aging and once after. This 80 proof whiskey has a silky finish laced with caramel, fruit, vanilla, and smoke. I like to call it our Tennessee cognac and often serve it in snifters after supper. Don't miss my favorite Classic Jack Mint Julep (page 14).

Jack Daniel's Tennessee Honey

Our newest product in a generation, Jack Daniel's Tennessee Honey, was introduced in 2010. Tennessee Honey is a lovely blend of honey liqueur and Jack Daniel's Tennessee Whiskey, and it's perfect for serving chilled in little shot glasses or over ice for sipping. At 70 proof, Tennessee Honey is a little lighter than Old No. 7. We often mix it with sparkling wine, ginger ale, iced tea, or lemonade. Or, try it in a Hot Buttered Whiskey Glaze (page 217). It's also a wonderful cooking ingredient, so pay close attention to the dessert chapter.

Heard around the TABLE

One day after dinner, a guest asked me if I knew the name of the man standing by the front door. I told her he was the undertaker from a funeral home in nearby Fayetteville. She looked at me and asked, "What does he do, just hang around in case someone eats himself to death?"

COCKTAILS

Setting Up the Bar

Jack Manhattans

Classic Jack Manhattan
Perfect Gentleman Jack Manhattan
Licorice Manhattan
Orange Manhattan
Tennessee Chocolate Almond Manhattans
Tennessee Chocolate Mint Manhattans
The Gentleman's Sour Apple Manhattan
Jack Daniel's Old Fashioned
Tennessee Cranberry Smash Manhattan

Tennessee Honey Sparklers

Tennessee Honey Royale
Tennessee Honey Bellini
Tennessee Cider

Official Taste Testers

Jack's Juleps

Classic Jack Mint Julep
Pineapple Jack Julep
Tennessee Honey Julep

Jack Daniel's Infused Whiskey

Ginger Jack
Orange Jack
Spiced Jack

Jack and Sodas

Jack and Cola
Jack and Cola Float or Jack Black Cow
Jack and Citrus Soda
Jack Attack

Meet Jeff Arnett

Jack Party Punches

Cool Jack Apple Mint Tea
Tolley Town Celebration Punch
Honey Milk Punch
Jack Daniel's Citrus Cider
Shoo Fly Punch

Jack Sours

Classic Tennessee Whiskey Sour
Pineapple Jack Sour
Jack Jajito Sour

Tall Cool Jack Cocktails

Hula Jack
ApriJack Nectar
Lynchburg Lemonade
Coconut Orange Jack
Madras Jacket
Jack's Pomegranate Lemonade
Iced Tennessee Honey Tea

Meet Jeff Norman

Warm Jack Cocktails

Hot Tennessee Toddy
Hot Tomato Jack
Jack Daniel's Warm Pear Nectar Sipper
Hound Dog Hot Bouillon
Mulled in Moore County
Hot Buttered Tennessee Honey
Tennessee Honey Hot Tea

Creamy Jack Cocktails

Bold Custard
Almond Jack Frost
Tennessee Honey Coffee Melt
Honey and Cream

Setting Up the Bar

I do believe in a well-stocked bar. In fact, since I live in two places—Lynchburg during the week and Nashville on the weekends—I was able to convert the laundry nook in my city town home into a wet bar. My husband, Tom, teases me about it and loves to tell people, "We have a lot of Jack Daniel's and a lot of dirty laundry!"

A well-stocked bar and a few simple tools are all you need for making great cocktails quickly and easily. I keep my bar equipment together to avoid that exasperating last minute, pre-party panic.

Shakers—Cocktail shakers are fun and showy, but for me the Boston Shaker used by professional bartenders for shaking and stirring drinks works just fine. It's a stainless steel mixing/stirring cup on the bottom with a smaller glass that fits snugly in the steel half. Mix the drink with ice in the metal cup for stirring and shaking. Insert the glass top to cover tightly and shake. Let the cocktail mixture cool in the cold metal cup on ice for a moment. Then use a wire strainer to pour your drink into the glass.

Wire strainer—Place this over the mixing glass to strain a cocktail from the ice into a glass.

Stirring spoon—A long handled spoon comes in handy for stirring a drink in the tall mixing glass.

Reliable combination bottle and can opener—When I was little, Daddy called this a church key. I don't know what kind of church he was talking about, but I believe he attended regularly. You can find one that includes a good cork screw.

Small cutting board and sharp paring knife—Small equipment is plenty adequate for cutting fruit garnishes. Don't fool with anything that's hard to store and takes up too much counter space.

Measuring cup and shot glass—I use a little six-ounce glass that's really handy for measuring the whiskey and the mixers.

Towels and cleaning supplies—No matter how tidy you are, bartending is sticky business. Keep things looking sharp with designated bar towels, paper towels, and a discreet bottle of all-purpose cleaner or bleach spray.

Punch Bowls

I love my mother's old crystal and silver punchbowls with matching little cups, but they're not for every punch occasion. An overly "frou-frou" style can put a damper on some real fun, especially when gentlemen are present. Remember "punch" is simply a cocktail made in a larger batch. I like to be inventive and let the occasion choose the bowl. Big crocks and pottery bowls fit in with an outdoor party. Mismatched icy pitchers can look handsome in a group. Even big glass vases work well with a long-handled ladle. Just be sure that whatever you choose for serving is food safe and easy to wash.

Glassware

Take it from me, the glass is just as important as the drink it holds. That doesn't necessarily mean expensive, but you need the correct glass for the drink *and* the occasion. Even when breaking the rules of glassware, the best bartenders stay true to the guiding principles and do it with confidence. I prefer clear glass to let the beautiful color of the cocktail shine through. The following glasses will do you nicely.

Rocks glasses—A good rocks glass (also called the old-fashioned) is small and sturdy in the hand, perfect for sipping whiskey neat or over ice with a splash of water.

Highball—This all-purpose glass can hold a good icy mixed drink like Jack and cola. Keep a few of the taller Collins glasses, perfect for Lynchburg Lemonade, if you have the space. Of course, we like to use chilled mason jars for fruity summer drinks with lots of ice.

Cocktail glasses—If you don't have the shelf space or patience for the v-shaped Manhattan-style up glass, serve strained chilled drinks in small wine glasses.

Wine glasses—Stemmed glassware shouldn't be confined to wines. Often, I'll serve an icy fruit punch in a stemmed glass for an especially elegant presentation.

Garnishes

Nothing ruins a drink's first impression faster than a badly cut garnish or a garnish that's past its prime.

Citrus fruits

For easy squeezing when you want just the juice in the drink, cut limes and lemons across in half through the fat middle and then cut each half into four chunks. Otherwise, cut festive wheels or half wheels, or cut lengthwise into long thin wedges. Oranges are typically cut into thin half or quarter wheels.

Twist—This is simply a thin slice of citrus rind, usually lemon or orange. You can buy a special tool or use a sharp paring knife. When zesting any citrus fruit, be sure to cut only deep enough to remove the colored peel without much of the bitter white pulp underneath. Twist the peel to release the oils and run it around the rim for flavor before dropping it in the drink.

Maraschino cherries—I prefer the stemless cherries so as not to inconvenience my guests with an annoying "now what do I do with this?" moment.

Other garnishes

Other interesting garnishes you can add to enhance or change the character of a drink (other than olives and onions) include thinly sliced green apple, cucumber, fresh peach slices, pineapple chunks, star fruit, raspberries, blueberries, strawberries, melon balls, crystallized ginger, fresh herbs, whole almonds, and even jelly beans and edible flowers.

Finishing Touches to a Well-served Cocktail

Little things matter like festive beverage napkins and coasters. Paper napkins are fine as long as they are beverage sized, not dinner. I love my old-fashioned lacey cocktail napkins even though they need a little pressing. I want my guests to feel special because they are special. Spread around plenty of drink coasters so guests can set down their drinks without worry. As for drink stirrers, I find they're a nuisance and unnecessary, especially if you've properly mixed the drinks.

Long ago my mother instilled in me the importance of a well-set table, whether casual or more formal. "Never just throw the silverware at the plates," she'd advise. I like to accent a room with lots of candles and lower the lighting so everyone looks their best. On a cocktail buffet, arrange foods neatly and combine serving dishes of different heights and shapes.

Jack Manhattans

Being the great-grandniece of Jasper Newton Daniel, my definition of a Manhattan must of necessity include all Jack Daniel's concoctions that are chilled and served straight up (no ice) in a cocktail glass. So many flavors combine beautifully with our Tennessee Whiskey, so the task of the maker of these elegant offerings is to never mask that unique charcoal mellowed taste.

Classic Jack Manhattan

> 2 ounces Jack Daniel's Tennessee Whiskey
> 1/2 ounce sweet vermouth
> Dash of bitters
> Maraschino cherry

Combine the Jack Daniel's, vermouth, and bitters in a mixing glass with ice. Stir to chill. Strain into a chilled cocktail glass or serve on the rocks. Garnish with a cherry.

Perfect Gentleman Jack Manhattan

> 2 ounces Gentleman Jack Rare Tennessee Whiskey
> 1/4 ounce dry vermouth
> 1/4 ounce sweet vermouth
> Dash of bitters
> Lemon twist

Combine the Gentleman Jack, vermouth, and bitters in a mixing glass with ice. Stir to chill. Strain into a chilled cocktail glass or serve on the rocks. Garnish with a lemon twist.

Licorice Manhattan

> 2 ounces Jack Daniel's Tennessee Whiskey
> 1/2 ounce anisette
> Dash of bitters
> Black jelly bean and orange twist

Combine the Jack Daniel's, anisette, and bitters in a mixing glass with ice. Stir to chill. Strain into a chilled cocktail glass or serve on the rocks. Garnish with a black jelly bean and an orange twist.

Orange Manhattan

> 1 1/2 ounces Jack Daniel's Tennessee Whiskey
> 1 ounce orange curacao
> 1 ounce fresh orange juice
> Dash of bitters
> Orange slice

Combine the Jack Daniel's, curacao, orange juice, and bitters in a mixing glass with ice. Stir to chill and strain into a chilled cocktail glass. Garnish with an orange slice.

Tennessee Chocolate Almond Manhattan

> 1 1/2 ounces Jack Daniel's Tennessee Whiskey
> 1 ounce white crème de cacao
> 1/2 ounce amaretto
> Whole almond (unsalted)

Combine the Jack Daniel's, crème de cacao, and amaretto in a mixing glass with ice. Stir to chill. Strain into a chilled cocktail glass or serve on the rocks. Garnish with one whole almond.

Tennessee Chocolate Mint Manhattan

> 1 1/2 ounces Jack Daniel's Tennessee Whiskey
> 1 ounce white crème de cacao
> 1/2 ounce white crème de menthe
> Fresh mint leaf

Combine the Jack Daniel's, crème de cacao, and crème de menthe in a mixing glass with ice. Stir to chill. Strain into a chilled cocktail glass or serve on the rocks. Garnish with a floating fresh mint leaf.

The Gentleman's Sour Apple Manhattan

1 ½ ounces Gentleman Jack Rare Tennessee Whiskey
½ ounce sour mix
½ ounce apple schnapps
Thin green apple slice

Combine the Jack Daniel's, sour mix, and schnapps in a shaker with ice. Shake and strain into a chilled cocktail glass. Garnish with a thin slice of green apple.

Jack Daniel's Old Fashioned

The Old Fashioned isn't technically a Manhattan, but it's so iconic it must be included here.

1 orange slice
Dash of bitters
1 teaspoon sugar
2 ounces Jack Daniel's Tennessee Whiskey

Muddle the orange slice, bitters, and sugar in the bottom of a rocks glass. Fill with ice. Top with 2 ounces of Jack Daniel's.

Tennessee Cranberry Smash Manhattan

1 orange slice
6 fresh or frozen thawed cranberries
Dash of bitters
1 heaping teaspoon sugar
2 ounces Jack Daniel's Tennessee Whiskey

Muddle the orange slice, cranberries, bitters, and sugar in the bottom of a rocks glass. Fill with ice. Top with 2 ounces of Jack Daniel's.

Heard around the TABLE

After making reservations just the day before, a couple from England visited us and sat at my table. While I was out of the room, the gentleman told everyone at the table that when he called to see if we had room for them, he got to laughing so hard that he could barely speak. He said that I sounded like someone from out of Gone with the Wind. *Said he never knew people actually talked like that —he thought it was just "movie talk."*

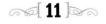

Tennessee Honey Sparklers

Jack Daniel's Tennessee Honey is our new blend of Jack Daniel's with a touch of honey. It presents all kinds of new possibilities for cocktails like these bright sparklers.

Tennessee Honey Royale

1 ounce chilled Jack Daniel's Tennessee Honey
4 ounces chilled sparkling wine
Lemon twist

Pour the Tennessee Honey into a champagne flute. Add the sparkling wine. Garnish with a lemon twist.

Tennessee Honey Bellini

1 ounce chilled Jack Daniel's Tennessee Honey
3 ounces chilled sparkling wine
1 ounce peach nectar

Pour the Tennessee Honey into a champagne flute. Add the sparkling wine. Spoon the peach nectar over the top.

Tennessee Cider

1 ounce chilled Jack Daniel's Tennessee Honey
4 ounces sparkling cider
Thin green apple slice

Pour the Tennessee Honey into a champagne flute. Add the sparkling cider. Garnish with a thin green apple slice.

Official Taste Testers

As a descendant of Jack Daniel and fourth generation Lynchburg native, I know it's in my blood to carry on the family tradition, and I gladly do my part. Every single Friday, I join twenty-three other distillery employees for the weekly taste-testing of the newest aged batches of Jack Daniel's. We compare the smell and taste of the current four-year-old Jack Daniel's whiskey to four-year-old batches from the previous year.

Our job is to find continuity from year to year so that every new bottle we sell tastes just as good as the last. We don't get paid extra for this work, but we do receive the coveted official duck decoy plaque after one year of service. No, I don't plan on quitting any time soon.

I have a business card that says I am a whiskey taster at the Jack Daniel Distillery. I love giving one to a stranger sitting next to me on an airplane. I immediately get twenty questions!

Jack's Juleps

Fresh mint drinks aren't just for Kentucky Derby time. Easy-to-grow mint makes for easy juleps. Legend has it that, instead of mint, Uncle Jack made his juleps with tansy (we know now that tansy is toxic). My other favorite juleps are made with the Jack Daniel's fresh orange or ginger infused whiskies on pages 15–16.

Classic Jack Mint Julep

Several sprigs of fresh mint (save one for garnish)
1 teaspoon sugar
2 ounces Gentleman Jack Tennessee Whiskey

Muddle the mint sprigs with the sugar in the bottom of a julep cup or rocks glass. Fill the glass with crushed or cracked ice. Add the Gentleman Jack. Garnish with a mint sprig.

Pineapple Jack Julep

Several sprigs of fresh mint (save one for garnish)
1 teaspoon superfine or granulated sugar
1 ½ ounces Jack Daniel's Tennessee Whiskey
2 ounces pineapple juice

Muddle the mint sprigs with the sugar in the bottom of a highball glass. Fill the glass with crushed or cracked ice. Add the Jack Daniel's and pineapple juice. Stir. Garnish with a mint sprig.

Tennessee Honey Julep

Several sprigs of fresh mint (save one for garnish)
2 ounces Jack Daniel's Tennessee Honey
Ginger ale

Muddle the mint sprigs in the bottom of a julep or rocks glass. Fill the glass with crushed or cracked ice. Add the Tennessee Honey. Top with a splash of ginger ale. Garnish with a mint sprig.

Jack Daniel's Infused Whiskey

Whiskey steeped with a complementary flavor is called an infusion. Just combine fresh ginger, orange peel, or spices with a bottle of Jack Daniel's in a big jar and leave it be for about a week or two. You won't believe the delicious complexity that develops.

We also add a little sugar water at the end to sweeten the mix. I've served these infusions as is over ice, in juleps, and blended with club soda, tonic, lemonade, ginger ale, and lemon-lime soda. Garnish the cocktails with orange slices, mint sprigs, or lime wedges. If you keep the infusions in the Jack Daniel's square bottle, be sure to label it accordingly.

Ginger Jack

1 cup peeled and coarsely chopped fresh ginger
1 bottle (750ml) Jack Daniel's Tennessee Whiskey
1 cup sugar
½ cup water

Combine the ginger and Jack Daniel's in a large jar. Store in a cool dark place for 1 to 2 weeks. Bring the sugar and water to a boil in a small saucepan over high heat and cook just until the sugar has dissolved. Cool. Strain the whiskey and discard the ginger. Stir the syrup into the flavored whiskey. Store in a container with a tight fitting lid or in a labeled Jack Daniel's bottle.

*I tell folks that
oftentimes we substitute
Jack Daniel's for vanilla
in our cooking, so I
encourage them to do
the same when that
pantry staple runs out.
One gentleman looked
up from his dinner and
said, "Honey, I'm gonna
run out of Jack Daniel's
long before I run out
of vanilla!"*

Orange Jack

4 or 5 large oranges
1 bottle (750ml) Jack Daniel's Tennessee Whiskey
1 cup sugar
$\frac{1}{2}$ cup water

With a sharp knife cut the zest, without any of the underlying white pith, off the oranges in wide strips. Combine the zest and Jack Daniel's in a large jar. Store in a cool dark place for 1 to 2 weeks. Bring the sugar and water to a boil in a small saucepan over high heat and cook just until the sugar has dissolved. Cool. Strain the whiskey and discard the orange peel. Stir the syrup into the flavored whiskey. Store in a container with a tight fitting lid or in a labeled Jack Daniel's bottle.

Spiced Jack

1 orange
1 cinnamon stick
1 vanilla bean, split
5 whole cloves
5 whole allspice berries
1 bottle (750ml) Jack Daniel's Tennessee Whiskey
1 cup sugar
$\frac{1}{2}$ cup water

With a sharp knife remove the zest , without any of the underlying white pith, from the orange in wide strips Combine the zest, cinnamon stick, vanilla bean, cloves, allspice, and Jack Daniel's in a large jar. Store in a cool dark place for 1 to 2 weeks. Bring the sugar and water to a boil in a small saucepan over high heat and cook just until the sugar has dissolved. Cool. Strain the whiskey and discard the seasonings. Stir the sugar syrup into the flavored whiskey. Store in a container with a tight fitting lid or in a labeled Jack Daniel's bottle.

Jack and Sodas

Folks in Lynchburg and all around the world enjoy a refreshing bubbly soda with a splash of Jack. Here are some of our favorites.

Jack and Cola

Jack and Coke® is the most popular Jack Daniel's cocktail of all time. In fact more than half of the Jack Daniel's consumed worldwide is mixed with cola. I especially love mine with a good healthy squeeze of fresh lime juice. It's right, every time.

> 2 ounces Jack Daniel's Tennessee Whiskey
> Cola
> Lime wedges

Combine Jack and Cola over ice in a highball glass. Garnish with lime wedges. You can also muddle a couple of lemon or lime wedges in the bottom of the glass. Add ice and Jack Daniel's. Top with Cola.

Jack and Cola Float or Jack Black Cow

Use whatever brown soda you like, even diet. I love a float made with root beer or cream soda. Talk about a fun afternoon sipper or casual dessert after a summer barbecue.

> Scoops of vanilla ice cream
> 2 ounces Jack Daniel's Tennessee Whiskey
> Cola, root beer, or cream soda

Put a scoop or two of ice cream in a tall glass. Top with Jack Daniel's and soda. Serve with a spoon and a straw.

Jack and Citrus Soda

A particular citrus soda has long been a Lynchburg favorite drink. It's yellow, very sweet and Lynchburg folks have been mixing for years. Must be why we're known for our sunny dispositions! It's not available everywhere, so my cousin in South Carolina takes it home by the case after a visit. We love to mix it with the Jack Daniel's Tennessee Honey too.

2 ounces Jack Daniel's Tennessee Whiskey
Citrus soda

Pour Jack Daniel's in a tall glass with ice. Top with Citrus Soda.

Jack Attack

This is a Jack and Ginger accented with a dash of bitters and a colorful garnish.

2 ounces Jack Daniel's Tennessee Whiskey
Dash of bitters
Ginger ale
Lime slice and maraschino cherry

Combine the Jack Daniel's, bitters, and ginger ale over ice in a tall glass. Garnish with the lime slice and a maraschino cherry.

Meet Jeff Arnett

I n 2008 Tennessean Jeff Arnett was named the seventh Master Distiller of the Jack Daniel Distillery. It's now Jeff's responsibility to make Uncle Jack's Tennessee Whiskey in strict adherence to Jack's guiding words: "Every day we make it, we'll make it the best we can."

With eighty barrel houses and nearly two million barrels of Tennessee whiskey to fill and look after, the job of Master Distiller is an enormous responsibility and surely one of the most enviable jobs in the world. Specializing in quality control at the distillery followed by managing Jack Daniel's Single Barrel Whiskey, Jeff is well prepared to take the helm. As he likes to say, "Seven is my lucky number. I became the seventh Master Distiller of Old No. 7 in my seventh year at Jack Daniel's."

Jeff loves American muscle cars and has had a bunch of them over the years, his two favorites being the 1967 Chevy Camaro and the 1965 Ford Mustang. These days as husband and father of two, you'll more likely find Jeff taking his two kids for rides around his ten-acre gentleman's farm in his "Jacked-up" golf cart, complete with Jack Daniel's emblems, a stereo, and a six-inch Jake's lift. Otherwise, he's working around the house or in the yard on one project or another, or relaxing in his barn loft Man Cave with a three barrel bar and flat screen TV.

There's also a chance you could run into Jeff anywhere in the world talking to folks about our hometown product in his role as a brand ambassador. "It's still amazes me how popular Jack Daniel's Tennessee whiskey is throughout the world and how many different ways people like to enjoy it," he says. "In England folks mix it with cloudy apple juice. In South Africa they make Jack Daniel's "Appletizers" with sparking apple juice."

"What's also interesting is that throughout the United Kingdom (our largest market outside of the U.S.), where the bar and pub shelves are lined with wonderful regional and local whiskeys, I always find a bottle of Old No. 7 among them. Always. And no matter where I travel,

I know that I'll know two words in whatever language they speak: "Jack Daniel's."

Since Uncle Jack passed on in 1911, only five other men have held the title "Master Distiller." They were my grandmother's brother Jess Motlow (1911–1941), my uncle Lem Tolley (1941–1964), Jess Gamble (1964–1966), Frank Bobo (1966–1992), and Jimmy Bedford (1992–2008).

Jeff remembers his predecessor, our sixth Master Distiller Jimmy Bedford, fondly and says that not a day goes by that he doesn't ask himself *what would Jimmy do?* in a particular situation. "To the world Jimmy was a rock star. To us, he was Jimmy—our friend, our neighbor, our coworker, and my mentor. We'll miss him always."

Jeff loves a dinner at Miss Mary Bobo's, and he's especially glad when we're serving Miss Mary's Chicken with Pastry. "And the okra," he says wistfully, "it's no better anywhere."

Jack Party Punches

A great party calls for a good-sized batch of your own "special cocktail punch," so these recipes call for "parts" rather than measured amounts. As my assistant manger Debbie Baxter's husband, Goose, says about cooking down his sorghum molasses, "Just eyeball it." Mix up a bit more than you think you'll need and keep it in a pitcher in the refrigerator. Then you can quickly refill the punch bowl.

Cool Jack Apple Mint Tea

> 1 part freshly brewed iced tea, sweetened to taste
> 2 parts apple cider
> 1 part Jack Daniel's Tennessee Whiskey
> Green apple slices, lemon slices, and fresh mint sprigs

Combine the tea, cider, and Jack Daniel's in a punch bowl or pitcher. Garnish with apple, lemon, and mint. Serve over ice.

Tolley Town Celebration Punch

> 4 parts cranberry juice
> 2 parts pineapple juice
> 1 part orange juice
> 3 parts Jack Daniel's Tennessee Whiskey
> Fresh cranberries, orange slices, and lemon slices

Combine the juices and the Jack Daniel's in a punch bowl or pitcher. Garnish with fresh cranberries and orange and lemon slices. Serve over ice.

Honey Milk Punch

> 2 cups whole milk
> 2 cups half and half cream
> 2 cups Jack Daniel's Tennessee Honey
> Nutmeg

Combine the milk, cream, and the Jack Daniel's Tennessee Honey in a pitcher. Chill or freeze until slushy. Serve sprinkled with nutmeg.

Jack Daniel's Citrus Cider

3 parts Jack Daniel's Tennessee Whiskey
2 parts apple cider
1 part orange juice
1 part lemon juice
4 parts ginger ale
Orange, lemon, and apple slices

Combine the Jack Daniel's, cider, orange and lemon juices, and ginger ale in a punch bowl or pitcher. Serve over ice. Garnish with orange, lemon, and apple slices. This cider punch is extra good in the fall when the air is crisp and cool.

Shoo Fly Punch

2 parts pineapple juice
1 part orange juice
1 part Jack Daniel's Tennessee Whiskey
¼ part Rose's lime juice
Splash of pomegranate juice, optional
Lime and orange slices and fresh mint sprigs

Combine the pineapple and orange juices, Jack Daniel's, and lime juice in a punchbowl or pitcher. Add a little pomegranate juice to give it a pinkish hue. Serve over ice. Garnish with lime and orange slices and mint.

Heard around the TABLE

A hostess enjoyed this encounter. As a Southern term of endearment and respect the title "Miss" applies to all our hostesses. As the hostess greeted her guests and led them to Miss Virginia, one lady appearing stunned turned to me and said, "But we're in Lynchburg, shouldn't we be seeing Miss Tennessee?" If only I'd been quick enough to respond, "You're talking to her!"

Jack Sours

The classic whiskey sour is a puckering blend of lightly sweetened lemon juice with whiskey and a dash of bitters garnished with a cherry and an orange slice. Whiskey sours require a good shaking to develop the distinctive foamy top. Serve them up or on the rocks. Experiment with the basic sour recipe by adding a splash of another fresh juice or a dash of liqueur. Here are a few of my favorites.

Classic Tennessee Whiskey Sour

>2 ounces Jack Daniel's Tennessee Whiskey
>1 ounce fresh lemon juice
>1 ounce simple syrup
>Orange or lemon slice and maraschino cherry

Combine the Jack Daniel's, lemon juice, and syrup in a shaker with ice. Shake vigorously. Serve up or on the rocks. Garnish with an orange or lemon slice and a cherry.

Pineapple Jack Sour

>2 ounces Jack Daniel's Tennessee Whiskey
>1 ounce Rose's lime juice
>2 ounces pineapple juice
>Fresh pineapple chunk and maraschino cherry

Combine the Jack Daniel's and lime and pineapple juices in a shaker with ice. Shake and strain into a cocktail or sour glass. Garnish with a chunk of fresh pineapple and a cherry.

Jack Jajito Sour

>2 ounces Jack Daniel's Tennessee Whiskey
>2 ounces fresh lime juice
>1 ounce simple syrup
>Fresh mint leaves

Combine the Jack Daniel's, lime juice, and syrup in a shaker with ice. Shake vigorously. Serve on the rocks with bruised mint leaves.

Tall Cool Jack Cocktails

Back in Uncle Jack's day, whiskey was enjoyed neat (no ice) followed by a chaser of cold water. He may have had a kind of lemonade, but not fresh ginger, pineapple, cranberry, apricot nectar, or ginger ale. If only he knew how smartly his Tennessee whiskey would blend with the flavors of the world today, including green tea in China, maple syrup in Vermont, and sparkling cider in England. The man was *of* his time and *ahead* of his time, all at the *same* time.

Hula Jack

> 1 teaspoon fresh grated ginger
> 1 teaspoon sugar
> Dash of bitters
> 2 ounces Jack Daniel's Tennessee Whiskey
> 1 ounce pineapple juice
> 4 ounces lemon-lime soda
> Lime wedge

Muddle the ginger, sugar, and bitters with a spoon in the bottom of a tall glass. Fill with ice. Add Jack Daniel's and pineapple juice. Top with soda. Garnish with a lime wedge.

ApriJack Nectar

> 2 ounces Jack Daniel's Tennessee Whiskey
> 3 ounces apricot nectar
> 1/2 ounce Rose's lime juice
> Lime wedge and mint sprig

Combine the Jack Daniel's, nectar, and lime juice in a tall glass with ice. Garnish with a lime wedge and a mint sprig.

Lynchburg Lemonade

If this Lynchburg, Tennessee, classic doesn't send you straight for your overalls and your banjo, I confess there's little more I can offer you! On really hot days keep your sweet & sour mix icy cold and use lots of ice in the glass. Shuffleboard is the recommended sporting event to accompany this cocktail. Please, shuffle responsibly.

1 part Jack Daniel's Tennessee Whiskey
1 part triple sec
1 part bottled sweet & sour mix
4 parts lemon-lime soda
Lemon slices
Maraschino cherries

Combine the Jack Daniel's, triple sec, sweet & sour, and lemon-lime soda. Serve over ice in tall glasses. Garnish with lemon slices and cherries.

Coconut Orange Jack

2 ounces Jack Daniel's Tennessee Whiskey
1 ounce cream of coconut
3 ounces orange juice
Squeeze of fresh lime juice
Orange slice

Combine the Jack Daniel's, cream of coconut, and orange and lime juices in a shaker with ice. Shake and pour into a tall glass with ice. Garnish with an orange slice. Or, combine all the ingredients in a blender ⅓ full of ice. Blend until slushy.

Madras Jacket

2 ounces Jack Daniel's Tennessee Whiskey
2 ounces orange juice
2 ounces cranberry juice
Lime wedge

Combine the Jack Daniel's and orange juice over ice in a tall glass. Top with cranberry juice. Garnish with a lime wedge.

Jack's Pomegranate Lemonade

2 ounces Jack Daniel's Tennessee Whiskey
1 ounce pomegranate juice
Lemonade or lemon-lime soda
Lemon wedge and mint sprig

Combine the Jack Daniel's and pomegranate juice over ice in a tall glass. Top with lemonade or lemon-lime soda. Garnish with a lemon wedge and mint sprig.

Iced Tennessee Honey Tea

Iced tea
Jack Daniel's Tennessee Honey

Pour iced tea into a tall glass with ice. Top with Tennessee Honey.

Meet Jeff Norman

What's the first question Master Taster Jeff Norman gets whenever he meets fans of Jack Daniel's? "So, how'd you get your job?" Well, a PhD in chemistry from Tennessee Tech might have something to do with it. Before being named Jack Daniel Master Taster, Jeff worked as a distillery operator whose responsibility it is to propagate the yeast, grind and cook the grains, combine grain slurry and yeast in the fermenters, and monitor the fermenters and distillers throughout the process.

"Tasting whiskey is part science and part art," Jeff says. "Sure, it sounds like a lot of fun, but it's real work." What better path to being a good whiskey taster is there than starting out as a Jack Daniel's whiskey maker.

Like me, Jeff is a proud Lynchburg native. He went to high school just down the road while both his mother and father worked for Jack Daniel's. His dad, Harry Norman, was a taster himself in the quality control department, and his mom Sara, an excellent cook, worked in engineering administration. Together, they have provided several decades of service to the distillery.

Jeff often pops by his family home at lunchtime for a visit and one of his mother's special Tennessee tomato, bacon, egg, and lettuce sandwiches in the summertime. When he's with us for dinner at Miss Mary's, Jeff is extra happy when we're serving his favorite fried chicken (although he says the catfish is a close second). He loves our fudge pie and says it's almost as good as his mother's!

"I always planned to return to Lynchburg ultimately," he says. "As Master Taster and a brand ambassador for Jack Daniel's, it means a great deal to me to have the opportunity in my work to promote the very thing that put food on our table as I grew up."

Warm Jack Cocktails

A warm Jack Daniel's toddy has been known to comfort many on a chilly day. Any of these are especially handy for cold weather and late-season tailgating. Keep a warm batch ready in a thermos at half-time.

Hot Tennessee Toddy

> 2 ounces Jack Daniel's Tennessee Whiskey
> Spoonful of honey
> Cinnamon stick
> A good squeeze of fresh lemon juice
> Boiling water

Pour Jack Daniel's into a mug. Add a spoonful of honey, the cinnamon stick, and lemon juice. Top with boiling water and stir. Sit down. Relax. Enjoy.

Hot Tomato Jack

> 3 ounces tomato juice
> 3 ounces beef broth
> Dash of Worcestershire sauce
> Dash of hot pepper sauce
> Squeeze of fresh lemon juice
> 2 ounces Jack Daniel's Tennessee Whiskey
> Lemon slice

Heat the tomato juice and beef broth in a saucepan or microwave-safe mug. Stir in the Worcestershire sauce, hot pepper sauce, and lemon juice. Pour Jack Daniel's into a mug and top with the hot tomato juice mixture. Garnish with a lemon slice.

Jack Daniel's Warm Pear Nectar Sipper

  4 ounces hot pear nectar
  2 ounces Jack Daniel's Tennessee Whiskey
  1 tablespoon maple syrup
  Nutmeg and lemon slice

Combine the nectar, Jack Daniel's, and maple syrup in a mug. Garnish with a sprinkle of nutmeg and a lemon slice.

Hound Dog Hot Bouillon

  1 cup hot beef bouillon
  1 ounce Jack Daniel's Tennessee Whiskey
  Dash hot pepper sauce
  Slice of lemon
  Finely chopped green onion

Combine the bouillon, Jack Daniel's, and hot pepper sauce in a big mug and enjoy the rich, steaming, brothy Jack with a slice of lemon and green onions.

Mulled in Moore County

Makes 16 servings

  1 quart apple cider
  1 cup orange juice
  1 lemon, sliced
  1 orange, sliced
  1 cinnamon stick
  1 tablespoon whole cloves
  3 cups Jack Daniel's Tennessee Whiskey

Combine the cider, orange juice, lemon and orange slices, cinnamon stick, and cloves in a large pot. Simmer about 10 minutes for the spices and juices to meld. Stir in Jack Daniel's and reheat. Serve in mugs.

  For a single serving: Place 2 ounces Jack Daniel's, a lemon slice, an orange slice, and cinnamon stick in a mug. Top with boiling apple cider.

Hot Buttered Tennessee Honey

2 ounces Jack Daniel's Tennessee Honey
Boiling water
Pat of butter
Nutmeg

Pour the Tennessee Honey in a mug. Top with boiling water. Top with a pat of butter. Garnish with a sprinkle of nutmeg.

Tennessee Honey Hot Tea

1 cup freshly brewed hot English breakfast tea
1 ounce Jack Daniel's Tennessee Honey

Combine the tea and Tennessee Honey in a mug and curl up with a good book.

Creamy Jack Cocktails

These creamy cocktails are more like little decadent desserts served in a glass. I like to serve them as a dessert or after dinner treat.

Bold Custard

Makes 6 servings

Holiday time in Lynchburg means boiled custard, never the store-bought eggnog (good as it is). I've named ours "Bold Custard" because that's what happens when you add a little Jack. Besides, most of us pronounce "boiled" and "bold" virtually the same anyway. We wouldn't think of serving our holiday coconut or fruitcake without punch cups of boiled custard.

> 1 quart whole milk or half-and-half
> 4 egg yolks
> ½ cup sugar
> Pinch of salt
> 1 teaspoon vanilla
> Jack Daniel's Tennessee Whiskey, served on the side

Heat the milk in a large saucepan until it just begins to simmer. Beat the egg yolks with the sugar and salt in a mixing bowl. Gradually stir in one cup of the hot milk to temper the egg yolks. Pour the tempered egg mixture into the remaining hot milk in the saucepan. Cook over low heat, stirring constantly, until thickened and the custard coats the back of a wooden spoon. Don't let it boil, or the eggs will curdle and you'll have to start over. Cool. Stir in the vanilla and chill before serving. Serve in cups or small glasses. Top with a dollop of whipped cream, if desired. Be sure to pass a little pitcher of Jack Daniel's on the side for everyone to add as they please.

Almond Jack Frost

1 1/2 ounces Jack Daniel's Tennessee Whiskey
1/2 ounce of amaretto
2 ounces half-and-half or light cream
1 teaspoon superfine sugar
Nutmeg

Combine the Jack Daniel's, amaretto, cream, and sugar in a shaker with ice. Shake and pour into a rocks glass. Sprinkle with nutmeg.

Tennessee Honey Coffee Melt

1/2 cup freshly brewed strong coffee
1 to 2 ounces Jack Daniel's Tennessee Honey
1 scoop vanilla ice cream

Pour the coffee into a medium mug. Add the Tennessee Honey and stir. Top with a generous scoop of vanilla ice cream.

Honey and Cream

2 ounces Jack Daniel's Tennessee Honey
2 ounces half-and-half or light cream

Combine the Tennessee Honey and cream over ice in a rocks glass.

COCKTAIL SNACKS

Quick Cocktail Snacks for the Busy Hostess

Hot Catfish Cocktail Sandwiches
Crispy Pecan Cheese Wafers
Jack Hot Wings

Pimiento Cheese . . . Let Us Count the Ways

Look No Further Pimiento Cheese
Really Good Deviled Eggs

Jack Shot Glass Sippers and One Slurp

Jackgrita Sippers
Peachy Jack Sippers
Tennessee Honey Lemon Drop Sippers
Jack Aphrodisiac Slurps

Helpful Hints for Cooking with Jack

Sweet, Hot, and Sour Mash Meatballs
Tennessee Smoked Trout Spread

Whiskey Dipping Sauces

Peppery Jack Blue Cheese Dipping Sauce
Hot Mustard Jack Dipping Sauce
Tennessee/Louisiana Border Dipping Sauce

Cornbread Barrel Bungs

Pepper Jack Barrel Bungs
Pimiento Cheese Barrel Bungs
Okra Barrel Bungs
Barbecue Barrel Bungs
Hot Artichoke Pimiento Cheese Dip
Hot Pimiento Cheese Dip

Uncle Jack the Man

Pickled Okra Party Shrimp
Peaches and Cream Country Ham Spread
Green Butter Bean Dip
Honey Blue Cheese Spread
Honey Jezebel Cheddar Spread
Jack's Sweet Hot Party Pecans
Barbecue Peanuts
Pumpkin Pie Honey Spiced Almonds
Bacon Grease Bruschetta

Quick Cocktail Snacks for the Busy Hostess

Smoky warm potato chips—Spread a bag of kettle potato chips on a baking sheet. Sprinkle them with smoked paprika. Warm them in a 350°F oven for about 10 minutes.

Corn nuts—Serve crunchy corn nuts in fancy bowls, the perfect complement to our corn whiskey.

Pork rinds—Serve big baskets of crispy pork rinds to snack on with cocktails. Think what you might, but pork rinds will start a conversation.

Grilled pimiento cheese sandwiches—Cut them into triangles for easy, one-bite cocktail party snacking.

Pimiento cheese bruschetta—Spread pimiento cheese on toasted Italian bread with a thin slice of fresh tomato.

Roasted okra—Pass a tray of oven-roasted whole okra pods with toothpicks. Serve them warm or at room temperature.

Crisp bacon strips—Cook thick-cut bacon on a baking sheet in the oven until crisp for flat, even slices. When cool, pack the strips standing up in a wide-mouth mason jar and serve with shots of icy cold Jack Daniel's Tennessee Honey. Sprinkle the bacon with a touch of brown sugar before cooking, if you like (see Foolproof Oven Bacon on page 86).

Tomato sandwiches—A Tennessee tomato with good mayonnaise on white bread is a summer party home run. Use a good quality loaf that can hold the juicy tomato. Quarter the sandwiches with crusts removed, if you like. For variety, make mini BLTs and add a thin slice of cucumber or a fresh basil leaf.

Smoked sausage slices and mustard—Slice smoked sausage into bite-size pieces. Serve with toothpicks and fancy mustard.

Oven fried potatoes—Oven roast a big bag of frozen tater tots or natural cut French fries. Serve with any of our dipping sauces (pages 47–48).

Muffaletta baguette—Slice a crispy baguette in half. Spread with prepared muffaletta olive mix found in the pickle section of the grocery store. Top with thinly sliced ham and cheeses. Cover and slice into thin fingers.

Hot Catfish Cocktail Sandwiches

Makes 12 servings

Few foods appeal to most any of us more than some kind of fried fish, be it New England haddock and chips in brown paper doused with salt and malt vinegar, or a frozen fish stick with tartar sauce while watching cartoons.

Fried fish is just behind fried potatoes as an all-time favorite food of people everywhere. Here in Tennessee we sure love a hot fish sandwich of cornmeal dredged catfish or whiting, fried to crispness, served with mustard, pickle chips, onion, and hot sauce on plain white bread. Delicious. It's such a part of our shared culture and so well loved that I refashioned this Southern essential into stylish cocktail fare dressed with yellow mustard slaw, a tangy substitution for tartar sauce.

Now when you're frying, be sure the oil is good and hot before you start. You want to sear the surface quickly before the oil can be absorbed. And fry the fish a few pieces at a time, in a few batches. A crowded pan lowers the oil temperature.

Serve these bite-size catfish nuggets with Jack's Red Dipping Sauce (page 241). Good as it is, shrimp cocktail could likely stand a little vacation from the party scene anyway.

> Vegetable oil
> 4 catfish fillets, cut into 2-inch pieces
> 1 cup self-rising cornmeal mix or plain cornmeal
> (season fish with salt, if using plain)
> 12 small, soft white dinner rolls
> 1 recipe Yellow Mustard Slaw (page 92)

Heat a good 2 inches of oil in a heavy iron skillet to 365°F. While the oil heats, carefully dredge the catfish in the cornmeal to coat all sides. Set the catfish pieces on a rack and let them rest for 15 to 20 minutes to allow the cornmeal to adhere before frying. Fry the fillets in the oil until golden brown and crisp. Drain the fillets on paper towels.

To serve: Fill a roll with hot fish, top with slaw, repeat!

Crispy Pecan Cheese Wafers

Makes about 36 wafers

There may be more cheese wafer recipes in the world than barrels of Tennessee whiskey aging in the hills of Lynchburg. Just about everyone has a favorite, including my mother who, after more than seventy years of baking, declared this recipe to be the best. Crispy rice cereal provides the extra special crunch. It's not required, but Mother adorns each wafer with a handsome pecan half that toasts during baking. When do we eat these? Every chance we get.

> 2 cups grated sharp Cheddar cheese
> 1 cup (2 sticks) salted butter, softened
> 2 cups all-purpose flour
> 2 cups crispy rice cereal
> Cayenne pepper, to taste
> About 36 pecan halves

Heat the oven to 375°F. Cream the cheese and butter in a large mixing bowl using an electric mixer. Slowly blend in the flour. Stir in the cereal and cayenne pepper. Drop the batter by teaspoonfuls onto a cookie sheet and flatten out with the back of a spoon or a fork to make round wafers. Top each with a pecan half. Bake for 10 minutes or until just lightly browned. Cool on a wire rack. Store in an airtight container.

Jack Hot Wings

Makes 6 to 8 servings

Smoking brisket and pork shoulder is an all-day affair, and whole hog is an all-night one, so Lynchburg barbecue fellas need plenty of snacks while they "work." After grilling or smoking the wings, they toss them in a big foil pan of special whiskey hot sauce and pass it around. These guys don't bother much with the blue cheese dressing, and I can't say I've ever seen a barbecue crew munching on carrot and celery sticks, either. I offer them anyway for folks like me who need to balance the hot wings with something cool.

For the Chicken
> Vegetable oil
> 3/4 cup all-purpose flour
> 1 1/2 teaspoons salt

¼ teaspoon black pepper

2 pounds chicken drumettes

For the Sauce

½ cup (1 stick) butter

½ cup Jack Daniel's Tennessee Whiskey

¼ cup ketchup

⅓ cup hot pepper sauce, or to taste

Blue cheese dressing

Carrot sticks, to garnish

Celery sticks, to garnish

To fry the wings: Heat 2 to 3 inches of oil in a fryer or heavy pot to 365° F. Combine the flour, salt, and pepper in a shallow bowl. Coat the wings with the flour mixture and gently place in the oil. Fry the wings, a few at a time, until they are cooked through and golden brown on all sides, 10 to 15 minutes. Drain the wings on paper towels.

To make the sauce: Combine the butter, Jack Daniel's, ketchup, and hot sauce in a small saucepan. Bring to a boil over medium heat. Remove from the heat and dip the cooked wings in the sauce. Serve with blue cheese dressing and fresh celery and carrot sticks.

To bake the wings: Heat the oven to 450°F. Place the drumettes in a roasting pan and brush with melted butter. Sprinkle with salt and pepper. Bake until lightly browned and cooked through, about 25 to 30 minutes. To grill the wings: Heat the grill to medium heat. Brush the drumettes with melted butter. Sprinkle with salt and pepper. Place the drumettes on the grill. Cook for about 30 minutes, turning frequently and keeping an eye out for flare-ups.

Heard around the TABLE

Several gentlemen at my table were musing about what to do upon their retirement. They agreed it wise to apply for host positions for dinner at Miss Mary's, and mattress testers in the afternoon.

Pimiento Cheese . . . Let Us Count the Ways

As I travel throughout the South and across the country and the world promoting Jack Daniel's, I can't help but smile when I see more and more chefs including some kind of pimiento cheese dish on their menus. How wonderful. It's not just cheese spread and crackers mind you, but all kinds of foods now showcase a pimiento cheese theme.

You, too, can do join the pimiento cheese movement at home. It might be as easy as adding a jar of pimientos to your weeknight mac and cheese. I'll bet you can come up with something pimiento cheesy even beyond these suggestions.

Pimiento cheese queso dip
Pimiento cheese on a burger
Pimiento cheese deviled eggs
Pimiento cheese mashed potatoes
Pimiento cheese au gratin
  potatoes
Pimiento cheese macaroni salad
Pimiento cheese squash casserole
Pimiento cheese soup
Pimiento cheese hushpuppies
Pimiento cheese cornbread
Pimiento cheese mac and chese
Pimiento cheese biscuits
Pimiento cheese muffins
Pimiento cheese in a baked potato
Pimiento cheese grits
Pimiento cheese potato soup
Pimiento cheese sauce
Pimiento cheese omelet or
  scrambled eggs

Pimiento cheese hash brown
  casserole
Pimiento cheese hominy or
  cabbage casserole
Pimiento cheese artichoke dip
Pimiento cheese spoonbread
Pimiento cheese strata
Pimiento cheese creamy corn
  salad
Pimiento cheese stuffed
  mushrooms
Pimiento cheese quiche
Pimiento cheese chopped salad
Pimiento cheese buttermilk salad
  dressing

Look No Further Pimiento Cheese

Makes about 4 cups

Like most home cooks, I'm always on the lookout for an appealing new trend or taste. When it comes to appetizers, though, absolutely nothing is more versatile, all-purpose, or delicious than the Southern classic, pimiento cheese. It's a tough one to top.

Real pimiento cheese is not even a close cousin to the supermarket tubs of the overly sweet, dull orange spread. After a taste of real pimiento cheese you'll never be tempted by store-bought again. In my house this pimiento cheese finds its way onto everything—from white bread to fancy crackers to toast and grilled bread. It's also delicious on celery stalks and Belgian endive spears. Do not allow pimiento cheese's apparent simplicity lull you into a sense of kitchen complacency. Good cheese (which you must shred yourself for the best flavor), real mayonnaise, and quality pimientos are essential. And don't forget the secret ingredient—a pinch of sugar. For variety, I occasionally add a few chopped green or black olives.

½ pound mild yellow Cheddar cheese, shredded (2 cups)
½ pound sharp white Cheddar cheese, shredded (2 cups)
Dash Worcestershire sauce
Dash hot pepper sauce
1 jar (4 ounces) diced pimientos, with juice
½ to ⅔ cup real mayonnaise
Pinch of sugar

Blend the cheeses, Worcestershire sauce, hot pepper, pimientos, mayonnaise, and sugar with a fork in a medium mixing bowl. Cover and store in the refrigerator for up to 1 week.

Heard around the TABLE

While on the phone, I asked the man making a reservation if anyone in his party had trouble with steps. He replied "only after dinner."

Really Good Deviled Eggs

Makes 24 deviled egg halves

There's no such thing as leftover deviled eggs, not good ones anyway. You certainly won't have any leftovers from this recipe either. Make more than you think you'll need because most folks have at least one more than they really should. Our little secret here is sweet pickle relish. Garnish each egg with whatever you like. I've used sliced black or green olives, capers, fresh herbs (like tiny fresh dill or parsley sprigs), a sliver of smoked salmon or country ham, crumbled crisp bacon, or a dusting of paprika.

> 12 hard cooked eggs, peeled and cut in half
> $\frac{1}{2}$ cup mayonnaise
> 2 tablespoons yellow or Dijon mustard
> $\frac{1}{3}$ cup sweet pickle relish
> $\frac{1}{2}$ teaspoon salt and black pepper, to taste
> Dashes of Worcestershire and hot sauces

Remove the yolks from the egg whites and place the yolks in a medium bowl. Set the whites aside. Mash the yolks with a fork. Stir in the mayonnaise, mustard, pickle relish, salt and pepper, and Worcestershire and hot sauces until smooth. Spoon the yolk mixture into the egg whites and arrange on a platter. Garnish as desired. Cover and refrigerate.

Jack Shot Glass Sippers and One Slurp

These three-sip "soups" served in little cups or shot glasses are always instant party conversation starters. Offer a tray as you greet and mingle with your guests, and in no time everyone will ask for the recipe—and another sip.

Jackgrita Sippers

Makes 12 servings

1 cup tomato juice
1 cup orange juice
½ cup lime juice
½ cup Jack Daniel's Tennessee Whiskey
2 tablespoons pomegranate juice
2 tablespoons sugar
Hot pepper sauce to taste
Fresh cilantro sprigs, for garnish

Combine the tomato, orange, and lime juices in a pitcher with the Jack Daniel's, pomegranate juice, sugar, and hot sauce. Chill and serve in shot glasses. Garnish with fresh cilantro sprigs.

Peachy Jack Sippers

Makes 12 servings

4 ripe peaches, pitted and peeled (or 4 cups frozen peach slices)
1 ½ cups orange juice
¼ cup lime juice
1 tablespoon sugar
½ cup Jack Daniel's Tennessee Whiskey
1 teaspoon almond extract
Mint sprigs, for garnish

Puree the peaches in a blender with the orange and lime juices and sugar. Stir in the Jack Daniel's and almond extract. Chill in a pitcher and serve in shot glasses. Garnish with mint sprigs.

Tennessee Honey Lemon Drop Sippers

Makes 12 servings

    1 pint Italian lemon ice or lemon sherbet
    Jack Daniel's Tennessee Honey
    Mint sprigs, for garnish

Fill shot glasses with a small scoop of lemon ice or orange sherbet. Top with Tennessee Honey and garnish with mint sprigs. Sip as the lemon ice or sherbet melts into the whiskey. Try this with other sorbet flavors like peach mango or raspberry.

Jack Aphrodisiac Slurps

Makes one slurp per oyster

    Freshly shucked oysters
    Jack Daniel's Tennessee Whiskey
    Hot pepper sauce
    Fresh lemon wedges

Shuck a fresh oyster and place the oyster and its juices in a shot glass. Top with a drizzle of Jack Daniel's, a dash of hot pepper sauce, and a squeeze of fresh lemon juice.

Helpful Hints for Cooking with Jack

Conventional wisdom advises pairing robust flavored foods with big wines and spirits and vice versa. Not so with Jack. Jack Daniel's Tennessee Whiskey offers sweet, spicy, woody, and caramel flavors that combine as well with hearty, flavorful foods like hickory-smoked barbecue as they do with more delicate dishes like silky smooth custard.

As a general note, when cooking with Jack Daniel's always allow enough time for the alcohol to mellow during the heating process. Many recipes call for bringing the liquid to a boil, which causes evaporation but preserves Jack's lovely aromas and flavors.

Heating the spirit is not always necessary. Some dishes, such as sweetened fresh fruits or dessert sauces, taste just fabulous with a splash of Jack as is. The golden rule (or, The Amber Rule as we like to say) of cooking with Jack is to find a balance of flavors by exercising a little restraint. As with salt, pepper, cinnamon, or any other seasoning, moderation is the key. The flavor of the Jack Daniel's should enhance and embrace a dish, never dominate it.

Flaming Jack. What everyone should know about flaming a dish.

Flaming or flambéing is simply a dish set to fire by igniting a small amount of liquor poured over it. This is useful cooking skill when a showy display of dancing blue flames is in order. Flaming enhances all kinds of foods, from smoky cocktail wieners to classic Bananas Foster. Here's how to feel confident about it:

The first word is caution. Remember that a modest fire is involved. Be constantly vigilant to protect your face, body, and anything flammable around the work area and the flames.

The second word is heat. The food to be ignited must be warm. The Jack Daniel's used to ignite the food must also be warm—but not boiling hot. Heat the whiskey directly on the surface of the food to be ignited just to the point where the alcohol starts to vaporize. Now it's ready to flame. Using a long-handled match or lighter, ignite the

Heard around the TABLE

One man asked "Tell me the truth. Do all the rooms really serve the same menu?"

whiskey by touching the edge of the pan with the flame. For warm desserts, sprinkle the top with sugar, then pour on the whiskey and ignite. The flames will die down by themselves in a short time.

Lynchburg Vanilla

We've been forever adding Jack Daniel's in recipes that call for vanilla because they are such flavorful companions. Whenever we're out of vanilla, we just use Jack Daniel's by itself. For the best of both worlds, make your own vanilla extract by combining 3 or 4 whole vanilla beans in a pint jar filled with Jack Daniel's Tennessee Whiskey. Seal it tight and leave it to infuse for a few weeks. Use it just as you would store-bought vanilla extract, but know that it's better, much better.

Sweet, Hot, and Sour Mash Meatballs

Makes about 50 meatballs

I think a moist, flavorful meatball starts with a combination of ground pork sausage and ground beef. It's another reason I watch out for local fresh pork sausage in the little country markets on the outskirts of town. Many of our farmers process their own hogs and are true sausage experts, each with his own special seasoning blend and smoking methods.

Apple butter adds some body and a bit of sweetness to this meatball sauce, an old favorite on the Lynchburg party circuit. You can also serve the sauce with cocktail wieners, slices of smoked sausage, any kind of grilled pork, or even store-bought pulled pork barbecue.

For the Meatballs

> 1 pound pork sausage
> 1 pound ground beef
> ½ cup plain dry breadcrumbs
> 2 eggs, beaten
> ¼ cup milk
> ½ cup finely chopped onion
> ½ teaspoon salt
> ½ teaspoon black pepper

For the Apple Butter Jack Sauce

> ¾ cup spicy brown mustard

½ cup apple butter

⅓ cup Jack Daniel's Tennessee Whiskey

¼ cup brown sugar

1 tablespoon cider vinegar

1 tablespoon Worcestershire sauce

Salt and black pepper, to taste

Hot pepper sauce, to taste

To make the meatballs: Heat the oven to 375°F. Combine the sausage, ground beef, breadcrumbs, eggs, milk, onion, salt, and pepper in a large mixing bowl. Blend well with your hands. Form the meat mixture into 1 ½-inch balls. Place them on an ungreased baking sheet (with sides to catch the grease) or on a jelly-roll pan. Bake about 30 minutes or until browned and cooked through.

To make the sauce: Combine the mustard, apple jelly, whiskey, brown sugar, cider vinegar, Worcestershire sauce, salt and pepper, and hot sauce in a large skillet. Stir until well blended. Stir in the cooked meatballs. Coat with the sauce and cook about 5 minutes until the sauce has thickened slightly. Serve with toothpicks.

Note: The meatballs may be frozen and reheated at 350°F for about 20 minutes.

Tennessee Smoked Trout Spread

Makes about 2 cups

A little seafood nibble is just the thing before a big steak or roast pork supper. Here I call for smoked trout, but you can substitute wood-smoked salmon with the same delicious results. Horseradish adds a tangy contrast to the smoky fish. Make the spread a day in advance so the flavors can mellow. I like it best with crunchy Melba toast or delicate water crackers.

⅓ cup grated fresh onion

1 tablespoon vegetable oil

2 tablespoons Jack Daniel's Tennessee Whiskey

Zest from 1 lemon

8 ounces smoked trout, skin removed, flaked into bite-size pieces

½ cup sour cream

2 tablespoons prepared horseradish

2 tablespoons chopped fresh parsley

2 teaspoons capers
Lemon slices, for garnish

Cook the onion in the oil in a small saucepan over medium heat until tender and lightly browned, about 5 minutes. Stir in the Jack Daniel's and lemon zest and cook until the liquid has evaporated, about 1 minute. Remove from the heat and cool. Combine the trout, sour cream, and horseradish in a medium bowl and blend well. Stir in the cooled onion mixture, parsley, and capers. Cover and refrigerate until serving time. Garnish with fresh lemon slices and additional parsley and capers.

Whiskey Dipping Sauces

Fried foods are one of life's greatest indulgences, and I cannot imagine a world without them. One of my all-time favorites is hand-cut homemade French fries. We cook big batches of fries in a turkey fryer outside and serve them with this cool trio of dipping sauces. Natural-cut frozen fries save time and are almost just as good as long as they're fried, not oven baked. Try these versatile sauces with other fried snacks like chicken wings or tenders or any fried vegetable.

Peppery Jack Blue Cheese Dipping Sauce

Makes about 2 1/2 cups

    1 cup mayonnaise
    1/2 cup sour cream
    1 cup (4 ounces) crumbled blue cheese
    1/4 teaspoon garlic powder
    1 teaspoon Worcestershire sauce
    2 tablespoons Jack Daniel's Tennessee Whiskey
    1 tablespoon hot pepper sauce, or to taste

Combine the mayonnaise, sour cream, blue cheese, garlic powder, Worcestershire sauce, whiskey, and hot sauce in medium bowl. Blend well. Cover and keep refrigerated.

Hot Mustard Jack Dipping Sauce

Makes about 2 1/2 cups

    1 cup coarse-grain mustard
    1 cup mayonnaise
    1/4 cup Jack Daniel's Tennessee Whiskey
    1/4 cup honey
    1 tablespoon hot pepper sauce, or to taste

Combine the mustard, mayonnaise, Jack Daniel's, honey, and hot sauce in medium bowl. Blend well. Cover and keep refrigerated.

Tennessee/Louisiana Border Dipping Sauce

Makes about 2 ½ cups

2 cups ketchup
¼ cup brown sugar
3 tablespoons Worcestershire sauce
½ cup Jack Daniel's Tennessee Whiskey
1 tablespoon hot pepper sauce, or to taste

Combine the ketchup, brown sugar, Worcestershire sauce, Jack Daniel's, and hot sauce in small saucepan. Bring to a boil over medium heat and simmer 2 to 3 minutes. Cool. Cover and keep refrigerated.

Cornbread Barrel Bungs

I t sounds funny, but little barrel bungs are vitally important in the making of whiskey. Wooden barrel bungs seal up whiskey barrels during the long aging process. These little cornbread mini muffins look just like them and are the ideal two-bite treat to serve with cocktails. I'm sure once you try any of these variations you'll be inventing a few of your own. Just remember this: "Every day you make them, make them the best you can," as Lem Motlow said about making our Tennessee Whiskey.

Pepper Jack Barrel Bungs

Makes 24 barrel bungs

3/4 cup self-rising cornmeal mix
3/4 cup buttermilk or about 1/2 cup milk
2 tablespoons vegetable oil
1 cup shredded Pepper Jack cheese

Heat the oven to 450° F. Grease 24 mini muffin cups. Combine the cornmeal mix, buttermilk, vegetable oil, and cheese in a small mixing bowl. The batter should be creamy and pourable. If it seems too thick, add a splash of water. Drop one teaspoonful of batter into each muffin cups. Each cup should be about half full. Bake 10 to 12 minutes or until golden brown. Cool the pan on a wire rack about 5 minutes. Remove the muffins from the pan and serve warm or at room temperature.

Variation: Add 1/2 cup cooked and crumbled pork sausage, or finely diced smoked sausage to the batter and bake as directed above. You can also vary the cheese. Jack and Cheddar are both delicious.

Heard around the TABLE

A lady from Texas said that her husband liked Jack Daniel so much that he kept some in a spray bottle in the refrigerator to spray on food. I asked her what he sprayed it on. She said "ice cream, brownies, pecan pie, and barbecue."

Pimiento Cheese Barrel Bungs

Makes 24 barrel bungs

> ³⁄₄ cup self-rising cornmeal mix
> ¹⁄₂ cup buttermilk or about ¹⁄₃ cup milk
> 2 tablespoons vegetable oil
> 1 (2-ounce) jar diced pimientos, drained and cut into tiny pieces
> 1 cup sharp Cheddar cheese
> Black pepper, to taste

Heat the oven to 450° F. Grease 24 mini muffin cups. Combine the cornmeal mix, buttermilk, vegetable oil, pimientos, cheese, and pepper in a small mixing bowl. The batter should be creamy and pourable. If it seems too thick, add a splash of water. Drop one teaspoonful of batter into each muffin cup. Each cup should be about half full. Bake 10 to 12 minutes or until golden brown. Cool the pan on a wire rack about 5 minutes. Remove the muffins from the pan and serve warm or at room temperature.

Okra Barrel Bungs

Makes 24 barrel bungs

> 1 cup fresh thinly sliced okra or thawed frozen okra slices
> ³⁄₄ cup self-rising cornmeal mix
> ³⁄₄ cup buttermilk or about ¹⁄₂ cup milk
> 2 tablespoons vegetable oil
> 1 cup shredded sharp Cheddar cheese
> Black pepper, to taste

Heat the oven to 450° F. Grease 24 mini muffin cups. If you're using fresh okra, place it in a microwave-safe bowl. Cover and microwave the slices about 1 minute until the pieces are slightly softened but still bright green. Combine the okra with the cornmeal mix, buttermilk, vegetable oil, cheese, and pepper in a small mixing bowl. The batter should be creamy and pourable. If it seems too thick, add a splash of water. Drop one teaspoonful of batter into each muffin cup. Each cup should be about half full.

Bake 10 to 12 minutes or until golden brown. Cool the pan on a wire rack about 5 minutes. Remove the muffins from the pan and serve warm or at room temperature.

Barbecue Barrel Bungs

Makes 24 barrel bungs

> ³⁄₄ cup self-rising cornmeal mix
> ¹⁄₂ cup buttermilk or about ¹⁄₃ cup milk
> 2 tablespoons vegetable oil
> 2 tablespoons dill pickle relish
> ¹⁄₂ cup finely chopped Shade Tree Pulled Pork Barbecue (see page 175)

Heat the oven to 450° F. Grease 24 mini muffin cups. Combine the cornmeal mix, buttermilk, vegetable oil, and pickle relish in a small mixing bowl. The batter should be creamy and pourable. If it seems too thick, add a splash of water. Drop one teaspoonful of batter into each muffin cup. Each cup should be about half full. Using your fingers, place pinches (about 1 teaspoon) of barbecue in the center of each muffin cup.

Bake 10 to 12 minutes or until golden brown. Cool the pan on a wire rack about 5 minutes. Remove the muffins from the pan and serve warm or at room temperature.

Hot Artichoke Pimiento Cheese Dip

Makes about 4 cups

Artichoke dip has become so restaurant regular that it doesn't seem special like it once was. To shine it back to life, let's combine the artichoke dip with the Southern super trend—pimiento cheese. Because this is filling and fun to scoop, your guests will appreciate small cocktail plates so they can double dip with abandon. If dinner is just heavy hors d'oeuvres, I always serve at least one special warm dish along with the usual fruits, vegetables, and cheeses. This one suits me fine. Serve with sturdy crackers.

> 1 can (13.75 ounces) artichoke hearts, drained and chopped
> 1 jar (4 ounces) diced pimientos or ¹⁄₂ cup roasted red bell peppers
> 2 cups grated sharp Cheddar cheese
> 1 cup mayonnaise
> Spoonful of sugar
> ¹⁄₄ cup grated Parmesan cheese

Heat the oven to 350°F. Combine the artichoke hearts, pimientos, Cheddar cheese, mayonnaise, sugar, and Parmesan cheese in a medium casserole. Bake 20 to 30 minutes or until bubbly.

*One table with guests
from Japan brought
a translator. As our
hostess gave her history
of the house talk, the
translator spoke and the
guests would ooh and
aah, all in perfect delay.*

Hot Pimiento Cheese Dip

Makes about 2 cups

*If I've learned anything about Southern food writers and Southern chefs, it's this:
we each have our own take on this classic combination of cheese and pimientos.*

*And as I've said, you can tweak just about any dish into a Southern specialty
by adding Cheddar cheese and pimientos. Here's a good place to start. Serve with
corn chips or crackers.*

8 ounces (2 cups) shredded sharp Cheddar cheese
4 ounces cream cheese, cut into small chunks
¼ cup mayonnaise
1 jar (4 ounces) diced pimientos, drained
Spoonful of sugar
Dashes of hot pepper and Worcestershire sauces

Heat the oven to 350°F. Combine the Cheddar cheese, cream cheese, mayonnaise, pimientos, sugar, and hot and Worcestershire sauces in a small
glass baking dish. Bake 20 to 30 minutes or until bubbly and hot. Stir
once halfway through cooking.

Note: This can also be prepared in the microwave. Cover a microwave-safe baking dish and microwave at 50 percent power for 2 minutes.
Stir until well blended.

Uncle Jack the Man

Folks frequently ask me about my Uncle Jack. Jasper Newton Daniel was a runaway at age six, a distiller by age thirteen, and a remarkable innovator his whole life. By all accounts, he was a real character.

At six, with his mother passed away, nine siblings at home, and his father newly married, Jack left the family. I guess he just wasn't getting enough attention. Jack went to live with the Call family headed by a Lutheran minister and whiskey maker, Dan Call. Mr. Call taught Jack how to make whiskey and even made him a partner in the operation. Mr. Call eventually sold the whiskey business to Uncle Jack after deciding to devote more time to his ministry.

Jack moved the distillery to a good source of limestone water flowing from the cave spring in Lynchburg. The cold water ran at a constant 56 degrees and was free of good whiskey's worst enemy, iron. Jack Daniel was the first distiller to register his distillery during the early 1860s when the federal government instituted the regulation and taxation of whiskey.

Quite an astute businessman, Jack sold his whiskey to both sides during the Civil War, a risky proposition at the time. Just as we do today, he also remained committed to the extra step of charcoal mellowing when other whiskey makers opted for quicker, cheaper methods after the war. Charcoal mellowing made his whiskey more expensive but ensured its unique, smooth character, unique enough that the U.S. government specially designated it as "Tennessee Whiskey," not bourbon.

Uncle Jack was a small man, standing only five feet-two inches tall, but was hardheaded about making charcoal mellowed Tennessee whiskey. When other whiskey makers opted for round bottles, he chose square. Jack Daniel came to world attention at the 1904 St. Louis World's Fair and Centennial Exposition. He traveled to the fair by train and returned four days later with the World's Fair Gold Medal for the best whiskey in the world. This was the first of seven gold medals his Old No. 7 whiskey would earn.

The story goes that it was his temper that killed him. One day he had trouble with the combination on his office safe and, out of frustration, gave it a good swift kick. At first he only suffered a limp, but blood poisoning eventually set in, and six years later, on October 10, 1911, Jack Daniel died. He's buried in Lynchburg Cemetery on the hill just above the town square.

Because Uncle Jack never married, the distillery passed to his nephew, Lem Motlow. Lem was responsible for seeing the distillery through the difficult twenty-nine years of Federal and State Prohibition. When Prohibition ended in Tennessee, he reopened the distillery and revived the charcoal mellowing tradition.

Pickled Okra Party Shrimp

Makes about 8 servings

Frozen bags of cooked shrimp with shells and tails removed make this a snap to pull together. The Pickled Okra Party Shrimp look especially fun in a big glass crock or jar with a lid. The vinegary onions and lemon slices are good eating, and that tangy bite of hot pickled okra will provide a pleasant surprise. Fresh saltine crackers are the only way to deliver a bite of this appetizer.

> 1 pound cooked medium shrimp, shells and tails removed
> 1 medium onion, cut into very thin slices
> 2 medium lemons, very thinly sliced
> ½ cup vegetable oil
> ½ cup cider vinegar
> 2 teaspoons celery seeds
> 1 tablespoon mustard seeds
> 10 bay leaves
> 1 ½ cups sliced pickled okra (mild or spicy)
> Black pepper and salt, to taste
> Cayenne pepper, to taste

Combine the shrimp, onion, lemons, vegetable oil, vinegar, celery seeds, mustard seeds, bay leaves, pickled okra, black pepper, salt, and cayenne in a large glass jar with a lid or a bowl with a lid. Refrigerate overnight. The shrimp will keep in the refrigerator for two weeks, but I bet they won't last that long!

Peaches and Cream Country Ham Dip

Makes about 2 cups

If ever there was a top-ten list of the first words spoken by a Southern child, I bet "country ham" would be on it. Country ham tastes like nothing else. This easy dip takes advantage of its unctuousness, while the peach preserves soften its roughness. I particularly like to surround the dip with green complements such as crisp celery sticks, green apple slices, green grapes, and endive scoops. Choose straightforward Melba toast or water cracker.

8 ounces cream cheese
4 ounces (about ½ cup) diced cooked country ham
3 tablespoons peach preserves
¼ cup green onion slices
1 tablespoon Dijon mustard
¼ cup chopped unsalted, roasted peanuts or unsalted, toasted pecans

Combine the cream cheese, ham, preserves, onion, and mustard in the bowl of a food processor. Process until almost smooth. Spoon the dip into a serving dish and garnish with the nuts.

Green Butter Bean Dip

Makes about 2 ½ cups

This easy butter bean dip takes on a green hue thanks to a handful of fresh herbs. I use whatever's fresh from the garden. If you don't keep one, a big fresh bunch of parsley will do nicely. You'll want to keep a couple of cans of butter beans in the pantry just for this dip. Serve with toasted pita triangles, crackers, or fresh dipping vegetables.

2 cans (16 ounces each) butter beans, drained
1 cup mixed fresh herbs (like parsley, basil, oregano, and chives) stems removed, plus extra for garnish
1 clove garlic, crushed with the side of a knife blade and peeled
1 to 2 tablespoons cider vinegar
2 tablespoons olive oil, plus more for serving
Hot pepper sauce, to taste
Chopped red onion for garnish

Combine the butter beans, fresh herbs, garlic, vinegar, olive oil, and hot sauce in the bowl of a food processor. Process until smooth. Pour into a serving bowl and garnish with a drizzle of olive oil, chopped red onion, and the reserved herbs.

Honey Blue Cheese Spread

Makes about 2 cups

Our newest member of the Jack family, Jack Daniel's Tennessee Honey, is a wonderful ingredient full of kitchen potential. Its sweet flavors are absorbed by the golden raisins to create the gentle softening a sharp blue cheese needs. Serve this spread surrounded by crackers and sliced fresh pears, apples, and grapes.

1/3 cup golden raisins
2 tablespoons Jack Daniel's Tennessee Honey
8 ounces cream cheese, softened
4 ounces crumbled blue cheese
1/3 cup chopped toasted walnuts (black walnuts are great too)
1/4 cup green onion slices
Black pepper, to taste

Combine the raisins and the Tennessee Honey in a small bowl and let sit about 30 minutes. Add the cream cheese and the blue cheese to the bowl and blend well. Stir in the walnuts and green onions. Add pepper to taste.

Honey Jezebel Cheddar Spread

Makes about 2 1/2 cups

Jezebel sauce is that old Southern concoction of jam, horseradish, and black pepper. In the old days it was the hot pepper jelly alternative for slathering over a block of cream cheese to serve with crackers. Here's our updated version with a little more punch thanks to sharp Cheddar cheese and a little sweetness from Jack Daniel's Tennessee Honey.

8 ounces cream cheese, softened
2 cups (8 ounces) sharp Cheddar cheese
1/4 cup pineapple or apricot preserves
1/4 cup prepared horseradish
1 tablespoon Jack Daniel's Tennessee Honey
1 teaspoon dry mustard
1 teaspoon coarsely ground black pepper

Combine the cream cheese, Cheddar cheese, preserves, horseradish, Tennessee Honey, dry mustard, and black pepper in a medium bowl. Pack in a crock or bowl and serve with your favorite crackers.

Jack's Sweet Hot Party Pecans

Makes 4 cups

Every great cocktail can be accessorized with a well put-together snack. My party pecans are a nice little bit of everything—salty, sweet, savory, and spicy. I keep a bag or two in the freezer at all times for last-minute entertaining, hostess gifts, or grabbing a handful at about 5:00 p.m. Go ahead and double the recipe. And try different nuts like raw walnuts, peanuts, or almonds.

> 4 tablespoons butter (not margarine)
> 3 tablespoons sugar
> ¼ cup Jack Daniel's Tennessee Whiskey
> ½ teaspoon cayenne pepper, or to taste
> 1 ½ teaspoons salt
> ½ teaspoon garlic powder
> 4 cups (about 1 pound) pecan halves

Heat the oven to 325°F. Combine the butter, sugar, Jack Daniel's, cayenne, salt, and garlic powder in a large saucepan. Bring to a boil over medium heat, stirring to blend. Boil 2 to 3 minutes or until the mixture is slightly thickened and syrupy. Stir in the pecans and toss well to coat. Spread the nuts in a single layer in a foil-lined (to make cleanup easier) jelly-roll or roasting pan. Bake about 30 minutes or until the nuts are crisp and golden brown, stirring occasionally. Cool. Store in an airtight container.

Barbecue Peanuts

Makes 4 cups

These barbecue nuts are extra handy to pass on the patio when your guests are anxious for the ribs to be ready. The oils in nuts take to smoke as readily as chicken, beef, and pork. Coat any variety of nut or a mixture of nuts with this simple blend—all the same ingredients that make barbecue taste great. Look for bags of raw peanuts in the nut section of your supermarket.

1 egg white
3 tablespoons brown sugar
2 teaspoons Dry County Dry Rub (page 182)
1 teaspoon liquid smoke
¼ to ½ teaspoon cayenne pepper, or to taste
4 cups raw (unroasted) peanuts

Heat the oven to 325°F. Line a rimmed baking sheet with foil and spray with cooking spray. In a medium bowl whisk the egg white until frothy. Stir in the brown sugar, dry rub, smoke, and cayenne pepper. Add the peanuts and stir until well coated with the mixture. Spread the peanuts in a single layer on the baking sheet.

Roast 30 minutes, stirring once or twice during cooking, until the nuts are golden brown and fragrant. Loosen the nuts from the pan while hot. Let cool. Store in an airtight container.

Pumpkin Pie Honey Spiced Almonds

Makes 4 cups

The spicy autumn seasonings that make pumpkin pie taste like pumpkin pie are also a nice complement to peanuts. Here again this sweet and spicy mix is held together with an egg white, the secret for beautifully coated nuts. Pack them in canning jars with a ribbon or in decorative bags for an attractive, thoughtful hostess gift.

1 egg white
½ cup sugar
2 tablespoons Jack Daniel's Tennessee Honey
1 ½ teaspoons salt
1 teaspoon cinnamon
½ teaspoon ground ginger
¼ teaspoon cloves
¼ teaspoon nutmeg
4 cups whole almonds*

Heat the oven to 325° F. Line a rimmed baking sheet with foil and spray with cooking spray. Whisk the egg white in a medium bowl until frothy. Stir in the sugar, Tennessee Honey, salt, cinnamon, ginger, cloves, and nutmeg. Add the almonds and stir until well-coated with the mixture. Spread the nuts in a single layer on the baking sheet.

Roast 30 minutes, stirring once or twice during cooking, until the nuts are golden brown and fragrant. Loosen the nuts from the pan while hot. Let cool. Store in an airtight container.

*Substitute pecans or walnuts for a twist.

Bacon Grease Bruschetta

Having enjoyed delicious grilled crusty breads rubbed with garlic and drizzled with olive oil in wonderful Italian restaurants, it finally occurred to me to grill some bread right at home. Instead of a lovely fruity olive oil, we're lightly brushing our bread with the succulent fat native to our region—bacon grease. Bacon grease gives the toast a lovely hint of salty smokiness. It's especially delicious topped with fresh chopped tomatoes.

Crusty Italian or French bread, cut into ½-inch thick slices
Melted bacon grease
Whole cloves of peeled garlic
Toppings of your choice such as chopped fresh tomatoes, crispy bacon, cooked lima or white beans, and slivers of Parmesan cheese

Brush one side of the bread slices with bacon grease. Grill over medium heat just until golden brown, flip and grill the other side. Rub the garlic on the bacon-greased side of the toasts. Eat as is or top with your favorite toppings.

BREADS AND BRUNCH

History of the Bobo Hotel

Old No. 7 Cooking Tips

Hominy Brunch Scramble
Cornbread Crepes
Miss Mary's Mayo Rolls
Apple Crisp Coffeecake

The Easy Way to Make Grits

Cheese Grits Bake
Homemade Buttermilk Biscuits
Pan Drippings Gravy
Redeye Gravy
Hash Brown Potato Bake
Fish Fry Hushpuppies

Plan Your Visit to Miss Mary Bobo's Boarding House

Self-Rising Cornmeal Mix

Cast Iron Cornbread
Corn Light Bread
Fully Loaded Cornbread
Muffin Cup Ham Biscuits
Southern Spoon Rolls
Baked Ham and Cheese French Toast
Game Day Sweet Potato Muffins
Foolproof Oven Bacon
Butter Pecan Coffee Cake Muffins
Blueberry Buckle Skillet Cake

History of the Bobo Hotel

The front of Miss Mary Bobo's was added in the 1850s, but the very oldest part of the house dates back to the 1820s. In those days folks built their homes on top of a source of good water if they could. Even though we're on municipal water now, a natural spring continues to run under the back of the house after all these years. Talk about location, location, location!

Miss Mary and her husband, Jack, bought the building in 1908, and until her death in 1983, just shy of the age of 102, Miss Mary boarded and fed her guests. Until a hip injury slowed Miss Mary down at age 98, she had actively managed her boarding house—supervising cooks, servers, and gardeners, buying groceries, paying bills, and greeting her guests at the front door.

Most of Miss Mary's boarders were single schoolteachers, traveling salesmen, and the United States tax revenue agents who were assigned to the distillery. Confirmed bachelor and bank president Tom Motlow (brother of Lem Motlow who inherited the distillery from Uncle Jack) lived in the boarding house until his death at age ninety-six. The gregarious leg-puller Roger Brashears who managed the distillery Visitor Center for years and is still Lynchburg's most colorful storyteller lived in the Boarding House during his younger days in the late 1960s and early 1970s. He laughs when he tells how he weighed 182 pounds when he moved into Miss Mary's and 287 pounds when he moved out—just six years later!

Mary Ruth Hall, a Moore County extension home economist, was also a boarder. In 1949 she moved to Lynchburg and paid $12.50 a week for room, board, and three meals a day. This amounted to one-fourth of her salary, and she had what was considered a good government job right after the war. In her retirement years Miss Mary Ruth was a popular table hostess at Miss Mary's.

And then there is Leola Dismukes, my second mother. Dill, or Dee Dee as we called her, took care of my brother, Jimmy Lee, and me when we were children. Later on, she cooked for Miss Mary for about twenty-five years beginning in the mid 1960s. I guess after Lee and I moved away to school, Dee needed new mouths to feed. She was our most beloved family friend.

When Miss Mary passed away, her children were in their seventies and not interested in running the property. When the house went for sale, folks in town were concerned that the Boarding House would close or, worse, be torn down. Thankfully, the distillery purchased Miss Mary's from her children and preserved its place in our rich history. I was hired to take over as proprietress, and we reopened on May 1, 1984. We've been busy serving noonday dinner ever since. I figure I'll last until I reach 102 since I'm eating the same food every day as Miss Mary did.

In 2006 we completed a two-year renovation and expansion of Miss Mary's because we simply hate to turn folks away who want to join us for dinner. The project included a renovation of our original buildings plus an expansion that grew us from seating for sixty in five dining rooms to ninety in eight dining rooms, plus a new kitchen, a new retail store, a meeting room, an elevator, and new entrances and restrooms.

We were careful to keep the workmanship and materials straightforward and simple so as to be consistent with the age and character of the house. You won't see anything too fancy or new looking. Many of the original details have been repeated throughout the work, like the wood cased columns, the handrails, the wooden porch, the ceiling, and brick pavers.

Some changes you can't see, but they are just as important. As you can imagine, a nearly 150-year-old building had a few surprises for the construction crew. For example, the existing brick and wood-sided structures were originally built directly on the dirt with no supporting foundation. I guess no one had thought up a building codes department yet! So, when digging out a pit for the new elevator, our guys had to slowly dig by hand and gently remove little bits of dirt so as not to disturb the structure. Also, because of years of settling, many of the floors and ceilings and some walls were less than level, shall we say. Our goal has been to make minor adjustments to stabilize the building without trying to make things "perfect."

Here's a little bit about each of our dining rooms.

Right Parlor

Left Parlor

Front Hall

The Jasper Room:

Jasper Newton Daniel, or Jack as he's better known, surely deserves a room given his reputation as the county's most gracious host. In fact, Mr. Jack took his noonday meal in this building around the turn of the twentieth century, when the Salmon Hotel was owned by Dr. E.Y. Salmon.

The Tolley Room:

This one may have a little something to do with me, but I'm not the only Tolley in the Lynchburg clan. My uncle Lem Tolley was the son of one of Mr. Jack's nieces and Jack Daniel's third Master Distiller (1941-1964). Uncle Lem's legacy lives on today through two of his great-grandsons, Dusty Dickey who works at the distillery as a guide during the summers, and Chris Dickey who runs our kitchen right here at Miss Mary's.

The Evans Room:

Before Miss Mary became a Bobo, she was an Evans. Her sister, Miss Ophelia Evans (later the wife of Lem Motlow, inheritor of the distillery from Uncle Jack in 1907), was Miss Mary's daily telephone chatter partner. They lived across town from each other, so the daily telephone visit was a handy way for them to keep up with the goings-on.

The Motlow Room:

Jack Daniel's Tennessee Whiskey owes a debt of gratitude to the Motlows. Lem Motlow kept our company going despite the twenty-nine years of National Prohibition. He even became a state-level politician to help get the distillery reopened in Lynchburg. Lem left the distillery to his four sons Reagor, Hap, Robert, and Conner Motlow, and daughter Mary Avon Motlow Boyd who ran things until they sold it to Brown-Forman in Louisville, Kentucky, in 1956.

The Crutcher Room:

Named after Miss Mary's only daughter Louise and her husband, Mr. Ervin Crutcher, the Crutchers were frequent guests of Miss Mary's since they lived right next door. Mr. Ervin was in charge of construction at the distillery for years and by all accounts a model son-in-law.

He built his bride a home on a patch of land given to them by Miss Mary and her husband, Jack.

The Parks Room:
Mr. Will Parks was one of Miss Mary's boarders and the owner of the Ford dealership in town. The story goes that Mr. Will didn't get along too well with Miss Mary's longest boarder, Mr. Tom Motlow, president of the local Farmer's Bank. Mr. Tom did not believe in going into debt to purchase an automobile, so he wouldn't loan money for a car. This must have put Miss Mary's creative hostessing skills to the test—all those years!

Tolley

The Fanning Room:
There are more than a few Fannings in Lynchburg, but there's only one Mr. Herb Fanning. Lem Motlow hired Herby in the 1940s following stints as a Depression-era hobo and baseball shortstop. To this day, Herby has appeared in more Jack Daniel's advertisements than anyone else. A beautiful bronze statue of him sits in front of the Lynchburg Hardware and General Store on the square where he enjoyed whittling, challenging friends at checkers, and entertaining everyone with stories.

Evans

The Roundtree Room:
This room honors the architect of not only Miss Mary Bobo's but also the town of Lynchburg as well. Mr. Thomas Roundtree lived in a log house on this site in 1818 when he laid out the town, and later he was the first to obtain a license to open a tavern here. In the 1850s he built the front section of Miss Mary's for Dr. Salmon and his wife who had ten children. When the children grew up and left home, Dr. Salmon turned the empty rooms into a boarding house back in Uncle Jack's time.

Fanning

Old No. 7 Cooking Tips

Common Ingredients

Grits

    Grits are simply coarsely ground corn cooked in water until creamy and soft. You'll most often find them ground from white corn, but yellow is also available. We like them best for breakfast with plenty of salt, pepper, and butter. Their versatile mild flavor makes them easy to pair and combine with all kinds of foods like cheeses, vegetables, and meats.

Self-Rising Flour and Self-Rising Cornmeal Mix

    These have been regular grocery store items in the South since the days when Southerners baked every day. These wonderful inventions make life easier because the salt and leavening are premixed with flour and cornmeal in the correct amounts for biscuits and cornbread. We also use the flour and cornmeal for anything that requires salt, like dredging meats, fish, and vegetables for frying.

Cornmeal

    In Tennessee we prefer white cornmeal ground from white corn. If you can't find self-rising cornmeal mix, blend 1 7/8 cups plain cornmeal (preferably white), 2 tablespoons all-purpose flour, 1 tablespoon baking powder, and 1/2 teaspoon salt.

Self-Rising Four

    Self-rising flour is all-purpose flour with added leavening and salt. To use all-purpose flour in a recipe that calls for self-rising, add 1 1/2 teaspoons baking powder and 1/4 teaspoon of salt per cup of flour.

Cooking with Cured Pork

Pork fat and cured pork products have been flavoring Southern foods for generations. Once it was all we had; now we know it just tastes good. In addition to keeping bacon drippings in a jar in the refrigerator (which I strongly recommend), here are the other kinds of cured pork cuts we often use.

Hog Jowl

Hog jowl is the cheek meat of the hog, and it's most often smoked, cured, and sliced thicker than bacon. Hog jowl packs plenty of fat and flavor. My mother prefers it to bacon when flavoring her beans and vegetables, and she even fries it for breakfast and serves it like bacon.

Sidemeat

Similar to hog jowl, side meat comes from the flank of the pig. It's smoked, cured, sliced, and sold as bacon. Packages labeled side meat are fattier, thick-sliced bacon used for seasoning.

Fat Back

Also known as salt pork, fat back comes from the side and belly fat of the pig. Fat back is salt cured but not smoked. Like all of the above, we use it to season soups, beans, and vegetables.

Ham Hocks

These are the ankle joints of the pig. They're available fresh, smoked, or cured. Add ham hocks to any slow cooked dish like greens, beans, and soups.

Cracklings

These are bits of fried pork skin. Around here they're sold already fried in small packages ready to add to cornbread batter for delicious cracklin' cornbread.

City Ham/Country Ham

Country ham is salted and dry cured for months and very typical of the South. It has a salty, rich meaty flavor and a dry texture. City ham is the everyday grocery store wet-cured variety. It's moist and less flavorful than country ham. Country ham is the only ham to use when adding a little rich flavor to foods like a pot of beans or greens.

Hambones

A good country hambone is ideal for flavoring all kinds of beans and greens. With all the country ham we serve in December, you can

imagine the hambones we have stockpiled in our freezers for winter pots of beans and greens. Just one of the many perks of the job! If you don't have a hambone handy, buy a little package of country ham scraps at the supermarket.

Iron Skillet Seasoning

Few utensils are as important in the Southern kitchen as a good cast iron skillet for frying meats and developing the all-important crispy cornbread crust. Cast iron requires regular but simple care to develop its natural non-stick finish.

Here's how to make and keep a slick skillet. Clean your new, un-seasoned, or rusty cast iron cookware with soapy hot water and a stiff brush. Sometimes I use steel wool if the pan is quite rusty. Dry the pan completely over a low heat on the stove. Spread a thin layer of vegetable oil or shortening on all cooking surfaces. Heat the cookware upside down in the oven at 350°F for about an hour. Place a sheet of foil on the rack below to keep the oven clean. Always clean your seasoned cast iron with hot water and a brush, never with soap or harsh detergent (and never in the dishwasher). Always dry it thoroughly after each use to prevent rust. As a long range rust preventative, fry as much bacon, sausage, and chicken as you can in your cast iron. Your cornbread will never stick.

The Business of Frying

Many folks' exposure to fried foods is only at restaurants. With a little care and attention, home frying is easy and fun now and again. The goal is to use enough hot fat, such as oil, lard, or shortening to quickly crisp the outside and cook the food throughout. Use plenty to cover the food completely. Be sure the fat is hot, about 365°F on a deep-fry thermometer.

If the fat is too hot, the food will burn on the outside and remain raw on the inside. If the fat is too cool, the food will be greasy, tough, and bland. Always fry foods in small batches in evenly cut pieces that have been thoroughly thawed and patted dry. Lower the pieces gently into the fat. Have a bowl or platter lined with paper towels ready for the hot cooked food. Let the hot fat fully cool before discarding.

Casserole Culture

At Miss Mary's we tend to bake lots of our vegetable dishes and desserts in convenient 9 x 13-inch baking dishes and pans. They are so easy to use. Steaming pans of creamy squash, broccoli, or cabbage casserole, fruit cobblers, sheet cakes, and even congealed salads became ingrained in our culture generations ago when much of small town socializing at church suppers, community meetings, and family gatherings required dishes to share. The 9 x 13-inch pan remains a kitchen essential when cooking for a crowd and can ensure plenty of delicious leftovers when cooking for more than one meal.

Beans

With nearly two dozen varieties of inexpensive, nutritious peas and beans available, our tables are seldom without one kind or another served as a side, a salad, a soup, or even as a main dish. White beans, pintos, and black-eyed peas top our list. We also cook a wide variety of limas and pea family members such as crowders, lady, speckled butter beans, and field peas. Whether fresh, frozen, or dried, we cook them all the same—in a big pot simmered and flavored with cured pork, the other vital Southern ingredient.

Pimientos in the Pantry

Back in the days before beautiful fresh red bell peppers were available year round, jarred pimientos became the pantry staple for cooks looking to add a little color to casseroles and salads. In spite of the modern pepper proliferation, pimientos have earned a permanent place in the Southern pantry. Thank goodness for the genius who combined the little red bits with shredded Cheddar cheese and mayonnaise for our traditional Southern sandwich spread—pimiento cheese.

The Tolley Chicken Broth Diet

I've found that a little calorie cutting is a much needed step when returning from traveling and indulging in rich meals. I've come up with a little diet of my own to put me back on track, and the key is chicken broth. We poach more than a few chickens for Miss Mary's Chicken and Pastry, so our freezers are teeming with broth. At home, we heat up the rich broth with cooked rice for a light but filling supper.

Watercress Out Back

A healthy crop of watercress grows on the banks of the little creek that meanders just behind Miss Mary's. I love it simply dressed with olive oil, a squeeze of lemon juice, and a sprinkling of salt. Its peppery crunch and tangy lemon flavor make a perfect bed for gelatin salads or for a pile of freshly fried catfish nuggets.

Tennessee Tomatoes

We have fabulous fresh tomatoes and a long growing season in Middle Tennessee thanks to the mild weather and the limey soil. The Bradley variety is the crown jewel that has a pinkish skin and sweet flavor. Often we're still eating fresh ripe tomatoes all the way to Halloween! Then it's time to get the remaining green tomatoes into the skillet.

Peppers, Onions, and Celery

You'll notice that many of our recipes are flavored with these simple vegetables, sometimes cooked, sometimes raw. Called the Holy Trinity in Louisiana cooking, I expect country cooks around here use them for the same reason. They give dishes an extra depth of flavor, and thankfully they are available year-round.

Hominy Brunch Scramble

Makes 4 servings

I love the rich corn flavor hominy adds to dishes. I'm also a Sunday brunch fan where an egg scramble lets me fold in just about anything that strikes my fancy (including any interesting leftovers). A can of hominy combined with a little cheese adds a lot of body to this simple scramble with bell pepper and onion. Swap the bell pepper for fresh or frozen spinach, but remember to squeeze the water out first.

> 2 tablespoons butter
> 1 small onion, chopped
> 1 small green bell pepper, chopped
> 1 can (15.5 ounces) white or yellow hominy, drained and rinsed
> 8 eggs, beaten
> ½ to 1 cup shredded sharp Cheddar cheese
> Salt and black pepper to taste

Place the butter in a large skillet over medium-high heat. Add the onion and green bell pepper and cook until the vegetables are soft, 7 to 8 minutes. Stir in the hominy and cook until it has warmed through, 1 to 2 minutes. Reduce the heat to medium. Pour in the eggs and cheese and season with salt and pepper. Cook and stir until the eggs are set.

Cornbread Crepes

Makes about 6 crepes

The word crepe may scare you off from attempting this dish. It shouldn't. All we're doing is making very thin cornbread pancakes that can be filled with all kinds of goodies. Treat them like cornbread omelets and fill them with ham, cheese, and chopped fresh vegetables. Or use them as a fancy foundation for chili or barbecue. All you really need is a good nonstick skillet, and the crepes will slide right out of the pan. The batter should have the consistency of thick cream or thin pancake batter.

> 4 eggs
> 1 ½ cups milk
> ¼ cup vegetable oil
> 1 cup self-rising cornmeal mix

Whisk the eggs and milk together in a medium mixing bowl. Whisk in the oil and cornmeal and mix until smooth. Let the batter sit for about 15 minutes. Heat a 12-inch nonstick skillet over medium heat. Lightly coat the bottom with oil or nonstick cooking spray. Add about ¼ to ⅓ cup of batter to the skillet. Immediately swirl the skillet to completely coat the bottom with the batter. Cook until the bottom side is golden brown. The top will be moist but cooked through and no longer runny. Loosen the edge with a rubber spatula and flip out onto a plate. Repeat with the remaining batter. Place the cooked crepes on a platter and cover with a towel to keep warm. Fill as desired.

Miss Mary's Mayo Rolls

Makes 12 rolls

My cousin Chris Dickey, our head cook at Miss Mary's, introduced his Mayo Rolls to our tables when he took the reins of the kitchen, and they have caught on like wildfire. So much so that Mayo Rolls may top the "most requested recipe" list.

Using mayonnaise instead of the usual shortening or butter became popular in the 1940s. I remember when folks in town were all making a mayo chocolate cake. Use just milk, or you can do what Chris prefers and substitute half buttermilk. If you like these, try the Muffin Cup Ham Biscuits on page 83.

2 cups self-rising flour

2 tablespoons sugar

Pinch of salt

1/3 cup mayonnaise

1 cup milk (or ½ cup buttermilk and ½ cup milk)

Heat the oven to 350°F. Grease a 12-cup muffin pan. Combine the flour, sugar, and salt in a medium mixing bowl. Stir in the mayonnaise and milk until a very soft dough forms. Spoon evenly into the muffin cups. Bake 15 to 20 minutes or until golden brown.

Variation: For mini muffins, grease 24 mini-muffin cups and bake them about 10 minutes.

Apple Crisp Coffeecake

Makes 16 to 20 servings

No matter how they take their coffee, family and guests will insist on seconds of this rich cake that's just as popular at breakfast and brunch as it is for an afternoon indulgence or late night snack. Make this coffeecake once and I guarantee this page will be dog-eared for all time. My mother insists on tossing in a handful of chopped fresh cranberries with the apples.

Crisp Topping

1 cup chopped pecans

¾ cup all-purpose flour

¾ cup brown sugar

½ cup (1 stick) butter, melted

½ teaspoon cinnamon

¼ teaspoon salt

Cake

2 cups self-rising flour

1 ½ cups sugar

½ cup (1 stick) butter, melted

1 cup sour cream

3 eggs, beaten

2 teaspoons vanilla

2 Granny Smith or Golden Delicious apples, peeled, cored, and diced

Heat the oven to 350°F. Grease a 9 x 13-inch baking pan.

To make the crisp topping: Add the chopped pecans, flour, brown sugar, melted butter, cinnamon, and salt to a mixing bowl and combine with a fork until crumbly. Set aside.

To make the cake: Combine the flour and sugar in a large mixing bowl. Blend well. Stir in the butter, sour cream, and eggs until smooth. Add the vanilla. Pour the mixture into the greased pan. Sprinkle with the apples and the crisp topping. Bake 30 to 45 minutes or until a toothpick inserted in the center comes out clean. Serve warm or at room temperature.

The Easy Way to Make Grits

You'll probably find the usual quick-cooking grits in your grocery store near the oatmeal. Quick grits are degerminated, fortified, rather bland, and as the label says, quick to cook. They work fine in all kinds of applications, and I like them just fine. However, if you can find a bag of stone-ground grits (you can order them online), don't pass up the chance to try them. They have triple the corn flavor, so much so that you won't believe the difference. And they take about an hour to cook, well worth the extra time.

My trick for making either stone-ground or quick-cooking grits without tending to the pot is to load them up in a slow cooker. That way I don't have to fret about them sticking to the pan or, worse, boiling over. Cook them on high an hour or two or three. Or you can cook them on low overnight. Add plenty of water, probably a cup or two more than called for. It doesn't matter. You cannot overcook grits. The corn never breaks down into mush like rice. Start them early Sunday morning when you put your coffee on, check the water and stir occasionally before you head for church, and they'll be ready when you are.

Cheese Grits Bake

Makes 10 servings

Many of the folks who visit Miss Mary's have never had the opportunity to try good Southern grits. The mere mention of this strange sounding word elicits jeers or fears from the uninitiated. Grits are nothing more than coarsely ground corn cooked in liquid and seasoned.

A good cheese grits casserole is as versatile as macaroni and cheese or potatoes au gratin. We love them for breakfast or dinner. Though the homely name often confines grits to country cooking, they can be quite sophisticated. Experiment with other good cheeses like Swiss, goat, or Parmesan and always add plenty of butter. Try serving these on the side with the Tennessee Barbecue Shrimp (page 158). Now you'll have your own style of shrimp and grits!

4 cups water
1 teaspoon salt
1 cup quick-cooking grits
¼ cup (½ stick) butter
2 ½ cups grated Cheddar cheese, divided
4 eggs, beaten
1 cup milk
1 clove garlic, minced
1 tablespoon Worcestershire sauce
Dash of hot pepper sauce

Heat the oven to 350°F. Grease a 9 x 13-inch baking dish. Combine the water and salt in a large saucepan. Bring to a boil. Stir in the grits. Reduce the heat to low, cover, and cook until thickened, about 5 minutes. Remove from the heat and stir in the butter and 2 cups of the cheese until melted. Stir in the eggs, milk, garlic, Worcestershire sauce, and hot pepper sauce. Pour into the greased baking dish. Sprinkle with the remaining ½ cup of cheese. Bake 45 minutes or until golden brown.

Homemade Buttermilk Biscuits

Makes about 12 biscuits

Good biscuits are best when the dough is not handled too much. By that I mean just enough kneading for the dough to hold together and to ensure nice flakey layers. I roll out my biscuits quite thin, about ½-inch thick if I'm planning to make country ham biscuits. Big fluffy biscuits may be more to your liking for breakfast. Roll those out about ¾-inch thick. Make them with any size cutter you like, or cut the dough into rough squares. I prefer tiny, two-bite biscuits to serve with cocktails.

⅓ cup lard or vegetable shortening
2 cups self-rising flour
1 cup buttermilk
Melted butter

Heat the oven to 450°F. Cut the shortening into the flour with a pastry blender or two knives until the mixture looks like coarse crumbs. Add the buttermilk and stir just until a soft dough forms. Turn the dough out onto a lightly floured board or pastry cloth. Knead gently just until

smooth, about 10 times. Roll or pat out the dough with your fingers to about ½ to ¾-inch thickness. Cut into rounds with a floured (2-inch) biscuit cutter. Place on a baking sheet. Bake 10 to 12 minutes or until golden brown. Rub the melted butter on the tops right when they come out of the oven.

Pan Drippings Gravy

Makes 2 to 3 cups

Whenever meat is frying in a Southern skillet, chances are a gravy will be made in the drippings and biscuits will already be in the oven. Whether it's pork chops, steak, chicken, sausage (or even squirrel), our skillet gravies are as important to country cooking as the Mother sauces are to French cuisine. The rule to remember is to use equal parts pan drippings to flour. The amount of liquid used depends on how thick you like your gravy. I use milk for sausage gravy and a combination of milk and broth for chicken gravy. Red Eye gravy made with country ham drippings isn't thickened at all. We prefer all water, but some folks I know add a little black coffee.

¼ cup pan drippings and browned bits from frying meat or chicken
¼ cup all-purpose flour
2 to 3 cups liquid (milk or broth)
Salt and black pepper, to taste

Pour the pan drippings into a skillet. Whisk in the flour with a fork to blend well. Cook over medium heat for about 1 minute. Gradually stir in the liquid. Bring the mixture to a boil, whisking constantly. Cook until thickened, about 2 to 3 minutes. Season with salt and pepper.

Redeye Gravy

Makes 1 ½ cups

Drippings from frying country ham
About 1 ½ cups water
Pinch of sugar

Remove the country ham from the skillet, add water to the skillet, and scrape up the browned bits from the bottom. Add a pinch of sugar. It's supposed to be thin and watery. Some folks add a little coffee at this point.

Heard around the TABLE

I was bragging at the table that adding a little Jack improves everything. We've never added it to anything yet that it hasn't made better. A man at my table said he agreed 100 percent. "Have you ever tried it on your cereal?" A man across the table said he'd never tried that but he had brushed his teeth with it a few times. An eighty-year-old woman chimed in that it would be good on oatmeal with a little brown sugar.

*A Swiss boy thought
sausage biscuits were
hamburgers.*

Hash Brown Potato Bake

Makes about 12 servings

Many of our guests request this simple potato bake recipe. Frozen hash browns and canned soup may not sound fancy, but you can't argue with the results. Whether it's dinner party-fancy, weeknight supper, or Sunday brunch, creamy, cheese potatoes are a great side to any chicken, red meat, or pork dish. For a little color stir in a small jar of pimientos. You can turn this into a main dish by adding chopped baked ham, country ham, cooked and crumbled pork sausage, Italian sausage, or Kielbasa. Cooked spinach, sautéed red and green peppers, and even a handful of corn kernels are colorful easy add-ins.

1 medium onion, chopped
$\frac{1}{2}$ cup (1 stick) butter
1 bag (30 ounces) frozen hash brown potatoes, thawed
1 $\frac{1}{2}$ cups sour cream
2 cups (8 ounces) grated sharp Cheddar cheese
1 can (10 $\frac{3}{4}$ ounces) condensed cream of mushroom soup
Fresh parsley, for garnish

Heat the oven to 350°F. Grease a 9 x 13-inch baking dish. Cook the onion in the butter in a skillet over medium heat until tender, 7 to 8 minutes. Combine the hash brown potatoes, sour cream, Cheddar cheese, and mushroom soup in a large mixing bowl and blend well. Stir in the onions and butter. Pour the mixture into the greased baking dish. Bake about 1 hour or until golden brown and hot. Garnish with a sprinkling of fresh parsley.

Variations:

Pimiento Cheese—Add a jar of drained, chopped pimientos
Green chile—Add a can or two of chopped green chiles
Sausage—Add a pound of cooked and crumbled country sausage
Ham—Add a couple of cups of chopped cooked ham

Fish Fry Hushpuppies

Makes about 20 hushpuppies

Why anyone would take the time to fry fish without making a side of hushpuppies is beyond me. A good hushpuppy is always deep golden brown, crisp, light in the center, and never greasy. Here we break our own rule against sugar in cornbread by adding just a little brown sugar to the batter. Hushpuppies are best eaten right out of the fryer. Cold ones are only fit for the dogs! In fact, country lore suggests that small balls of dough were fed to the dogs to keep them from begging when other dishes were being prepared in the kitchen.

2 cups self-rising cornmeal mix
2 tablespoons self-rising flour
2 tablespoons brown sugar
2 tablespoons finely chopped onion
2 tablespoons finely chopped green bell pepper
1 cup milk
2 eggs, beaten
Vegetable oil for frying

Combine the cornmeal, flour, sugar, onion, and green pepper in a medium mixing bowl. Stir in the milk and eggs and blend well. Set aside for 5 minutes; do not stir. Pour about 3 inches of vegetable oil into a Dutch oven and heat to 365°F. Drop the dough by heaping teaspoonfuls into the hot oil. Fry until golden brown, 3 to 5 minutes, and drain on paper towels.

Heard around the TABLE

When I explained to my table how hard it is to get reservations sometimes, a funny gentleman from Rhode Island asked if anyone ever "scalped" reservations. He observed that he could have easily made some money by selling his seat to some folks on the front porch who were hoping for no-shows.

Plan Your Visit to Miss Mary Bobo's Boarding House

In Lynchburg and throughout the South we call the midday meal "dinner," not lunch, and in the evening we sit down to "supper." Just as in Uncle Jack's day, we serve family-style dinner in our boarding-house dining rooms from Monday through Saturday.

Reservations are essential, so most folks call us well in advance of their visit. We certainly do not want to have to turn you away (and will try very hard not to), so please call ahead. Add us to your address book and follow us on Facebook to keep up with the Lynchburg goings-on.

Miss Mary Bobo's Boarding House
Lynchburg, Tennessee, USA 37352
(931) 759-7394
We are closed on Sunday and all major holidays.

Self-Rising Cornmeal Mix

Self-rising cornmeal mix is a wonderful, premixed, everyday pantry staple here in Lynchburg and across the South. If you can't find it (I recommend you look), use 1 ¾ cups plain white or yellow cornmeal blended with ¼ cup all-purpose flour, 1 tablespoon of baking powder, and ½ teaspoon salt.

Once you master the basic cornbread recipe, try adding one or more of these ingredients:

1 cup shredded Cheddar or Jack cheese
½ cup crumbled bacon, pork cracklings, or diced country ham
1 cup crumbled cooked sausage
1 small can or two of chopped green chiles
A small can of cream-style corn
½ cup sautéed onions and diced green bell peppers
½ cup sugar (Don't even think about it!)

Cast Iron Cornbread

Makes about 8 servings

Southern cornbread is all about developing a golden brown crust. Good cornbread is crisp on the outside and moist, never dry, on the inside. Anyone who doesn't like cornbread has only been served bad cornbread, plain and simple. For our Southern cornbread, we always use white self-rising cornmeal mix (a wonderful Southern product that is mostly cornmeal with just a touch of flour and the perfect amount of leavening). We don't add sugar. We do add buttermilk for its characteristic tang and moisture-enhancing properties, although regular milk works too.

Use any size cast iron skillet you like, but my mother and I like cornbread best when made in a large skillet so the bread is thin and crusty. If you don't have a good cast iron skillet, it's time to get one and season it with lots of bacon frying. Flip the cornbread out of the pan onto a cutting board and serve it crusty brown-side up. You can use this same recipe for griddle corn cakes, muffins, or corn sticks. Keep leftovers in the freezer and you're ready to make Real Southern Cornbread Dressing (page 114) any time.

1 egg
¼ cup bacon drippings or vegetable oil
2 cups self-rising cornmeal mix
About 1 ⅓ cups milk or 1 ⅔ cups buttermilk

Heat the oven to 450°F. Grease a 9-, 10-, or 12-inch cast iron skillet and place it in the oven to get it good and hot. Combine the egg and oil in a medium mixing bowl and blend well. Stir in the cornmeal mix and milk until smooth and creamy. The batter should be pourable like pancake batter. If it seems a little thick, add a little more milk or water. Carefully pour the batter into the hot skillet and bake until the crust is golden brown. The 9-inch skillet will take about 20 to 25 minutes to bake, the large skillet will take about 15 to 18 minutes to bake, and the medium skillet will take somewhere in between.

Corn Light Bread

Makes one loaf or about 10 servings

Corn Light Bread is the one big exception to the established rule that Southerner's don't care for sugar in their cornbread. This dense loaf of sweet cornbread is a favorite barbecue side indigenous to Middle Tennessee that I don't see anywhere else. The sweetness works in this cornbread because it can hold its own next to sweet/tangy barbecue sauces and smoky meats. It also has a sturdy texture that's easy to eat.

2 cups self-rising cornmeal mix
1 cup self-rising flour
½ cup sugar
1 large egg, beaten
1 ½ cups buttermilk
½ cup vegetable oil

Heat the oven to 375°F. Grease a 9 x 5 x 3-inch loaf pan. Stir the cornmeal, flour, and sugar together in a large mixing bowl. Add the egg, buttermilk, and oil. Stir until well blended. The batter should be creamy and pourable. If it seems too thick, add a shot of water. Pour the batter into the loaf pan. Bake 45 minutes, until golden brown. Cool about 5 to 10 minutes in the pan. Remove from the pan and cool on a wire rack. Store wrapped tightly in foil.

Fully Loaded Cornbread

Makes 16 servings

I call this the carrot cake of cornbread because of its consistently moist texture and crowd appeal even at room temperature. You can take it to a potluck or lay it out on a sideboard without the slightest worry. It will surely be gone. Use as many jalapenos as your folks can take. You never know how hot your particular jalapenos will be, so try a tiny taste first. Sometimes a jalapeno is burning hot; other times they don't even offer the slightest buzz of heat.

1 can (14 3/4 ounces) cream-style corn
1 1/2 cups buttermilk
1 large egg
1/3 cup vegetable oil
3 cups self-rising cornmeal mix
2 cups shredded sharp Cheddar cheese
1 can chopped green chiles
3 fresh jalapeno peppers, seeded and finely diced

Heat the oven to 400°F. Grease a 9 x 13-inch baking pan. Stir together the corn, buttermilk, egg, and oil in a large mixing bowl. Stir in the cornmeal until well blended. Stir in the cheese, chiles, and jalapenos. Pour the batter into the prepared pan. Bake 30 to 35 minutes or until golden brown.

Muffin Cup Ham Biscuits

Makes 12 regular size or 24 mini muffins

Debbie Baxter, my assistant manager at Miss Mary's, regularly stirs up batches of these muffin/biscuits for a big weekend breakfast. Debbie loves that they're easier than rolled-out biscuits, plus they have terrific country ham flavor. Instead of ham, make them with a pound of cooked and crumbled pork sausage. There's nothing better with a pot of stone-ground grits and fried eggs.

These muffins reheat so well that Debbie keeps some in the freezer for a quick weekday breakfast. Mayonnaise replaces the usual shortening and creates a cake-like texture and rich flavor. When I have a cocktail party in Nashville, my city friends love a mini cocktail version of these with their splash of Jack.

2 cups self-rising flour
1 cup milk
½ cup mayonnaise
2 cups chopped country ham

Heat the oven to 425°F. Grease 12 regular or 24 mini muffin cups. Combine the flour, milk, mayonnaise, and country ham in a large mixing bowl. Stir with a fork to make a soft dough. Drop by spoonfuls into the greased muffin cups. Bake until golden brown, about 15 minutes for regular or 8 to 10 minutes for mini muffins.

Southern Spoon Rolls

Makes about 24 rolls

I once brought Mother a dozen authentic bagels from New York City. She gave them a good try but declared bagels much too chewy and cold for her. The bread tradition of the South has long been soft and white. We serve these soft yeast rolls at Miss Mary's whenever cornbread or biscuits don't already have a place at the table.

1 package active dry yeast
2 cups warm water
½ cup sugar
½ cup (1 stick butter), melted plus extra for coating
1 egg, beaten
4 cups self-rising flour

Grease 24 muffin cups. Combine the yeast and warm water in a large mixing bowl and stir until the yeast has dissolved. Stir in the sugar, butter, and egg and blend well. Add the flour, stirring vigorously until a soft dough forms, about 2 minutes. At this point you can cover and refrigerate the dough overnight and then bake the rolls the next day. Or loosely cover the mixing bowl and let the dough rest on the countertop for about 20 minutes.

Heat the oven to 400°F. Fill the muffin cups evenly, about ½ full. Bake for 15 to 20 minutes or until golden brown. Brush the hot rolls with additional melted butter and serve immediately.

Baked Ham and Cheese French Toast

Makes 6 servings

Brunch gatherings are a relaxed way to visit with friends when you want to entertain but are not up for a fancy dinner party. And brunch dishes are more often than not make-ahead so you can really enjoy your party too.

You'll not attend a proper brunch anywhere in the South and not find a cheese grits casserole and an eggy overnight strata on the sideboard. All that's needed to complete the menu is a basket of muffins or biscuits and a platter of fresh fruit. For drinks, try a round of Honey Milk Punch *(page 21) laced with Jack Daniel's.*

16 slices (about ½-inch thick) French bread
2 to 3 tablespoons softened butter
6 ounces Cheddar or Swiss cheese, sliced into 14 pieces
4 to 6 ounces thinly sliced ham, cut into 14 thin pieces
5 eggs
2 cups milk
Pinch of salt

Butter an 8 x 8-inch (2 quart) casserole dish. Lightly butter one side of the bread slices. Arrange the bread slices like fallen dominos in 2 rows of 8 in the casserole, Place a slice of cheese and ham between the bread slices. In a medium bowl whisk together the eggs, milk, and salt. Pour the mixture over the bread. Cover tightly with plastic wrap and press down on the bread to help keep it submerged. Refrigerate overnight (or at least a couple hours). Heat the oven to 350°F. Bake about 1 hour or until puffy and golden brown.

Game Day Sweet Potato Muffins

Makes 12 regular or 24 mini muffins

Some of the most elaborate cooking I've ever seen has been performed in crowded parking lots on game day. When it's my turn, I go for finger foods, good sandwiches, and a crock of steaming soup, all things I can prepare ahead.

These moist mini sweet potato or pumpkin muffins are an annual fall tailgate favorite that pack and travel exceptionally well. Add a drop or two of Jack Daniel's to the batter for fun.

1 ½ cups self-rising flour
¾ cup plus 2 tablespoons sugar
1 teaspoon cinnamon
¼ teaspoon nutmeg
¼ teaspoon ginger
1/3 cup oil
2 eggs, beaten
2 tablespoons Jack Daniel's Tennessee Whiskey, optional
1 cup mashed cooked sweet potato or pumpkin puree
½ cup chopped toasted pecans

Heat the oven to 375°F. Grease 12 muffin cups or 24 mini muffin cups. Combine the flour, ¾ cup of sugar, cinnamon, nutmeg, and ginger in a large mixing bowl and blend well. Stir in the oil, eggs, Jack Daniel's, and sweet potatoes until well blended. Spoon into the muffin cups. Sprinkle with the pecans and remaining 2 tablespoons sugar. Bake for 15 to 20 minutes for regular size muffins, 10 to 13 minutes for mini muffins.

Foolproof Oven Bacon

Frying bacon in your cast iron skillet is about the best way to season the pan and keep it ready for cornbread. If you're like me, though, and tend to juggle multiple kitchen tasks at once, baking your bacon in the oven is a miracle. The strips turn out straight and flat, not uneven and curly. Thick-cut oven cooked bacon strips are sturdy enough to stand up in a jar like bread sticks. For your next party, surprise your guests by passing a mason jar of bacon strips and a tray of shot glasses filled with chilled Tennessee Honey. It's lots of fun.

1 pound thick-cut bacon
Black pepper, to taste
¼ cup brown sugar, optional

Line a large, rimmed baking pan with foil for easy clean up. Lay the bacon strips snuggly side by side on the pan. They should just fit. Sprinkle the bacon with the brown sugar and black pepper, if you like. Place the baking sheet in the cold oven and turn the heat to 400 F. Bake 35 to 40 minutes or until the bacon is nicely browned, turning the pan around once during the cook time for even cooking. The exact timing depends on how thick the bacon is and how crispy you like it.

Butter Pecan Coffee Cake Muffins

Makes 12 muffins

Muffins are the easiest treat in the world to make, easier than cookies, a cake, or brownies. In the old days talented home economies teachers would teach the valuable muffin method of baking quick breads—stir together the dry ingredients, stir together the wet ingredients, then combine and stir until a lumpy batter forms. You don't want to overmix a muffin batter, or the muffins will be tough and tunneled. A tunnel is a long, strange looking air pocket that has no place in a well-made muffin.

Streusel Topping

½ cup firmly packed brown sugar
½ cup chopped pecans
1 teaspoon cinnamon

Batter

1 ½ cups self-rising flour
½ cup sugar
1 egg
¾ cup milk
¼ cup melted butter

Heat the oven to 425°F. Grease a 12-cup muffin pan or place 12 paper baking cups in the muffin pan and coat lightly with cooking spray.

To make the streusel topping: Combine the brown sugar, pecans, and cinnamon in a small bowl and set aside.

To make the batter: Combine the flour and sugar in a medium mixing bowl. In a small bowl whisk together the egg, milk, and butter. Pour the liquid over the flour mixture. Stir with a fork just until the flour is moistened and a lumpy batter forms.

To make the muffins: Spoon 1 tablespoon of the batter into each of the cups; sprinkle with half of the sugar/nut mixture. Top evenly with the remaining batter. Sprinkle each with the remaining sugar/nut mixture. Bake 20 to 24 minutes or until golden brown. Cool on a wire rack about 10 minutes before removing the muffins from the pan.

Blueberry Buckle Skillet Cake

Makes 8 servings

A traditional blueberry buckle consists of a soft cake batter topped with blueberries that the batter bakes around, then topped with a crumbly sweet topping. Our skillet version is a little more substantial, almost like a muffin cake. You can easily substitute other fruits or whatever's in season. My favorite part of the recipe is the sandy textured crumb topping.

Crumb Topping

> $\frac{1}{2}$ cup sugar
> $\frac{3}{4}$ cup self-rising flour
> 1 teaspoon cinnamon
> $\frac{1}{4}$ cup butter, softened

Buckle

> 1 $\frac{1}{2}$ cups self-rising flour
> $\frac{3}{4}$ cup sugar
> 1 egg
> $\frac{1}{2}$ cup milk
> $\frac{1}{4}$ cup butter, melted

1 teaspoon vanilla

2 cups fresh or frozen blueberries

Heat the oven to 375° F. Grease a 9-inch cast iron skillet or 11 x 7-inch baking dish.

For the crumb topping: Combine the sugar, flour, and cinnamon in a small bowl. Rub the butter into the flour with your fingers until crumbly. Set aside.

To make the buckle: Combine the flour and sugar in a medium mixing bowl. In a small bowl whisk together the egg, milk, butter, and vanilla. Pour the liquid over the flour mixture and stir with a fork just until the flour is moistened and a lumpy batter forms. Pour the batter into the greased skillet. Scatter the blueberries over the top. Sprinkle with the crumb topping. Bake 40 to 45 minutes or until golden brown. Serve warm.

Buckle Variations: Replace the blueberries with two cups peeled, cored, and diced apple; peeled and diced fresh peaches; raspberries; blackberries; or fresh chopped cranberries.

Heard around the TABLE

An energetic guest from New York reached across the table and asked, "What would happen if I started spinning this Lazy Susan loaded with food?" Our hostess was stunned. Her husband later told her she should have replied, "The last person who did that is buried out back." She keeps waiting to use that line someday.

SALADS

The Four Slaws of Lynchburg

Yellow Mustard
White Mayo
Clear Vinegar
Lynchburg
Succotash Salad with Lemon Dressing

Lynchburg Hostess Tips and Tricks

Baby Spinach and Beets with Hog Jowl Dressing
Country Citrus Fruit Salad

Fruit Salad

Toasted Pecans

Creamy Shoepeg Corn Salad and Creamy English Pea Salad

Creamy Shoepeg Corn Salad
Creamy English Pea Salad
Early Spring Greens with Warm Bacon Dripping Dressing
Cranberry Fruit Fluff

Debbie's Tips on Making Naturally Fermented Kraut in Canning Jars

Crispy Kraut Salad
Bobo's Carrot Raisin Salad
Tennessee Tomato White Bean Cornbread Salad
Pepper Jack Mac Salad
Tangy Sweet Summer Garden Salad
Lynchburg Lemonade Congealed Salad
Carrot Ambrosia Gelatin Salad

The Four Slaws of Lynchburg

No one slaw does it all, but I believe four just might. The Yellow Mustard Slaw is like the one served on the slaw burgers at Honey's Pool Room in nearby Fayetteville. It's also really good on grilled hot dogs and sausages.

White Mayo Slaw is the creamy one, dressed with a simple combination of mayo, vinegar, and sugar. It's perfect with catfish.

Clear Vinegar Slaw is my first choice to go with barbecue ribs and pulled pork because it cuts through the fat. Rich meat doesn't pair as well with creamy mayonnaise. We use finely grated cabbage so that the slaw sits nicely on a pulled pork sandwich.

Our Lynchburg Slaw is loaded with carrots, green pepper, and onion. Serve it as a luscious cabbage salad with just about anything. That's why it's our choice at Miss Mary's since we serve at least eight different dishes per day.

Yellow Mustard

Makes 8 servings

¼ cup grated onion (about 1 medium onion)
¼ cup sugar
¼ cup cider vinegar
¼ cup sweet pickle relish
¼ cup prepared yellow mustard
½ teaspoon celery seed
½ teaspoon salt
Dash of hot pepper sauce
16 ounces (about 8 cups) finely shredded cabbage or packaged slaw mix

Combine the onion, sugar, vinegar, pickle relish, mustard, salt, celery seed, and hot pepper sauce in a small bowl. Blend well. Place the shredded cabbage in a large bowl and stir the dressing over the top. Stir thoroughly. The more you stir the more the cabbage packs down and the saucier it gets. Refrigerate until serving.

White Mayo

Makes 8 servings

¼ cup mayonnaise
¼ cup cider vinegar
¼ cup sugar
½ teaspoon salt
½ teaspoon celery seed, optional
16 ounces (about 8 cups) finely shredded cabbage or packaged slaw mix

Combine the mayonnaise, vinegar, sugar, salt, and celery seed in a small bowl. Blend well. Place the shredded cabbage in a large bowl and pour the dressing over top. Stir thoroughly. Refrigerate until serving.

Clear Vinegar

Makes 8 servings

½ cup cider vinegar
½ cup sugar
½ cup water
1 teaspoon salt
16 ounces (about 8 cups) grated or finely shredded cabbage or packaged slaw mix

Combine the vinegar, sugar, water, and salt in a small bowl. Blend well, but don't worry that the sugar hasn't dissolved completely. Place the shredded cabbage in a large bowl and pour the dressing over the top. Stir thoroughly. Refrigerate until serving.

Lynchburg

Makes 10 servings

1 ½ cups mayonnaise
½ cup cider vinegar
2 tablespoons sugar
16 ounces (about 8 cups) grated or finely shredded cabbage or packaged slaw mix
2 carrots, peeled and grated
1 medium onion, finely chopped

1 medium green pepper, finely chopped
Salt and black pepper, to taste

Combine the mayonnaise, vinegar, and sugar in a small bowl. Blend well. Place the shredded cabbage in a large bowl and add the carrots, onion, and green pepper. Pour the dressing over the mixture and blend well. Season with salt and pepper. Refrigerate until serving.

Succotash Salad with Lemon Dressing

Makes 10 servings

The variety of color in this salad may be its best feature. All the lovely greens— lima, parsley, pepper, and celery—are nicely accented with yellow and red. The creamy dressing is made with olive oil and lemon juice, with a spoonful of mayonnaise added for body. Omit the mayonnaise if you prefer a classic vinaigrette. Both styles are delicious.

Salad

1 bag (16 ounces) frozen baby lima beans (or use fresh when you can find them)
1 bag (12 ounces) frozen corn kernels (or the kernels from three ears of fresh corn)
1 cup chopped fresh parsley
½ cup chopped celery
¼ to ½ cup chopped onion, green, red, or white

1 small green bell pepper, chopped
2 medium tomatoes, diced or 1 pint cherry tomatoes, cut in half

Dressing

¼ cup olive or vegetable oil
Juice of one large lemon (2 to 3 tablespoons)
2 tablespoons mayonnaise
Salt and black pepper, to taste
Tomatoes

To make the salad: simmer the lima beans in salted boiling water until tender according to the package directions, being careful not to overcook them. Cook the frozen corn just until tender according to package directions, or simmer the fresh corn in salted water about 3 minutes. Drain the beans and corn. Transfer the drained vegetables to a large mixing bowl and allow to cool. Add the parsley, celery, onion, and bell pepper.

To make the dressing: combine the olive oil, lemon juice, and mayonnaise in a small bowl. Whisk until smooth. Season generously with salt and pepper.

Toss the salad with the dressing. Season with additional salt and pepper, if necessary. Chill until serving.

Just before serving, scatter the salad with the tomatoes.

Lynchburg Hostess Tips and Tricks

Y ou can plan and plan and cook forever, but if host and guest don't do their parts, good food and drink can't save an occasion. At Miss Mary's, each table is led by a seasoned hostess who does her very best to ensure a good time for all. It's not always easy, but it is always rewarding.

Our Lynchburg hostesses are mostly retired ladies who love to talk to and be with people. Many hostesses had teaching careers or served in public in some way and still enjoy greeting and learning from our guests who visit from all across the country and the world. The ladies know more than a thing or two about good country cooking too. Many are excellent home cooks with years of experience entertaining friends and raising families.

In the many years I've been at Miss Mary's, we've had more than a hundred wonderful hostesses, including my mother and the mothers of some of our hostesses today. They all tell me it's the best job for anyone who loves to talk and eat! We've had many guests announce that upon retirement they'll be moving to Lynchburg and filling out a hostess job application.

Keep our simple approach in mind for all gatherings. Simply put, a good hostess uses good manners and common sense.

Introductions break the ice. We ask each guest to introduce themselves before beginning the meal. Conversation comes easier when you know a first name and hometown. Suddenly, there's plenty to talk about. Our hostesses look our guests in the eye and give them a smile.

Talk up the menu. We want our guests to appreciate the specially chosen menu. You will at your party too. As the bowls are passed to the left, we talk a little about each dish and encourage generous helpings. At home I do the same, taking care to point out the bar and share highlights of the buffet or dinner. Many of our guests have never seen or tasted Southern food, so our hostesses get a big kick out of explaining dishes like grits casserole and fried okra.

Get conversation rolling. Be prepared to ask lots of good questions and help your guests find common ground. Our hostesses are excellent talkers who enjoy asking, asking, and asking, and giving a few answers too. They ask about your hometown, your weather, your local cooking, your career, your travel plans, your children, your grandchildren, your hobbies, your visit to the distillery and the town square, and your favorite dish. Our table hostesses always keep a few funny stories and local lore in mind to jumpstart a quiet table. Good listening makes better conversation.

Go with the flow. A seasoned hostess expects the unexpected. Even at Miss Mary's, we've weathered plenty of dinner dilemmas with a laugh and a smile. That's part of the fun. You never know what the next group of guests will bring to the table. Your good guests will always be ready to jump in and help.

You can imagine after all these years our hostesses have lots of funny stories to tell, and they do. The laughter that comes out of the hostess break room proves it. They call it their own version of group therapy. I heard one say, "If we could bottle the laughter and joy in here, we'd have another spirit to sell!"

Baby Spinach and Beets with Hog Jowl Dressing

Makes 8 servings

Everything is better with bacon (and Jack Daniel's), including rich, earthy beets. Our favorite "bacon" is actually hog jowl that we buy sliced by the pound. I also buy hog jowl in a big piece that I cut into golf ball-size pieces and freeze and it's ready to season a pot of beans or greens anytime. Canned beets are convenient, but fresh ones roasted in the oven or in a foil packet on the grill are even better. I also microwave fresh unpeeled beets in a covered dish with a splash of water. Microwave them for a few minutes until tender. The skins will peel right off when cool. Sprinkle the salad with blue cheese crumbles if you like.

1 pound baby spinach
1 can (14 ½ ounces) sliced beets, drained
6 slices hog jowl or bacon
1 medium Vidalia onion, chopped
2 teaspoons sugar
3 tablespoons cider vinegar

2 tablespoons Jack Daniel's Tennessee Whiskey

Salt and black pepper, to taste

Blue cheese crumbles, optional

Croutons

Combine the spinach and beets in a salad bowl. Cook the hog jowl in a skillet over medium heat until crisp. Remove, cool, and crumble. Add the onion and sugar to the drippings in the skillet and cook until the onion is softened. Stir in the vinegar and Jack Daniel's. Cook and stir until slightly thickened. Pour over the spinach and beets, and season with salt and pepper. Toss to combine. Sprinkle with the crumbled hog jowl, blue cheese, and croutons. Serve immediately.

Country Citrus Fruit Salad

Makes 8 servings

Brown sugar blended with a little Jack Daniel's is a marvelous complement to fresh fruits. The flavor is rich but doesn't overpower the fruit. Don't worry if you're lacking a fruit or two called for in the recipe. Mix it up with what's in season and what's in the refrigerator crisper drawer. We love a handful of mini marshmallows thrown in and occasionally some toasted chopped pecans.

3 seedless oranges, peeled and cut into bite-size chunks

1 small fresh pineapple, cut into 1-inch cubes

2 firm, ripe bananas, sliced

1 medium bunch red seedless grapes

1 pint fresh strawberries, halved

3/4 cup brown sugar, or to taste

1/4 cup Jack Daniel's Tennessee Whiskey

1/2 cup shredded coconut

1 cup chopped toasted pecans, optional

Combine the oranges, pineapple, bananas, grapes, and strawberries in a large bowl. In a small bowl combine the sugar and Jack Daniel's. Blend well and gently stir the mixture into the fruit. Sprinkle with coconut and pecans.

*A Nashville man said
that he had been on the
internet that morning
chatting with a fellow
from Copenhagen but
had to sign off because
he was headed to
Lynchburg for a tour of
the Jack Daniel Distillery.
The man in Copenhagen
asked, "Will you be
eating at Miss Mary
Bobo's?" He answered
back, "Yes, how do
you know about Miss
Mary's?" The man replied
that he'd eaten here
and said, "Hope they're
serving Lynchburg
Candied Apples!"*

Fruit Salad

Southern fruit salads, congealed or not, are often creamy, very sweet, and can be served for dessert. Here's a simple fruit salad you'll find at Miss Mary's. Combine 8 ounces of cream cheese with about ¼ cup of heavy cream and blend until fluffy. Stir in a can of drained fruit cocktail and some drained crushed pineapple. Chill and serve.

Toasted Pecans

Toasted pecans make all the difference in many of our recipes. To toast nuts, place them in a dry skillet over medium-low heat, stirring frequently, about 5 minutes. When you begin to smell their aroma, the nuts are ready. Toast extra and keep them in the freezer for up to 6 months.

Creamy Shoepeg Corn Salad and Creamy English Pea Salad

Creamy Shoepeg Corn Salad and Creamy English Pea Salad are Southern classics and popular sides at Miss Mary's. Both are dressed with a blend of sour cream and mayonnaise and the all-important pinch of sugar. Serve either one when a leafy green salad just won't do, such as for covered dish suppers, picnics, and buffet sideboards.

Creamy Shoepeg Corn Salad

Makes 8 servings

White, sweet shoepeg is our favorite corn. The small, elongated kernels resemble the small pegs used to attach soles to boots back in the 1800s.

> 3 cups cooked and cooled shoepeg corn (you'll need two 10-ounce packages of frozen corn)
> 1 small green bell pepper, chopped
> ¼ cup chopped red onion
> ½ cup sour cream
> 1 tablespoon mayonnaise
> 1 tablespoon vinegar
> ¼ teaspoon celery salt
> Pinch of sugar
> Salt and black pepper to taste

Combine the corn, bell pepper, onion, sour cream, mayonnaise, vinegar, celery salt, sugar, and salt and pepper in a medium bowl. Blend well. Cover and refrigerate until serving time.

Creamy English Pea Salad

Makes 8 servings

At Miss Mary's we often make English Pea Salad with frozen peas and pearl onions and omit the red onion. Don't bother with mushy canned peas. Instead, cook frozen

Heard around the TABLE

A gentleman asked one hostess, "How often do you work?" Before she could reply another guest replied, "Whenever she gets hungry."

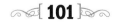

peas just a couple of minutes to retain their gorgeous green color and fresh texture. Feel free to use a small jar of diced pimientos instead of the red bell pepper. I've also enjoyed many pea salad variations that include chopped hard-boiled egg and diced Cheddar cheese.

3 cups frozen green peas, cooked until just tender
(use one 16-ounce bag of frozen peas)
½ cup sliced celery
½ cup chopped red bell pepper
¼ cup chopped red onion
½ cup sour cream
1 tablespoon mayonnaise
¼ cup celery salt
Pinch of sugar

Combine the peas, celery, bell pepper, onion, sour cream, mayonnaise, celery salt, and sugar in a medium bowl. Blend well. Cover and refrigerate until serving time.

Early Spring Greens with Warm Bacon Dripping Dressing

Makes 6 servings

Green tossed salads are a relatively recent arrival to the South. Growing up, the only time we enjoyed lettuce was when the baby greens came up in the spring garden along with the radishes and green onions. We'd toss together a big batch of this salad wilted with plenty of salty sweet bacon dripping dressing. We loved it so much that on occasion it was all we'd have for supper. Make the dressing from saved bacon drippings, or cook some bacon, use the drippings, and crumble the bacon on the salad.

1 pound baby lettuce, rinsed and dried
8 green onions, sliced
10 radishes, thinly sliced
8 slices of bacon
¼ cup cider vinegar
1 tablespoon sugar
Salt and black pepper, to taste
2 hard boiled eggs, chopped

Toss the lettuce, onions, and radishes in a large salad bowl and set aside. Cook the bacon in a large skillet over medium heat until crisp. Remove and crumble the bacon; set aside. Remove all but ¼ cup of the bacon drippings from the skillet. Stir in the vinegar and sugar. Cook over medium heat until the sugar has dissolved. Pour the warm dressing over the salad and toss. Season with salt and pepper. Top with the crumbled bacon and eggs.

Cranberry Fruit Fluff

Makes 8 servings

Why confine cranberries to the holidays? My mother loves cranberries so much she's likely to add them to almost anything and not just during the holiday season. She was so delighted the time I ordered too many fresh cranberries for Miss Mary's one year. Mother rescued the extras and stashed them in freezer bags to use all year long.

This old favorite is like a showy cousin to the Waldorf salad. It's a gorgeous pink color, fluffy, and decadent. Mother insists on the overnight rest for the cranberries, marshmallows, and sugar. The next day, the marshmallows have nearly disappeared into the creamy mix. Experiment with seasonal fruits such as clementines, plums, and pears. Yes, the only dressing is whipped cream. And no, we don't eat it for dessert. It's a salad!

2 cups fresh cranberries, ground in a food processor
3 cups miniature marshmallows
¾ cup sugar
2 medium crisp apples, cored and diced
½ cup seedless green or red grapes, cut in half
½ cup toasted pecans or walnuts
Pinch of salt
1 cup heavy cream, whipped

Combine the cranberries, marshmallows, and sugar in a mixing bowl. Cover and chill overnight. Stir in the apples, grapes, nuts, and a pinch of salt. Fold in the whipped cream and chill before serving.

Debbie's Tips on Making Naturally Fermented Kraut in Canning Jars

Always consult the *The Old Farmer's Almanac* for nature's signs that it's time to get busy making kraut. Choose firm Flat Dutch cabbage heads. Hybrid cabbages just don't work right.

- Trim up the stalks to poke down into the mason jars later on.
- Shred the cabbage and chop it up.
- Combine 1 gallon of chopped cabbage in a large bowl with 2 tablespoons of salt and 1 tablespoon of sugar. Mix it all up thoroughly.
- Put the mixture in quart glass jars, packed lightly, leaving about an inch of headspace. One gallon of cabbage should fit into 3 quart-size canning jars. Stick the trimmed stalks down in the center of the jars.
- Place the lids on the jars, firmly but not tight, so the built up gases can escape.
- Store the jars in a cool, dark place where the temperature is between 65° and 70°F.
- After 14 days tighten the lids. The process should be complete in 30 to 60 days.

Crispy Kraut Salad

Makes 8 servings

Debbie Baxter's parents, David and Ola Cleek, have been making sauerkraut from homegrown Firm Flat Dutch cabbage heads (they say the hybrid cabbage just doesn't work) since Debbie was a child. The age-old process of brining and preserving cabbage packed in canning jars takes 30 to 60 days. Even now the grown kids fight over the tender cabbage stalks that her mother inserts in the center of each jar.

The Cleeks tend a big vegetable garden, and luckily Debbie's husband, Goose, likes to do the same (although she says he works her to death). It doesn't take long in the spring for the family competition over "whose got what in the garden and how big is it" heats up. "Daddy calls Goose all the time to boast about the first corn, cabbage, beans, or tomatoes they're having for supper," Debbie says. "'Haven't you had that yet?' Daddy gloats!"

Kraut salad is another Miss Mary's favorite even though it often seems a little unusual to many of our guests. Surprisingly good, the crisp texture and sweet/sour flavor is a first-rate match for pork. It's also a great winter salad when tomatoes aren't worth buying.

4 cups sauerkraut, rinsed and drained
1 cup sliced celery
½ cup chopped green bell pepper
½ cup chopped red bell pepper
½ cup chopped red onion
1 cup sugar
1 cup vinegar
¼ cup vegetable oil
Salt and black pepper, to taste

Combine the sauerkraut, celery, green and red bell pepper, and onion in a large bowl. In a small bowl whisk together the sugar, vinegar, and oil. Season with salt and pepper. Pour the dressing over the salad ingredients and blend well. Chill before serving.

Bobo's Carrot Raisin Salad

Makes 8 servings

Here's an old fashioned recipe worth reconsidering. When Miss Mary's guests get a chance to have it, more often than not a guest will wonder out loud why she doesn't make this more often. I agree. It's worth the effort to grate your own whole carrots (or use a food processor). I avoid precut carrot slivers and "baby carrots" as they are too coarse and tasteless to bother with. Many guests also comment on our carrot raisin salad thanks to the toasted pecans. They give the salad an earthy taste that beautifully ties it all together.

4 cups grated carrots (about 1 pound or 5 medium-large carrots)
1 can (8 ounces) crushed pineapple

½ cup shredded sweetened coconut
½ cup raisins
2 tablespoons to ¼ cup sugar
½ cup mayonnaise or until creamy
½ cup toasted pecans (page 100)

Combine the carrots, pineapple, coconut, raisins, and sugar in a medium bowl. Stir in the mayonnaise until creamy. Cover and refrigerate until well chilled. Top with toasted pecans just before serving.

Tennessee Tomato White Bean Cornbread Salad

Makes 10 servings

As I've mentioned a time or two already, leftover cornbread is important to country cooking. A little slice warmed in the toaster oven is among my favorite afternoon snacks, and old-timers often ate cornbread from a bowl doused with buttermilk. Cornbread is the basis for cornbread dressing, and it's a lovely crisp topping for casseroles. We also make salads with it because it is sturdy enough to handle juicy tomatoes and creamy dressing. This is one of my favorite summer salads.

Salad

4 cups crumbled Cast Iron Cornbread (page 81)
3 cups diced ripe tomatoes (use any combination of colors and sizes)
1 can (15.5 ounces) white beans, rinsed and drained
1 cup sliced celery
½ cup sliced green onions
½ cup chopped fresh parsley

Dressing

1 cup mayonnaise
½ cup buttermilk
2 tablespoons fresh lemon juice
2 cloves garlic, mashed into a paste
Generous amount of black pepper to taste
Salt to taste

To make the salad: Combine the cornbread, tomatoes, white beans, celery, green onions, and parsley in a large bowl. Toss to blend.

To make the dressing: Combine the mayonnaise, buttermilk, lemon juice, garlic, pepper, and salt in a small bowl. Toss the dressing with the salad just before serving or serve on the side.

Pepper Jack Mac Salad

Makes about 10 servings

Pepper Jack cheese in a classic macaroni salad gives the usually mild-flavored dish a little zing. I prefer a good amount of crunchy, fresh, chopped vegetables to contrast with the pasta. Plus, the cheese is named Jack, always a plus.

  8 ounces macaroni, cooked and cooled
  1 cup grated Pepper Jack cheese or Cheddar cheese
  1 cup chopped red bell pepper
  1 cup chopped green bell pepper
  1 cup sliced celery
  ½ cup sliced green onion or chopped red onion, or to taste
  1 cup mayonnaise, or to taste
  Salt and black pepper, to taste

Combine the macaroni, cheese, bell peppers, celery, onion, mayonnaise, and salt and pepper in a large bowl. Cover and chill before serving.

Tangy Sweet Summer Garden Salad

Makes 8 to 10 servings

Great for a hot summer day, this salad features the most popular garden vegetables that are coming out of our ears by late July. Is it a vegetable or a relish? Well, we went with salad because we soon noticed that our guests tend to pile it on their plates like a salad, not spoon it sparingly like a relish. The people have spoken! Add hot pepper if you're a fan.

  2 large cucumbers, peeled and thinly sliced
  4 medium tomatoes, cut into wedges
  1 large onion, cut into thin slivers
  1 large sweet pepper, cut into slivers
  ½ cup vegetable oil
  ½ cup cider vinegar

¼ cup sugar
1 teaspoon celery seed
Salt and black pepper, to taste

Combine the cucumbers, tomatoes, onion, and pepper in a large bowl. In a small bowl whisk together the oil, vinegar, sugar, and celery seed. Season generously with salt and pepper. Pour the dressing over the vegetables and blend well. Chill before serving.

Lynchburg Lemonade Congealed Salad

Makes 8 servings

My mother's generation of home cooks went wild over congealed salads. Hardworking homemakers considered them a modern miracle for adding color and fun to the country Southern table. The explosion of readily available canned fruits and vegetables that they didn't have to put up encouraged congealed creativity in every shade of color and texture. Sweet, savory, creamy, or tart, we had them all the time with everything. This adults-only salad inspired by one of our favorite summer drinks will have you reconsidering this time-honored tradition. Be sure to zest the lemon before squeezing the juice.

2 packets (4 ½ teaspoons) unflavored gelatin
1/3 cup Jack Daniel's Tennessee Whiskey
1 ½ cups boiling water
¾ cups sugar
Zest from one fresh lemon
½ cup fresh lemon juice
1 cup orange juice
1 can (15.4 ounces) crushed pineapple in juice
2 cups miniature marshmallows
1 cup chopped toasted pecans
Orange slices, for garnish

Sprinkle the gelatin over the Jack Daniel's in a medium bowl to soften. Let stand about 5 minutes. Add boiling water, sugar, and lemon zest. Stir until the sugar and gelatin are completely dissolved, about 1 minute. Add lemon and orange juices. Chill in a 2-quart casserole or bowl until slightly thickened. Stir in the pineapple and its juices, marshmallows, and pecans. Cover and chill until firm. Garnish with orange slices.

Carrot Ambrosia Gelatin Salad

Makes about 12 servings

This gorgeous salad features grated fresh carrots in a fresh orange juice gelatin. Make sure you save a place for this winter salad on the holiday sideboard. Remember that fresh pineapple in a gelatin salad won't work because the enzymes in the fruit prevent the gelling process—use canned pineapple only. Use a gelatin mold* if you have one. I often serve this on a bed of tangy watercress. Toasted pecans and a dollop of mayonnaise aren't necessary, but they add a nice touch.

> 1 can (20 ounces) pineapple tidbits in juice
> 2 packets unflavored gelatin
> 3 cups orange juice, divided
> ¼ cup sugar
> 2 cups grated carrots
> 1 can (29 ounces) mandarin orange segments, drained
> ½ cup shredded coconut
> Toasted pecans, watercress, and mayo for serving

Drain the juice from the pineapple tidbits, reserving ½ cup of the juice. Pour the reserved juice in a medium bowl. Sprinkle the gelatin over the juice to soften. Bring 1 cup of the orange juice to a boil and pour over the gelatin. Add the sugar and stir until the gelatin is completely dissolved, 1 to 2 minutes. Stir in the remaining 2 cups of orange juice. Pour the gelatin into a 9 x 13-inch baking dish or an 8-cup mold. Refrigerate until slightly thickened, say the consistency of egg whites, about 1 hour. Remove from the refrigerator and stir in the pineapple tidbits, carrots, mandarin oranges, and coconut. Cover with plastic wrap. Refrigerate until set. Cut into squares and serve on a bed of watercress. Add a dollop of mayonnaise and sprinkle with toasted pecans, if desired.

   *To remove the gelatin from a mold, dip the bottom of the mold in warm water for about 10 seconds. Invert onto a serving platter. Use your finger to press the edge of the gelatin to help release the air lock if necessary.

VEGETABLES AND SIDES

Miss Mary Bobo's Dinner Menu Planning Guidelines

Boarding House Baked Macaroni and Cheese
Real Southern Cornbread Dressing

Dressing with a Twist

Giblet Gravy

Creole Red and Green Beans
Easy Country Greens
Creamy Hominy Spinach Casserole

Everyday Lynchburg Candied Apples

Baked Lynchburg Candied Apples
Skillet Lynchburg Candied Apples
Mashed Potatoes Au Gratin
Mother's Best Fried Corn

Things Taste Better with Jack

Pepper Jack Rice Bake

Not Up to Frying Tonight Oven Roasted Okra

Everyday Southern Fried Okra
Sweet Tomato Supper Pudding
Tennessee Butternut Squash
Sour Mash Sweet Potatoes
Squash Casserole with Cheddar Cornbread Crumbs

Easy Cabbage Casserole Additions

Dry County Cabbage Casserole
Apricot Dinner Casserole
Pineapple Cheddar Dinner Casserole
Jack in the Beans
Low and Slow Baked Beans

Miss Mary Bobo's Dinner Menu Planning Guidelines

Two meats, six sides, one bread, one dessert every day!
One white meat—chicken or catfish.
One red meat—beef or pork.
Lynchburg Candied Apples—every day except Thanksgiving week and the entire month of December. That's when we swap the apples for Sour Mash Sweet Potatoes.
Fried okra—every single day.
One starch or vegetable—potatoes, creamed corn, turnip greens, or cauliflower with cheese sauce. We serve our cornbread dressing during the holidays.
One casserole—Squash (in the summer), mac and cheese, cheese grits, hash brown potatoes, cabbage, broccoli rice, or green chili rice.
One bean—green, pinto, navy, crowder peas, black-eyed peas, limas, field peas, and snaps.
One salad or relish—red pepper relish, kraut salad (delicious with pinto beans), corn salad, or green pea salad. In the summer it's fresh tomato relish and carrot raisin salad.
Bread—cornbread muffins, mayo rolls, or yeast rolls.
Dessert—pie, cake, cobbler, or shortcake.
Drinks—fresh iced tea or coffee.

Boarding House Baked Macaroni and Cheese

Makes 8 to 10 servings

*We may not be pasta experts, but macaroni and cheese is ever-present on South-
ern dinner tables. Here we serve it all year long, even during the holidays. Boarding House mac and cheese is among our most requested recipes, and our simple
method usually comes as a surprise.*

*We use good ol' processed American cheese combined with the Italian cooking
trick of adding some starchy pasta water to the sauce. Processed cheese makes a
creamy, reliable sauce unlike aged Cheddar that turns clumpy and rubbery when
combined with water. Instead, sprinkle a little sharp Cheddar on the top and a few
breadcrumbs, if you like. Kids love it too.*

1 box (16 ounces) elbow macaroni
2 pounds processed American cheese, cubed or shredded
1 teaspoon dry mustard
Salt and black pepper, to taste
1 cup grated sharp Cheddar cheese
3/4 cup coarse breadcrumbs, optional

Heat the oven to 375°F. Grease a 9 x 13-inch baking dish. Cook the macaroni in salted water according to package directions. When the macaroni is cooked, but before straining, use a ladle to remove 3 cups of the
macaroni water and set aside. Strain the macaroni and return it to the
pot. Add the reserved water and processed cheese to the pot. Stir the
macaroni over low heat until the cheese melts. It will seem a bit watery,
but the macaroni will absorb most of the liquid during baking. Add the
dry mustard, salt, and pepper and stir to combine. Pour the mixture into
the greased dish. Bake for 20 minutes or until hot and bubbly. Top with
Cheddar cheese and breadcrumbs and return to the oven for 10 minutes,
or until the Cheddar cheese has melted.

Real Southern Cornbread Dressing

Makes 10 to 12 servings

Down here in the country a cornbread dressing casserole is an absolute companion to the holiday roast turkey and the Sunday roast chicken. Because we make it in a casserole, we don't call it "stuffing." A stuffed bird takes longer to cook which risks drying out the breast meat. Besides, you can make a lot more dressing in a 9 x 13-inch pan.

For my Real Southern Cornbread Dressing you must start with your own cornbread (no store-bought "cornbread stuffing" crumbs). A batch of Cast Iron Cornbread (page 81) is all it takes. A sealed bag of leftover cornbread and biscuits in the freezer makes the rest of the dish a snap.

Our basic dressing includes the traditional celery, onions, and sage, and often a good pork sausage. Soft on the inside and crispy on top, good cornbread dressing holds up well under gravy. My mother folds an egg or two into the broth for a lighter, puffier texture. Believe me, this dish is the most passed around for seconds and thirds that we offer.

6 cups crumbled skillet cornbread
3 cups toasted bread cubes or leftover biscuit cubes
¼ cup plus 2 tablespoons butter, divided
1 cup chopped celery
1 cup chopped onion
1 tablespoon dried sage
2 teaspoons black pepper
2 to 3 cups turkey or chicken broth

Combine the cornbread and bread cubes in a large mixing bowl. Melt ¼ cup butter in a large skillet over medium heat and add the celery and onion. Cook until softened, 7 to 8 minutes. Add the cooked vegetables, sage, and pepper to the cornbread. Stir in enough broth to moisten the cornbread and blend well. Spoon the mixture into a generously buttered 9 x 13-inch baking dish. Dot the top with the remaining 2 tablespoons of butter. Bake the casserole until golden brown and heated through, 35 to 40 minutes.

Dressing with a Twist

Cornbread dressing offers plenty of room to roam too. Start with the basic recipe and experiment with any of these ingredients to create a new holiday favorite side dish for your family.

Chopped toasted pecans
Fresh chopped parsley
Chopped fresh apple
Raisins and other dried fruits
Bits of country ham
Cooked pork sausage like hot or mild Italian
Any cooked smoked sausage like kielbasa, andouille, or chorizo
Sautéed red and green bell peppers
Shredded cooked greens
Crisp crumbled bacon
Herbs such as rosemary, thyme, marjoram, and oregano

Giblet Gravy

The rich giblet gravy we serve with our holiday turkey and dressing often includes chopped hard-cooked eggs. It's an old Tennessee tradition that dates back to when folks killed their own hens for dinner. The fresh hen would often contain an unlayed egg or two that we'd use to enrich the gravy. Quite a delicacy, the developing soft eggs are almost all yolk with a mild buttery flavor.

Make a quick gravy just by thickening chicken or turkey broth. Whisk together ¼ cup cold water with ¼ cup flour in a small bowl for every 2 cups of broth. Stir the flour mixture into the broth in a saucepan. Bring to a boil and simmer a few minutes until thickened. Add cooked chopped giblets, and to enrich the broth further add the accumulated drippings from the pan of a roast turkey or chicken. Add that unlayed egg too! Season with sage, salt, and pepper.

Creole Red and Green Beans

Makes 8 servings

Our little secret when cooking vegetables the Southern way is a pinch, well, a big pinch of sugar. No kidding, we tend to add some sugar to most everything at Miss Mary's, from pinto beans to turnip greens. Not always enough to taste, but enough to balance the flavors. My mother has been making these Creole green beans my whole life, usually with home-canned tomatoes and green beans. Now it's a boarding house classic during the holiday season. Like all good Southerners, we cook our green beans a little longer than most. You can cook the beans until bright green and crisp tender, about 5 minutes, or like us for at least 20 minutes.

> 1 pound fresh or frozen green beans, trimmed and cut in half
> 1 medium green bell pepper, finely chopped
> 2 stalks celery, finely chopped
> 1 medium onion, finely chopped
> 3 tablespoons bacon drippings or butter
> 1 can (28 ounces) diced tomatoes
> A pinch to ¼ cup sugar, to taste
> Salt and black pepper, to taste

Cook the green beans in boiling salted water in a large saucepan until tender. Drain, return to the pot, and set aside. Cook the bell pepper, celery, and onion in the drippings in a large skillet until tender, about 10 minutes. Stir in the tomatoes and simmer, uncovered, 10 to 15 minutes, or until thickened. Gently stir the tomato mixture into the green beans. Season with sugar, salt, and pepper. Heat through.

Easy Country Greens

Makes 6 servings

These days more and more in-town folks are signing up with CSA (Community Supported Agriculture) farmers for their seasonal produce. Funny that turnip greens have been growing wild in the field behind my house all these years, but never once did I consider going into the greens business!

We grew up on bitter turnip and tangy mustard greens, but you can fix this dish with kale or collards just as well. Heartier than soft spinach, traditional Southern greens are cooked until tender in a rich pork broth called pot likker. A smoked ham

During turnip green season one year, a hostess told her table that she had been washing fresh greens in her washing machine. A Northern guest asked, "Doesn't it make a mess?" "No," she replied, "It was a bushel."

hock usually flavors the broth, but these days I often find it easier to use diced pork side meat, a chunk of hog jowl, country ham scraps, sliced bacon, or even bacon drippings.

Any cured pork will nicely flavor the greens, but stay clear of any sweet flavored bacon. If you use a ham hock, simmer it in water for about 30 minutes and you'll have a lovely flavorful broth. Then remove the meat from the bone and return the meat to the pot when adding the greens. At the table pass the pepper vinegar and don't forget a hot skillet of Cast Iron Cornbread (page 81).

4 strips of bacon, diced, ⅓ cup diced salt pork or diced country ham, or 3 tablespoons bacon drippings
4 cups water
1 pound turnip, mustard, kale, or collard greens, washed, tough stems removed, and cut into 2-inch pieces
Pinch of dried red pepper flakes
Pinch of sugar
Salt to taste
3 hard-boiled eggs, sliced or quartered
Pepper sauce or vinegar, to serve

Fry the bacon or salt pork (if using) in a large pot until crisp. Add water to the pot and bring to a boil. If using country ham or bacon drippings add it to the hot water. Stir in the greens, dried red pepper flakes, and sugar. Cover and simmer over low heat for 20 to 30 minutes or until the greens are tender. Season with salt to taste. Garnish the serving bowl with the eggs. Serve with pepper sauce or vinegar.

Creamy Hominy Spinach Casserole

Makes 8 servings

Hominy is without question the most polarizing ingredient used at Miss Mary's. Poll our hostesses and the only consensus you'll find is universal disagreement. Either our Lynchburg ladies love hominy, or they would outlaw it if they could, corny as that may sound.

If you're in the "love it" camp, as I am, you will simply flip over this combination of hominy with creamy spinach. For a real steakhouse meal at home, substitute my hominy spinach casserole for the predictable baked potato, whether it's a juicy grilled steak, chicken, pork tenderloin or chops, or grilled fish. To make our Miss Mary's version, leave out the spinach for a pure hominy casserole. Just add a second 15-ounce can of hominy.

1 medium onion, finely chopped
¼ cup plus 2 tablespoons butter
1 clove garlic, minced
¼ cup all-purpose flour
3 cups milk
1 large can (29 ounces, or two 15-ounce cans) hominy, drained
1 box (10 ounces) chopped frozen spinach, thawed and squeezed of excess moisture
1 ½ cups shredded white Cheddar or Swiss cheese
Salt and black pepper, to taste
1 cup crushed saltine or butter cracker crumbs or coarse breadcrumbs

Heat the oven to 375°F. Cook the onion in the ¼ cup of butter over medium heat until tender, 7 to 8 minutes. Add the garlic, and cook two minutes more to soften (but not burn) the garlic. Stir in the flour and cook about 1 minute. Stir in the milk, bring to a boil, and cook, stirring constantly, until thickened. Stir in the hominy, spinach, and cheese. Season with salt and pepper, to taste. Pour the mixture into a greased 9 x 13-inch baking dish. Sprinkle with the crumbs and dot with the remaining 2 tablespoons butter. Bake 30 minutes, or until hot and bubbly.

Everyday Lynchburg Candied Apples

Other than our Everyday Southern Fried Okra, this is the only dish we serve every day. These apples are so rich and sweet I suggest a nice spoonful of them on your biscuit instead of jam. And Sunday brunch is such a nice occasion for this dish at home with family.

We're lucky most years to have available to us a spring crop of small tart green apples perfect for frying. You can peel them or not. For candied apples I recommend a good crisp Granny Smith or a Golden Delicious apple. We tend to prepare ours extra sweet, but you add sugar to your liking. It's also fun and old timey to fry them in a cast iron skillet at home.

Some time ago the usual pre-dinner chaos in the kitchen picked up, and it so happened that three different cooks, unaware of what the others had done, added some hometown product to the dish. At dinner that day, a gentleman guest took one bite and said, "Honey, these apples are gonna need a chaser!"

Baked Lynchburg Candied Apples

Makes about 16 servings

6 cups peeled and sliced tart green apples
3 cups sugar
½ cup Jack Daniel's Tennessee Whiskey
½ cup (1 stick) butter, cut into slices

Heat the oven to 375°F. Place the apples in a greased 9 x 13-inch baking dish. Sprinkle the sugar over the apples. Pour in the Jack Daniel's and dot with butter. Bake 45 minutes or until the apples are tender and the sauce is bubbly.

Skillet Lynchburg Candied Apples

Makes 8 servings

3 tablespoons butter
6 cups peeled and sliced tart green apples
½ cup sugar
¼ cup Jack Daniel's Tennessee Whiskey

Melt the butter in a large skillet over medium heat. Cook the apples in butter until just tender, about 5 minutes. Stir in the sugar and Jack Daniel's. Continue to cook until the juice has thickened, about 5 minutes. Serve warm.

Mashed Potatoes Au Gratin

Makes 8 servings

Long before "hybrid" became hip, was this easy hybrid casserole of potatoes au gratin and mashed potatoes. For the mashed portion, be sure to use russet potatoes for their light fluffiness. The eggs lighten the texture of the potatoes while the top develops a handsome golden crust. Before serving, dress the dish with fresh chives and either bits of country ham or crumbled bacon.

Occasionally I'll turn this into dinner by adding some cooked chopped onion and sausage or a little chopped baked ham. Use other cheeses if you like, or try a spoonful or two of prepared horseradish, a jar of drained pimientos, or a little Dijon mustard.

4 pounds russet baking potatoes, peeled and cut into 1 ½-inch chunks
1 tablespoon salt, plus more for seasoning
1 cup hot milk
1 cup sour cream
¼ cup butter
3 eggs, beaten
2 cups grated sharp Cheddar cheese, divided

Heat the oven to 400°F. Grease a 2-quart shallow casserole dish. Cover the potatoes with water in a large pot. Add about a tablespoon of salt. Bring the water to a boil and simmer the potatoes until tender, about 20 minutes. Drain and return the potatoes to the pot. Mash the potatoes

Our hostess Lila told her table of Yankee guests that in the South we split the biscuit and put chicken gravy over it. The man on her right picked up his biscuit, split it, and while holding it in his hand, dabbed it with a quarter-size spot of gravy on the bottom, replaced the top and set it on his plate.

with the milk, sour cream, and butter until smooth. Season with salt. Stir in the eggs and 1 ½ cups of the cheese. Spread the potatoes in the greased dish leaving the top bumpy. Sprinkle with the remaining ½ cup cheese. Bake for 30 minutes or until heated through and the top begins to brown.

Mother's Best Fried Corn

Makes 6 servings

My daddy so loved that he married a good country cook. Many a time he'd come home for midday dinner escorting an unexpected guest or two, just to show off Mother's cooking. She never knew how many places to set, but she did begin to notice that oftentimes a few certain salesmen, and one particular preacher, would pay a sudden visit to Daddy's store just before noon.

Today, her fried corn is still the specialty most often requested by her grand-children. Fried corn is not really fried but simply cooked in bacon drippings or butter until creamy and thickened. Mother says to do at least a dozen ears if you're going to the trouble. We prefer any white corn over yellow. We believe it to be sweeter, whether it is or not!

> ¼ cup (½ stick) butter or bacon drippings
> 12 ears of sweet corn, kernels removed and cobs scraped*
> 1 cup water
> Pinch or two of sugar
> 1 tablespoon cornstarch, if necessary
> Salt to taste

Melt the butter in a large skillet over medium high heat. Add the corn, water, and sugar. Cook and stir about 20 minutes or until the corn mix-ture turns milky and thickens. If it seems too thin, dissolve the corn-starch in 3 tablespoons of water and add to the pan. Continue to cook until bubbly and thickened.

*When cutting corn off the cob, stand the cob on its end and care-fully cut half the kernels with a very sharp knife. Next, scrape down the cob with the back of the knife to extract the rest of the kernel and the juices without dulling the knife blade.

Things Taste Better with Jack

A kitchen table brainstorm session is behind this little list meant to inspire you while working in your kitchen.

Savory Flavors

Grilled meats—beef, pork, lamb, chicken
Deglazed pan drippings from pan-frying beef, pork, or chicken
Au jus pan drippings from roasted meats
Barbecue sauces
Hot wings
Sweet potatoes
Winter squash
Salmon with sweet teriyaki sauce
Buttery sautéed mushrooms
Creamy rich foie gras
Blue cheese dips and spreads
Liver pate
Shrimp, crab, and lobster—barbecued or in a creamy sauce
Sweet and savory meatballs or sausages
French onion soup
Creamy mushroom bisque
Cocktail sauce
Glazed duckling or goose
Venison and all kinds of game
Cranberry relish
Fried apples
Baked beans
Sweet relishes and chutneys
Chili
Sugar glazed baked ham
Beef stew
Caramelized onions

Heard around the TABLE

A Lynchburg couple on a tour of England got in the habit of stopping at pubs for directions. The lady would go in and ask if they had Jack Daniel's, they would say yes, and she'd say, "Well, that's where I came from. Can you give me directions?" They were always so friendly and nice.

Sweet Flavors

Flaming warm fruits such as bananas, apples, cherries, pineapple, or peaches

Caramel sauce

Pecan praline

Dried fruits of all kinds

Citrus desserts

Crème Anglaise and boiled custard

Buttery baked or sautéed apple desserts

Gingerbread

Chocolate sauces, cakes, and ice cream

Rich sponge cake trifle or tiramisu

Desserts with all kinds of nuts

Pecan pie

Bread pudding

Poached pears or peaches

Maple syrup

Molasses

Vanilla

Fruitcake—soak the cakes in Jack instead of brandy

Coffee desserts

Sweetened whipped cream

Pumpkin or sweet potato pie

Cheesecake

Brown sugar

Pepper Jack Rice Bake

Makes 8 to 10 servings

Country cooks are experts at making the most of everything, especially leftovers. Sort of like sour mash, a little of last night's supper usually appears in the next day's meal. This rice casserole is just one of those happy accidents that occurred when I found myself with a few extra ears of roasted corn. This peppery variation of a popular Miss Mary's casserole includes roasted corn kernels and a little red bell pepper that you can roast or cook in a pan with onion. The Pepper Jack cheese adds a nice kick. Use hot green chiles, too, if you like a southwestern taste.

2 tablespoons oil

1 medium red bell pepper, chopped

1 medium onion, chopped

1 ½ cups rice, cooked according to package directions (6 cups cooked)

8 ounces sour cream

1 can (10.75 ounces) condensed cream of celery soup

2 cans (4.5 ounces each) chopped green chiles

1 cup roasted corn kernels

2 cups shredded Pepper Jack or Monterey Jack cheese, divided

Salt and black pepper, to taste

Heat the oven to 375°F. Grease a 9 x 13-inch baking dish. Heat the oil in a large skillet over medium-high heat. Add the bell pepper and onion and cook until softened, 7 to 8 minutes. Combine the cooked rice, sour cream, soup, green chiles, corn, and cooked peppers and onion, and 1 cup of the cheese in a large mixing bowl. Blend well. Season with salt and pepper.

Pour the mixture into the greased baking dish. Cover the dish with foil and bake 30 minutes. Remove the foil cover and sprinkle the remaining 1 cup of cheese on top. Bake uncovered for 10 minutes or until the cheese is melted and the casserole is bubbly.

Not Up to Frying Tonight
Oven Roasted Okra

Heat the oven to 400°F. Arrange whole fresh okra pods in a single layer on a rimmed baking sheet or in a 9 x 13-inch baking pan. Drizzle with olive oil and sprinkle with salt. Toss well to blend. Bake about 30 minutes or until the okra pieces are lightly charred. The baking time will vary according to the size of the okra pods. Serve hot or at room temperature. You can even serve them with toothpicks as a fun cocktail appetizer.

Oven Roasted Okra, Tomatoes and Onions—Proceed as above, but add a handful of cherry tomatoes and an onion cut into slivers and toss well before baking.

Everyday Southern Fried Okra

Makes 8 servings

At Miss Mary's we put fried okra on the dinner tables every single day. If we changed our minds about this, I believe the okra market would react instantly and most unfavorably! The secret to our exceptional fried okra is always to "dry" the okra in the cornmeal for at least 30 minutes before frying. Once it's "set," the cornmeal adheres to the okra much better during the frying process.

Many of our guests from beyond the South (and beyond the country too) have never seen okra, so I (and the hostesses) offer extra encouragement to the wary not to miss out on such an opportunity as this. A gentleman guest once confided that the sum total of his okra experience was spying a single piece floating in a bowl of canned vegetable soup. So unappealing, he set it aside. You can't blame him, certainly not after enjoying our delicious Miss Mary dinner table staple.

When entertaining friends at home, I serve fried okra in little baskets for a hot tidbit with cocktails. This treat instantly starts fun party conversation, as does a basket of pork rinds sprinkled with a little hot sauce and warmed in the oven, by the way.

> 2 boxes (10 ounces each) frozen sliced okra or 3 cups sliced fresh or frozen okra
> 2 cups self-rising cornmeal mix
> Black pepper to taste (optional)
> Vegetable oil for frying
> Salt, to taste

Thaw and drain the frozen okra in a colander. Gently roll the okra a few at a time in cornmeal and coat each piece evenly. Set aside about 30 minutes to 1 hour to dry. Heat ½ inch of oil in a large skillet to 365°F. Add batches of okra to the hot oil in a single layer. Gently roll the pieces with a fork or slotted spoon until the okra is browned on all sides. Remove with a slotted spoon and drain on paper towels. Season with salt and serve immediately.

Sweet Tomato Supper Pudding

Makes 8 to 10 servings

Grilled pork chops (or nearly any grilled meats or vegetables) are well balanced by a side of this sweet tomato pudding. Lynchburg folks have long made sweet stewed tomato side dishes with stale bread and home-canned tomatoes during the winter and spring months to add a little color to the table. We always make it extra sweet with at least one generous cup of sugar. The Bobo version is always pure, absent onion or cheese. For entertaining at home, I prefer the tomatoes adorned with onions and cheese. I might even toss fresh basil on top.

½ cup (1 stick) butter
1 medium onion, chopped
2 cans (28 ounces each) whole tomatoes with the juice
½ cup to 1 cup sugar
1 teaspoon dried basil
4 cups toasted white bread cubes
Black pepper, to taste
1 ½ cups grated sharp white or yellow Cheddar cheese or ½ cup grated Parmesan cheese, optional

Heat the oven to 375°F. Grease a 9 x 13-inch baking dish. Heat the butter in a large saucepan over medium heat. Add the onion and cook the onion until softened, 7 to 8 minutes. Stir in the tomatoes and sugar. Cook and stir until the sugar has dissolved. Stir in the basil, bread cubes, and pepper. Pour the mixture into the greased baking dish. Bake uncovered for 20 minutes. Sprinkle with cheese and return to the oven for 10 minutes.

Years ago we'd bring our jars and bushels of fruits and vegetables down to the extension service cannery where they'd provide rural families with a roomy shared kitchen, canning equipment, and plenty of free advice. It was a great service that kept our own kitchens clean. My mother always canned the best tomatoes and sweetest tomato juice which we enjoyed well into the cool, dreary season. Her secret, which she learned from her mother, was a pinch of sugar and salt in each jar. "Otherwise, they're not fit to eat, don't you think?" Mother would ask confidently.

Tennessee Butternut Squash

Makes 8 to 10 servings

If you think that winter squash is not worth fixing without pools of butter and brown sugar, this recipe might change your mind. Combining creamy butternut squash with savory onions, acidic tomatoes, and earthy sharp Cheddar cheese confirms that opposites do attract. It's a chic, colorful cold weather side that can be assembled ahead and baked just before serving. We love it with all kinds of poultry and pork. I've demonstrated this dish on television time and again, always receiving a hearty response from the appreciative and hungry television crew.

2 ½ to 3 pounds butternut squash (about two medium)
Pinch of sugar
Salt and pepper, to taste
3 tablespoons butter
1 medium onion, chopped
2 cloves garlic, minced
¼ cup Jack Daniel's Tennessee Whiskey
1 can (14 ounces) diced tomatoes, drained
1 ½ cups sharp white Cheddar or Gruyere cheese

Heat the oven to 400°F. Grease a 9 x 13-inch baking dish. Split the squash in half and scoop out the seeds. Place the squash halves cut side down in the baking dish. Cover the dish lightly with foil and bake until tender, about 45 minutes. Remove from the oven and cool enough to handle. Scoop out the squash and place the halves back in the dish. Season the squash with a pinch of sugar, salt, and pepper; set aside.

Heat the butter in a skillet over medium heat. Add the onion and garlic and cook until tender, about 7 minutes. Add the Jack Daniel's and continue to cook until the liquid has evaporated. Spoon the onion mixture over the squash. Top with tomatoes and bake 20 minutes. Sprinkle the top with cheese and return the dish to the oven for 10 minutes or until the cheese is melted and bubbly.

Sour Mash Sweet Potatoes

Makes 8 servings

Here is our most requested holiday dinner recipe. *You will find Sour Mashed Sweet Potatoes on Miss Mary's tables at both seatings from December 1st through the 24th. By the New Year our hostesses and cooks are quite ready to retire sweet potatoes in any form until the next December. Delicious as they are, I have to agree. One year we all voted to celebrate our holiday gathering at a Tullahoma pizza parlor in January. Even we need a little change from time to time.*

Stay away from the can! Always cook fresh sweet potatoes for the most delicious results. You will be pleased by the huge difference in flavor. Boil the sweet potatoes in their jackets and the skins will slide right off when cooked. It's up to your family tradition whether to top the sweet potatoes with toasted chopped pecans (I'm a pecan gal myself) or marshmallows. Or both.

> 4 large sweet potatoes
> ¼ cup butter
> ¾ cup brown sugar
> ⅛ teaspoon salt
> 1 tablespoon fresh orange zest, optional
> ¼ cup Jack Daniel's Tennessee Whiskey
> ½ cup lightly toasted chopped pecans

Place the sweet potatoes in a large pot and cover completely with water. Add a little salt to the water. Bring to a boil, cover, and cook until tender, about 35 minutes. Drain and cool enough to handle.

Heat the oven to 350°F. Peel off the skins and place the potatoes in a large mixing bowl. Mash the potatoes with the butter until slightly lumpy. Stir in the sugar, salt, orange zest, and Jack Daniel's. Spoon half of the sweet potato mixture into a buttered 2-quart casserole dish. Sprinkle with half of the pecans. Repeat with another layer. Bake for about 30 minutes or until heated through.

Squash Casserole with Cheddar Cornbread Crumbs

Makes 8 to 10 servings

I can't imagine what we'd do without leftover cornbread at Miss Mary's. Cornbread crumbs find their way onto so many of our vegetable casseroles because cornbread and vegetables together make a wonderful taste and texture combination, as this squash casserole proves.

At the risk of repeating myself, this casserole is yet another dish improved by the flavorful qualities of country ham bits. Substitute bacon drippings for the butter when cooking the vegetables, if you like. When adding country ham, be careful with salt and always taste first. I know plenty of folks who would top this popular casserole with buttery cracker crumbs, too, and others who prefer to stir the cheese right into the squash. Both are delicious.

6 tablespoons butter, divided
1 large onion, chopped
10 cups sliced yellow squash
½ cup water
1 jar (2 ounces) chopped pimientos, undrained
¼ to ½ cup finely chopped country ham, optional
Salt and black pepper, to taste
2 to 3 cups coarsely crumbled cornbread or 2 cups cracker crumbs
2 cups grated Cheddar cheese

Heat the oven to 375°F. Grease a 9 x 13-inch baking dish. Melt 4 tablespoons of the butter in a large saucepan over medium heat. Stir in the onion and cook until tender, stirring occasionally, 7 to 8 minutes. Add the squash and water. Reduce the heat; cover, and simmer about 20 minutes. Mash the squash with a fork to break up large pieces. Stir in the pimientos and the country ham, if desired. Season with salt and pepper. Pour the squash into the greased baking dish. Combine the crumbled cornbread and the cheese and sprinkle evenly over the top. Dot with the remaining 2 tablespoons of butter and bake 20 to 30 minutes or until bubbly and the topping is golden brown.

Easy Cabbage Casserole Additions

Add ½ cup minced country ham or make it a main dish with 2 cups of chopped regular "city" ham or sliced cooked smoked sausage.

Dry County Cabbage Casserole

Makes 8 to 10 servings

Green cabbage is central to Southern country cooking. Cabbage is inexpensive and versatile, and it possesses exceptional keeping qualities. You do not have to grow your own crop, as my assistant manager Debbie and her husband, Goose, do. Count on it being in any grocery store.

Cabbage offers so many side dish options it should receive a diversity award. Cabbage can be boiled, baked, roasted, fermented, sweetened, and soured. You'll find it in hot side dishes, a tangy relish, the basis for a soup, and salads. Country cooks make sweet relishes, creamy casseroles, kraut, and gallons of slaw from this humble vegetable that unfortunately never quite makes it onto the fashionable foods list. We love it just the same, and when it does top the charts, you heard it here first.

If you're not a fan then perhaps you've just been unlucky with restaurant slaws and haven't yet enjoyed this creamy casserole. We've converted many cabbage doubters into real believers with this one, very old-fashioned recipe.

12 cups sliced cabbage (cut into ¼-inch-thick slices)
½ cup (1 stick) butter, divided
1 large onion, chopped
1 medium bell pepper (any color), chopped
6 tablespoons all-purpose flour
3 cups milk
Salt and black pepper, to taste
1 cup grated Cheddar cheese
1 cup cornbread crumbs, cracker crumbs, or coarse breadcrumbs

Heat the oven to 350°F. Grease a 9 x 13-inch baking dish.

Bring a large pot of salted water to boil. Add the cabbage and cook until tender but still bright green, 7 to 10 minutes. Drain well in a colander and set aside. Heat 6 tablespoons of the butter in a medium saucepan over medium-low heat. Add the onion and bell pepper and cook until the vegetables are tender, 7 to 10 minutes. Stir in the flour and blend well, cooking and stirring about 1 minute to allow the flour to cook in the butter. Add the milk and stir until smooth. Cook, stirring constantly, over medium heat until thick and bubbly. Remove from the heat. Season with salt and pepper, to taste. Stir in the cheese until it is melted.

Place the drained cabbage in the prepared dish. Pour the cheese sauce over the cabbage. Stir to evenly coat the cabbage with the sauce. Top with the crumbs and dot with the remaining 2 tablespoons of butter. Bake for 30 minutes.

Apricot Dinner Casserole

Makes 10 to 12 servings

Have you caught on yet to the rather generous number of sweet side dishes in this chapter? We Southerners consider this among our most endearing qualities. Are those congealed salads actually salads, or are they congealed desserts? My moth-

er's cranberry fluff holds its own as a side dish or a dessert, so it's easy to remain undecided.

Casseroles made with canned fruit are another wonderful, and frugal, country way to transform ordinary canned fruit into elegant sides, especially when appearing on holiday sideboards. Add the additional festive touch of dried cherries, dried cranberries, or golden raisins sprinkled into the apricots.

4 cans (15.25 ounces each) apricot halves in heavy syrup, drained
1 ½ cups brown sugar
2 cups butter cracker crumbs
½ cup (1 stick) butter, melted
¼ cup Jack Daniel's Tennessee Whiskey, optional
Cinnamon to taste

Heat the oven to 350°F. Grease a 9 x 13-inch casserole dish. Place the apricots cut-side up in the dish. Sprinkle with the brown sugar and the cracker crumbs. Drizzle with the melted butter and Jack Daniel's. Bake 45 minutes or until the casserole is bubbly and golden brown. Season with cinnamon to taste.

Pineapple Cheddar Dinner Casserole

Makes 10 to 12 servings

This casserole is just right with a big baked ham for Easter.

3 cans (20 ounces each) pineapple chunks, packed in juice
¼ cup all-purpose flour
½ cup sugar
2 cups shredded sharp Cheddar cheese
2 cups butter cracker crumbs
¼ cup (½ stick) butter, melted

Heat the oven to 350°F. Grease a 9 x 13-inch casserole dish. Drain the pineapple, reserving ½ cup of the juice. Place the pineapple chunks in the dish. Combine the flour and sugar in a small bowl and sprinkle over the fruit. Drizzle with the reserved juice. Sprinkle with the cheese and cracker crumbs. Drizzle with the butter. Bake 45 minutes or until the casserole is bubbly and golden brown.

Jack in the Beans

Makes 6 servings

Around here you can't have barbecue, or even a good grilled hamburger, without beans. This easy-to-doctor bean recipe has come in handy more times than I can remember. Make it with or without a little smoky flavor courtesy of liquid smoke, but I always use bacon drippings for added richness and flavor.

2 tablespoons bacon drippings or oil
1 small onion, chopped
2 tablespoons brown sugar
⅓ cup Jack Daniel's Tennessee Whiskey, optional
1 can (28 ounces) baked beans
1 tablespoon spicy brown mustard
2 tablespoons Worcestershire sauce
1 teaspoon liquid smoke, optional

Heat the drippings in a large saucepan. Stir in the onion and brown sugar. Cook over medium heat, stirring frequently, until the onion is soft and golden brown, about 5 minutes. Stir in the Jack Daniel's, baked beans, brown mustard, Worcestershire sauce, and liquid smoke. Simmer 20 to 30 minutes.

Low and Slow Baked Beans

Makes 10 to 12 servings

If the first rule of barbecue is "low and slow" and the first side of barbecue is baked beans, the most consistent route to success is an electric slow cooker. Not only do the beans cook gently and beautifully, but a slow cooker frees you to be elsewhere with no worries about a scorched pot on the stove. Canned beans save you an extra step, and the sorghum with a touch of Worcestershire sauce adds the sweet, rich unctuousness so important to good baked beans.

1 to 2 tablespoons oil
1 large onion, chopped
1 clove garlic, minced
¼ pound salt pork
4 cans (15.5 ounces each) navy or great Northern beans
½ cup Jack Daniel's Tennessee Whiskey, optional

1 can (6 ounces) tomato paste
1 cup sorghum or mild-flavored molasses
½ cup prepared yellow mustard
1 tablespoon Worcestershire sauce
Salt and black pepper, to taste

Heat the oil in a skillet over medium heat. Add the onion and garlic and cook until the onions are translucent. Combine the onion mixture, salt pork, beans, whiskey, tomato paste, molasses, mustard, and Worcestershire sauce in a large slow cooker and cook on high 4 to 6 hours or on low about 8 hours. Add salt and pepper to taste.

DINNER

Three Keys to Fried Chicken Success

Miss Margaret's Best Southern Fried Chicken
Jimmy Bedford's Country Ham Glaze

How to Bake a Tennessee Country Ham in a Bag or on a Rack in a Roaster

Lazy Hunters

Tennessee Walking Horse National Celebration

Pan-Fried Tennessee Whiskey Chicken Breasts
Skillet Steaks with Lynchburg Pan Sauce
Tolley Town Pot Roast
Kitchen Beef Brisket
Oven Barbecue Tennessee Pork Tenderloin
Miss Mary's Chicken with Pastry or Biscuit Dumplings

Biscuit Dumpling Variation

Bobo's Pork Roast
Pantry Salmon Croquettes with Creole Mustard Sauce
Crispy Fried Catfish or Crappie
Miss Mary's Famous Meatloaf
Crispy Oven Fried Chicken with Pork Rind Crust

The Jack Daniel Distillery Tour

Tennessee Barbecued Shrimp
Chicken and Dressing Skillet Cake
Slow Simmered Marinated Chuck Roast
Sauer Mash Smoked Sausage Pot
Sausage Cornbread Supper Pudding
Country Stuffed Peppers

Three Keys to Fried Chicken Success

Small birds—Supermarket chickens these days tend to be large, four to five pounds. Look for the smallest bird labeled "fryer" (avoid the big roasters when frying) and cut it up yourself at home. The smaller breast pieces cook evenly, don't dry out as quickly, and have a good ratio of crispy skin to juicy meat. When using larger chicken breasts, cut them in half before frying.

Cast iron skillet—Even heating throughout a pan or skillet is essential for good frying, and heavy cast iron heats more evenly than other metals. Frying chicken (and plenty of bacon) keeps an iron pan well-seasoned, which also makes the best cornbread.

Lard—Unlike vegetable oils, lard gives fried chicken the proper, slightly earthy flavor and crisp texture you need for real Southern fried chicken. There's just nothing like it.

How to Make Perfect Southern Fried Chicken

Pick small whole birds weighing 3 ½ to 4 pounds (not the big roasting birds) and cut them up yourself.

Cut 11 pieces including a pulley bone (wishbone). Cut off the wings, legs, and thighs. Cut around the pulley bone so you have a long skinny piece with two meaty ends of breast meat. Cut the breast in two, and cut two side breasts (more like backs).

Rinse and dry the pieces. Season with salt. Dip each piece in a beaten egg, if you like (some folks dip in egg, buttermilk, sweet milk, or nothing). Then simply coat each piece in seasoned flour. Allow the floured pieces to dry for about 15 minutes so that the coating will stay on the skin during the frying process.

Use an iron skillet. Fry the pieces in about ½ to 1 inch of hot lard (365°F on a deep fry thermometer) and do not crowd the skillet. Cook the chicken in smaller batches to allow room among all the pieces.

Brown the chicken pieces on both sides. Then reduce the heat and cover the skillet to help the meat cook all the way through so that the juices run clear when the meat is pierced with a fork. About five minutes before it's fully cooked, remove the lid, return the heat to high, and crisp both sides. Remove the chicken to a platter covered with paper towels to absorb excess oil. Fried chicken out of the pan is exceptionally hot, so allow it to cool slightly before handling.

Miss Margaret's Best Southern Fried Chicken

Makes about 7 pieces of chicken

Every spring Daddy used to buy a cage full of baby chicks down at his general store and raise them in the chicken yard out back until they weighed about two pounds. Mother simply cut the tender little dressed birds in half, dusted them with seasoned flour, and tossed them in a skillet of hot lard.

Our sixth Master Distiller, Jimmy Bedford, grew up watching his mother, Wilma, snag a little fryer, pecking and scratching out in the yard, and have it fried and on the table for breakfast within the hour. Dip the chicken in egg before flouring for a thicker crust.

Here's to the original "free-range" chicken fried in lard that we serve at Miss Mary's today. We cut up the chicken to include a piece called the pulley bone. It's the wishbone with meat from the top of the breast.

1 ½ to 3 pound chicken (the smaller the better)
Salt
2 eggs, beaten
¼ cup milk or buttermilk
2 cups flour, seasoned with salt and black pepper
3 cups lard (you can use vegetable or peanut oil)

Cut the chicken into pieces such as 2 thighs, 2 drumsticks, 2 breast halves, and 1 pulley bone.

Rinse and pat dry. Season the chicken with salt. Beat the eggs in a shallow bowl with the milk. Place the seasoned flour in another shallow bowl. Dip the chicken pieces into the egg wash and then in the flour, coating well. Set aside to dry for about 15 minutes.

Heat the lard in a large high-sided skillet with a lid, preferably a cast iron chicken fryer. When the oil is hot (365° to 375° F), carefully place the chicken pieces in the skillet, but don't overcrowd the skillet. Cook until the chicken is golden brown on one side, about 10 minutes. Turn and brown on the other side. Reduce the heat to medium-low. Cover the pan and cook for 10 minutes per side. Uncover, increase the heat, and cook 5 minutes to allow the chicken to get crispy. The chicken is done when the meat juices run clear when pierced with the tip of a knife. The smaller the pieces, the faster the cooking time.

Jimmy Bedford's Country Ham Glaze

Our much-loved sixth Master Distiller, the late Jimmy Bedford, was well known throughout Moore County for more than just his good tasting whiskey. Jimmy cured and smoked his own country hams in the smokehouse on his farm just down the road. These days country hams are more readily available than ever. Here's Jimmy's quick ham glaze that I like because it complements the saltiness of a good country ham.

3/4 cup brown sugar
1/4 cup Jack Daniel's Tennessee Whiskey
1/2 cup coarse-grain mustard
1 whole country ham (about 15 pounds)

Combine the brown sugar, Jack Daniel's, and mustard in a small bowl. Follow the manufacturer's directions for cooking your ham. Cool slightly. Cut the thick layer of skin and fat off the cooked ham with a sharp knife. Brush the cooked ham with the glaze. Bake at 400°F about 20 minutes or until the glaze caramelizes on the ham.

We serve country ham at room temperature very thinly sliced. An electric knife makes the neatest slices. We carve up such a ham-storm at Miss Mary's that our electric knives often burn out from exhaustion throughout the year.

How to Bake a Tennessee Country Ham in a Bag or on a Rack in a Roaster

Scrub all the mold off the ham. Soak overnight in cold water. Saw off the hock, if you like.

Place the ham (skin-side up so it will baste itself) in an oven cooking bag. Pour in about 1 quart of water. Tie the bag tightly around the ham so that the water rises about halfway up the ham.*

Place in a shallow roasting pan that the ham will comfortably fit in—not too big or too small.

Roast 20 minutes per pound at 325°F. The internal temperature should be 160°F when the ham is done, and the bone will feel loose. Remove the bone and save it for a pot of beans.

Cool slightly. Cut the skin and fat off the ham, if desired. Coat with Jimmy Bedford's Country Ham Glaze (page 141) and bake at 400°F about 20 minutes or until the glaze caramelizes on the ham. Wrap securely in foil. Store in the refrigerator.

*Or place the trimmed ham fat-side up on a rack in a roasting pan with 2 inches of water. Cover tightly with foil. Bake as directed above.

Lazy Hunters

Goose Baxter, a seasoned tour guide at the distillery and avid hunter, says squirrel hunting is a lazy man's sport because you don't go anywhere. "Find yourself a hickory, beech, or white oak tree where they're feeding on the nuts. Go lean up on a nearby tree and wait. We call it 'still' hunting because you sit real still." Sounds good to me—just relaxing and enjoying the scenery. Squirrel hunters like Goose enjoy a big fried squirrel breakfast with fried potatoes, gravy, and biscuits after an early morning hunt. All the *real*, lazy hunters like me just serve fried chicken.

Tennessee Walking Horse National Celebration

ncredible as it may sound, country ham is a major topic of discussion at the annual Tennessee Walking Horse National Celebration held down the road in Shelbyville during the week before Labor Day. The horses are magnificent, but it's the country ham sandwiches (sliced salty ham always served on soft hamburger buns) sold by a variety of vendors that sustain the crowd of thousands through long days of events. My family and plenty of our friends have held box seats for the celebration as long as I can remember. And every year it doesn't take long for word to get around about who's making the best sandwiches. We feel obliged to try them all.

Pan-Fried Tennessee Whiskey Chicken Breasts

Makes 6 servings

Some folks prefer pan-frying boneless, skinless chicken breasts instead of frying the whole bird. I'll admit, it's a lot easier. Dress them up with a savory sauce featuring a little Jack and mustard or add a spoonful of orange marmalade for an exotic sweetness. You'll also have good luck using the more flavorful boneless, skinless chicken thighs in this recipe.

6 boneless, skinless chicken breast halves
Salt and black pepper
½ cup all-purpose flour
5 tablespoons butter, divided
2 tablespoons oil
2 tablespoons minced onion
1 cup chicken broth
¼ cup Jack Daniel's Tennessee Whiskey
1 tablespoon coarse-grain Dijon mustard

Sprinkle the chicken with salt and pepper. Place the flour in a shallow bowl. Coat the chicken pieces evenly with flour, shaking off the excess.

Heat 2 tablespoons of the butter and the oil in a large cast iron or non-stick skillet until hot. Place half the chicken pieces in the skillet. Cook 4 to 5 minutes without turning. Flip the chicken over and cook 4 to 5 minutes. Remove to a platter and keep the chicken warm. Cook the remaining chicken and remove to the platter.

Add the onion to the drippings in the skillet. Cook over medium heat until soft, about 3 minutes. Stir in the broth and Jack Daniel's. Increase the heat to high and boil the liquid until thickened, stirring frequently, about 5 minutes. Stir in the mustard and the remaining butter. Pour the sauce over the chicken. Serve immediately.

Skillet Steaks with Lynchburg Pan Sauce

Makes 2 to 4 servings

In Tennessee, we grill steaks all twelve months of the year, but there's nothing like the crust you can only get from pan-frying meat in a hot, hot iron skillet. A well-ventilated kitchen is the key to success. To keep the smoke outside, use your gas grill side burner or turkey fryer burner. This is about as man-pleasing a recipe as I know. Get to know your butcher, and cut those steaks nice and thick.

> 2 porterhouse or T-bone steaks, about 1 ½ to 2 inches thick
> Vegetable oil
> Salt and pepper
> 2 tablespoons butter
> 1 tablespoon Worcestershire sauce
> ¼ cup Jack Daniel's Tennessee Whiskey

Heat a large cast iron skillet over high heat until very hot, about 10 minutes. Generously rub the steaks with oil and sprinkle with salt and pepper. Cook the steaks one at a time. Sear on one side, about 5 minutes. Flip and cook an additional 5 minutes for medium-rare; 6 minutes for medium. Remove the steak from the skillet and keep it warm while you sear the second steak. Remove the steak from the skillet and reduce the heat to medium. Melt the butter in the skillet, stir in the Worcestershire sauce and Jack Daniel's, and bring to a boil. Cook about 2 minutes until thickened. Pour the sauce over the steaks and serve immediately.

Tolley Town Pot Roast

Makes 10 servings

This is my down-home version of France's famous Boeuf Bourguignon, and it's a make-ahead, party home run for stress-free entertaining. Shape the theme of the dinner with side dishes beyond the usual green beans, salad, and mashed potatoes. Try creamy grits or wide egg noodles, make a wintery salad with watercress, and swap the green beans for roasted Brussels sprouts.

4 pounds beef chuck roast, cut into 2-inch chunks
½ cup all-purpose flour
About ¼ cup bacon drippings or oil
3 medium onions, chopped
2 ribs celery, chopped
2 large carrots, chopped
4 cloves garlic, minced
1 can (14.5 ounces) diced tomatoes, undrained
½ cup Jack Daniel's Tennessee Whiskey
2 cups beef broth
2 tablespoons Dijon mustard
2 bay leaves
1 package (16 ounces) mushrooms, halved or quartered
1 package (16 ounces) frozen pearl onions
Salt and pepper, to taste
Chopped fresh parsley

Heat the oven to 350°F. Toss the meat with the flour in a medium bowl. Heat 2 tablespoons of the bacon drippings in a large Dutch oven with an oven-proof lid over medium-high. In 3 batches, brown the meat on all sides . Add more drippings as necessary. Set the meat aside. Reduce the heat to medium and add the onion, celery, and carrots. Cook until the onions become tender and just begin to brown, about 8 minutes. Stir in the garlic and continue to cook an additional 2 minutes. Return the meat to the pan and add the tomatoes, Jack Daniel's, beef broth, mustard, and bay leaves. Bring to a boil. Cover and cook in the oven for 2 hours. Stir in the mushrooms and pearl onions. Season with salt and pepper. Cover and return to the oven and cook 1 hour or until the meat and vegetables are fork tender. Serve with egg noodles, grits, or potatoes. Sprinkle with parsley.

Kitchen Beef Brisket

Makes 10 servings

The Jack Daniel's World Championship Invitational Barbecue contestants who compete in Lynchburg in October may dismiss oven-cooked brisket with a wave of the tongs. Not me. A brisket needs steady, warm, moist heat, so why not take advantage of the oven? After slow oven roasting, grill the brisket for a little smoky char. I usually cook the brisket in the oven with a dash of liquid smoke slipped into the marinade. Be sure to get a flat brisket with a nice layer of fat to help tenderize the meat as it cooks.

1 (5 to 6 pound) beef brisket
1 medium onion, cut into thin wedges
¼ cup Jack Daniel's Tennessee Whiskey
¼ cup soy sauce
¼ cup ketchup
¼ cup brown sugar
¼ cup cider vinegar
2 tablespoons Dijon mustard
1 tablespoon Worcestershire sauce
2 cloves garlic, minced
1 tablespoon liquid smoke, optional
Black pepper, to taste

Heat the oven to 300°F. Put the brisket fat-side up in a roasting pan and sprinkle with the onions. Combine the Jack Daniel's, soy sauce, ketchup, brown sugar, cider vinegar, mustard, Worcestershire sauce, garlic, liquid smoke, and pepper in a large measuring cup. Pour the mixture over the brisket. Cover the pan tightly with heavy duty aluminum foil. Bake about 4 hours or until the internal temperature reaches 190°F and the meat is tender.* Let the meat rest at least 10 minutes before carving across the grain into thin slices with a sharp knife. Serve with pan drippings.

*Even better, cook the brisket a day before serving. Remove the cooked brisket from the drippings. Cover tightly with foil and refrigerate overnight. Refrigerate the drippings and skim off the hardened fat the next day. Before serving, slice the brisket while it's cold for a much neater cut. Combine the meat with the pan drippings in a baking dish. Cover and reheat at 325°F for about 30 minutes or until thoroughly warm.

Oven Barbecue Tennessee Pork Tenderloin

Makes 6 servings

When outdoor grilling is just out of the question, barbecued oven-roasted pork tenderloin is a clever alternative. This basting sauce is terrific on oven-baked (or grilled) ribs as well. The sauce is very sticky, so remember to line a baking or roasting pan with foil for easy cleanup. Serve the sliced pork with Cast Iron Cornbread (page 81), white beans, and either creamy White Mayo or Clear Vinegar Slaw (page 93). Now that's not a bad indoor picnic—even without the hickory smoke.

¼ cup Jack Daniel's Tennessee Whiskey
¼ cup soy sauce
¼ cup ketchup
½ cup brown sugar
½ teaspoon garlic powder
2 pounds pork tenderloin

Heat the oven to 450°F. Combine the Jack Daniel's, soy sauce, ketchup, brown sugar, and garlic powder in a small saucepan. Bring to a boil and simmer until slightly thickened, about 5 minutes. Place the tenderloin on a foil-lined baking or roasting pan. Brush with the sauce. Roast for about 30 minutes until the internal temperature is 155°F. Remove from the oven and let the meat rest about 10 minutes before slicing.

Miss Mary's Chicken with Pastry or Biscuit Dumplings

Makes 8 servings

This is one of our all-time favorites at Miss Mary's. You'll see that the creamy chicken mixture is pretty standard. What makes this dish so special is the delicious pastry made with lard. Our recipes may continue to evolve, but one thing we'll never give up is our loyalty to this historic tradition. Lard gives foods a savory richness that shortening lacks. We've shocked plenty of guests with the mention of the "L" word. I like to remind everyone that Miss Mary lived to be 102 and many of the old boarding house regulars lived well into their nineties. We like to attribute that to good wholesome eating—including lard. I certainly plan on following in their footsteps.

Make the pastry while the chicken is cooking, and don't throw out your pastry scraps. Cut them into pieces and place them on a cookie sheet. Brush with egg wash

and sprinkle with cinnamon and sugar. Bake them in the oven with the casserole until golden brown. Treat the kids and yourself with sweet pastry strips right out of the oven.

> 1 (2 ½ to 3-pound) chicken
> 1 large onion
> 1 rib celery
> 1 teaspoon salt
> ¼ cup all-purpose flour
> ¼ cup water
> Salt and black pepper to taste
> 1 Basic Pie Pastry (page 206)

Place the chicken, onion, celery, and salt in a large pot. Add enough water to completely cover the chicken. Bring to a boil; reduce the heat, and simmer until the chicken is tender and cooked through, about 1 hour. Skim away any foam that forms during cooking. Remove the chicken from the broth so the chicken can cool enough to handle. Pick the chicken off the bones, discarding bones and skin. Spread the chicken in a greased 9 x 13-inch baking dish and set aside.

Heat the oven to 400°F. Remove the celery and onion from the broth. Pour all but 3 cups of the broth from the pot and save the rest for another use. Combine the flour with the water in a small bowl. Blend to make a smooth paste and then stir it into the hot broth. Cook 5 to 7 minutes or until the broth is thickened. Season with salt and pepper. Pour over the chicken. Roll the pastry out in a rectangle about ¼-inch thick. Cut into strips about 2 inches wide and 13 inches long. Lay the strips over the chicken. Bake for 30 minutes or until the pastry is golden brown.

Biscuit Dumpling Variation

If making pastry isn't for you, make easy drop biscuit dumplings. Follow the recipe for Homemade Buttermilk Biscuits (page 76) but use 1 cup of regular milk. Drop the soft dough by spoonfuls over the warm chicken mixture and bake at 400°F for 20 to 25 minutes or until golden brown.

Bobo's Pork Roast

Makes about 12 servings

Traditional boarding house food is not about "one-dish" dinners of meats swimming together with vegetables in the same casserole. Our tables are crowded with platters of meats and gravy, bowls and casseroles of vegetable sides, and often a relish or two. The boarding house rule is to help yourself to the dish in front of you and pass to the left. By the time folks are starting on seconds, they're calling out for or offering a dish to the other end of the table.

Our pork roast is popular for seconds and thirds along with mashed potatoes and our tangy Crispy Kraut Salad (page 104). We slice it very thinly, which adds to the tenderness. Any size roast will do, just alter the seasonings and vegetable amounts.

1 (5 pound) pork loin roast, cut in half lengthwise
Meat tenderizer, such as Adolph's
Salt and black pepper to taste
Onion powder to taste
Garlic powder to taste
Lemon pepper to taste
3 stalks celery, coarsely chopped
3 carrots, peeled and coarsely chopped
2 onions, cut into wedges
⅓ cup flour
⅓ cup water

Sprinkle the roast with meat tenderizer and let it rest in the refrigerator at least 3 hours or overnight.

Heat the oven to 450°F. Sprinkle all sides of the two roast pieces with salt, pepper, onion powder, garlic powder, and lemon pepper. Arrange the celery, carrots, and onions in the bottom of a roasting pan. Add about 1 inch of hot water to the pan. Place a rack over the vegetables and place the pork roast pieces on the rack. If you don't have a rack, place the roast pieces directly on the vegetables. Cover tightly with foil and place the roast in the oven. Bake 1 ½ to 2 hours or until fork tender and registering 175°F on a meat thermometer. Remove the roast from the pan and let it rest on a board before slicing.

To make gravy, strain the drippings into a saucepan and discard the vegetables. Combine the flour and water in a small bowl to make a paste. Whisk the flour mixture into the drippings. Bring to a boil over medium heat and simmer until the gravy is bubbly and thickened, about 5 minutes. Season with salt and pepper. Thinly slice the roast and serve it on a platter covered with the gravy.

Pantry Salmon Croquettes with Creole Mustard Sauce

Makes about 13 croquettes and 3 cups of sauce

Canned is the only form of salmon anyone in land-locked Lynchburg had ever tasted back in Miss Mary's day and throughout my childhood. It's still an economical, convenient, and delicious pantry staple. Having canned salmon in the pantry is most of the work, that and crushing a few crackers. Unlike most fried foods, you don't have to enjoy the croquettes right away. They'll keep crisp and hot in a warm oven until serving time. Make the Creole Mustard Sauce as tangy as you like and pass the sauce at the table (always to the left, of course, like we do it at Miss Mary's). Use one can of salmon and cut the recipe in half for about six croquettes, but you'll miss the leftovers.

Croquettes

2 cans (14.75 ounces each) salmon, drained
1/2 cup grated onion
1 cup finely chopped celery
Juice of half a lemon (about 2 tablespoons)
1 tablespoon Worcestershire sauce
2 eggs, beaten
3/4 cup milk
3 cups cracker crumbs, divided (about 2 sleeves of saltines)
Vegetable oil for frying

Creole Mustard Sauce

5 tablespoons butter
5 tablespoons all-purpose flour
1 cup chicken broth
1 cup milk
2 tablespoons Creole mustard or other coarse-grain mustard to taste
1 cup frozen green peas
Salt and black pepper to taste

To make the croquettes: Place the salmon in a large bowl and remove the skin and large bones. Flake with a fork. Stir in the onion, celery, lemon juice, Worcestershire sauce, eggs, milk, and 1 1/2 cups cracker crumbs. Blend well. Scoop 1/3 cup of the mixture for each croquette. Gently coat with the remaining cracker crumbs, flatten slightly, and let rest on a cookie sheet. Heat 1/2 inch of oil in a large skillet over medium-high heat. Fry a few croquettes at a time until golden brown and crisp, 3 to 4 minutes per side. Keep the cooked croquettes in a warm oven while frying the rest.

To make the Creole Mustard Sauce: Melt the butter in a small saucepan over medium heat. Stir in the flour and cook until smooth and bubbly, about 1 minute. Gradually stir in the broth and milk. Bring the sauce to a boil and simmer until thickened. Stir in the mustard and peas. Season with salt and pepper. Cook until the peas are heated through. Serve with the croquettes.

Crispy Fried Catfish or Crappie

Makes 6 servings

Crappie fishing on nearby Tims Ford Lake is a high-priority pastime in Lynchburg, so you can bet our expert anglers keep freezers full. It's true, we don't bother with fish too much if it isn't fried. There's just something about the steaming white, moist flaky meat wrapped in a delicate crisp crust. Many folks don't bother with egg wash like we do with catfish at Miss Mary's. You can simply dredge the fillets in cornmeal and pan-fry them in a skillet. The self-rising cornmeal works great because it's already perfectly seasoned with salt.

> Vegetable oil for frying
> 1 cup self-rising cornmeal mix
> ¼ cup flour
> 2 eggs
> ½ cup milk
> Salt and black pepper to taste
> 6 to 10 catfish fillets or about 3 pounds crappie fillets

Heat about 1 to 2 inches of oil in a heavy iron skillet to 365°F. Combine the cornmeal and flour in a shallow bowl. In a separate bowl, beat the eggs and milk and blend well. Season the fish with salt and pepper. Dip the fish in the egg mixture and then the cornmeal mixture, coating all sides. Shake off the excess. Repeat for a double-dipped thicker crust, if you like. Let the coated fillets rest a few minutes before cooking.

Fry a few pieces of fish at a time in the hot oil until golden brown on all sides. Cooking time depends on the thickness of the fish. Test for doneness by piercing it with a fork or the tip of a knife into the thickest part of the fish. The fish is cooked through if the center is opaque and the flesh flakes easily. Drain on paper towels. Serve with Fish Fry Hushpuppies (page 79) and Jack's Red Dipping Sauce (page 241).

Miss Mary's Famous Meatloaf

Makes 6 servings

If you ever find yourself dragging a dish through the spice rack, consider Miss Mary's Famous Meatloaf—a testament to simplicity. Our guests love our meatloaf, not because it's spicy or exotic or heirloom or a fusion of flavors, but because it is

perfectly simple. So simple that the ingredient list might surprise you. No fancy seasonings, just our reliable onion and bell pepper flavor in both the meatloaf and our famous ketchup meatloaf sauce. Double the recipe because you'll need left-overs for sandwiches.

Appetizer suggestion? Serve the meatloaf as a true Tennessee country pâté—chilled and thinly sliced with fancy mustard, pickles, and crackers.

Meatloaf

1 ½ pounds ground beef
¾ cup quick-cooking oatmeal
1 ½ teaspoons salt
¼ cup finely chopped onion
¼ cup finely chopped bell pepper
¼ cup ketchup
2 eggs, beaten
1 tablespoon Worcestershire sauce
Dash of garlic powder
Dash of onion powder

Sauce

¾ cup ketchup
¼ cup brown sugar
2 tablespoons finely chopped onion

2 tablespoons finely chopped bell pepper

1 tablespoon Worcestershire sauce

1 tablespoon cider or white vinegar

Heat the oven to 350°F. Grease a 9 x 3-inch loaf pan or an 8-inch square casserole dish. Using your hands, combine the ground beef, oatmeal, salt, onion, bell pepper, ketchup, eggs, Worcestershire sauce, garlic powder, and onion powder in a large mixing bowl until well blended. Shape into a loaf that fits your prepared pan. Bake for 1 hour.

While the meatloaf bakes, prepare the sauce. Combine the ketchup, brown sugar, onion, bell pepper, Worcestershire sauce, and vinegar in a small saucepan and simmer until the vegetables are tender, about 10 minutes.

Remove the meatloaf from the oven. Pour off the excess juice in the pan and spread the top with some of the sauce. Return to the oven and bake for 10 minutes. Remove from the oven and let it rest 10 minutes before slicing. Serve slices on a platter drizzled with the remaining sauce.

Crispy Oven-Fried Chicken with Pork Rind Crust

Makes 4 to 6 servings

When you don't feel like frying chicken in lard in a skillet, you can get a darn good crust with a hint of its characteristic flavor thanks to crushed pork rinds. Yes, pork rinds. What a discovery—crushed pork rinds have the same delicate crunchiness as fancy panko bread crumbs. Together they make a dynamite crispy oven-fried chicken breading.

2 pounds boneless, skinless chicken breast halves (about 4 pieces)

1 ½ cups finely crushed pork rinds (1 bag (3 ¾-ounce) will make about 2 crushed cups)

1 ½ cups panko bread crumbs

1 teaspoon seasoned salt (like Lawry's)

Black pepper, to taste

2 eggs, beaten

2 tablespoons mayonnaise

2 tablespoons water

Heat the oven to 400°F. Cut the chicken breast halves crosswise into about 1 ½ inch wide strips. Combine the pork rind crumbs with the

panko bread crumbs, seasoned salt, and black pepper in a wide shallow bowl. Blend well with your fingers. Whisk together the eggs, mayonnaise, and water in a separate bowl. Dip the chicken pieces in the egg mixture and then the crumbs. Place the coated pieces on a greased, rimmed baking sheet. Bake 30 minutes or until golden brown and crisp. The internal temperature of the chicken should be at least 160°F on an instant read thermometer.

Heard around the TABLE

Miss Mary's was filled to the brim with fifth graders from Murfreesboro, Tennessee, led by a teacher who was interested in teaching manners. The children had prepared for weeks and wrote thank you letters when they got back to school. One young man wrote, "P.S. Give the cooks a raise." Another said "Miss Mary Bobo's is the best restaurant I've ever eaten in my life, and I'm ten years old."

The Jack Daniel Distillery Tour

Established in the 1830s and registered with the U.S. government in 1866 by Jack Daniel, the Jack Daniel Distillery is the oldest registered distillery in the United States (registered No. 1). The distillery is also included on the National Register of Historic Places.

Every year roughly 250,000 people from around the world visit Lynchburg and tour the distillery. The distillery offers guided tours from 9 a.m. to 4:30 p.m. seven days a week, except Thanksgiving Day, Christmas Day, and New Year's Day. Just pull into the lot in front of the Visitor Center and sign up for your tour at the front desk. It's just to the right of Uncle Jack. You can't miss him.

A distillery tour takes about an hour. Our tour guides are wonderful storytellers who will walk you through our Tennessee whiskey-making process. You'll meet plenty of friendly people along the way who will be glad to see you and proud to introduce you to our Lynchburg way of life.

Highlights of the Jack Daniel Distillery Tour

Visit the rickyard where we burn the cords and cords of hard sugar maple into the famous charcoal that mellows our Tennessee whiskey, one drop at a time.

Peer into the underground cave spring that inspired and encouraged Uncle Jack to locate his distillery here. The spring is the source of the pure, virtually iron-free water that goes into our whiskey. Cave spring water runs at a constant 56°F.

Take your picture with Uncle Jack at a few spots along the tour—at his life-size bronze statue where he stands guard at the cave spring; at two places in the Visitor Center—by his historic white marble statue in the center of the room, or next to the life-size black and white photograph of Jack on the wall; and in Jack Daniel's first office which bears the plaque designating the distillery as a National Historic Register site.

Watch and smell whiskey-making underway, including the whiskey stills; the fermenting tanks filled with the finest corn, rye, and barley malt; and the charcoal mellowing vats where our whiskey drips through the charcoal beds during the ten-day process.

Wander around a quiet barrel house where the whiskey spends four years aging. Each barrel house stores more than twenty thousand barrels of whiskey, each barrel holding about fifty gallons and weighing more than four hundred pounds. Just about anywhere you look, you'll spot a barrel house in the hillsides of Lynchburg.

If you'd like more information about Miss Bobo's, drop a line to Bob Babel, Jack Daniel Distillery, Lynchburg, TN 37352.

AFTER A TOUR of Jack Daniel's Distillery, we recommend lunch with Lynne Tolley.

Lynne is proprietress of Miss Mary Bobo's Boarding House right here in Lynchburg. And, each noon she has a tableful of country cooking awaiting anyone with a healthy appetite. So we hope you'll pay us a call some day soon. There's never been a distillery like Mr. Jack's. And from what our visitors tell us, there aren't many lunches like Miss Lynne's.

CHARCOAL MELLOWED DROP BY DROP

Enjoy the White Rabbit Saloon, a reconstruction of a saloon Uncle Jack operated in Lynchburg before Prohibition. There we'll serve you a glass of lemonade or coffee while you visit the little shop that sells commemorative bottles of Jack Daniel's Tennessee Whiskey, the only location in Moore County where whiskey can be sold.

While you're with us, be sure to take in our beautiful town square. It's a short walk from the distillery, and you'll find a variety of local merchants and shops, including the old Lynchburg Jail that's now a museum. The Lynchburg Hardware and General Store, originally

opened by Jack Daniel's nephew Lem Motlow so he could make a living during Prohibition, offers the whole line of Jack Daniel's merchandise; and the Barrel Shop sells all kinds of furniture and creative household items crafted from used Jack Daniel oak barrels.

The centerpiece of our town square is a red brick courthouse (Lynchburg is the Moore county seat) built in 1884 from brick made right here in Moore County. Miss Mary Bobo's is just a few houses down from the square, just past the gazebo at the corner.

Visit the Lynchburg cemetery up the hill where you can see my Uncle Jack's grave. Look for the two cast-iron chairs originally placed near his headstone for local ladies who mourned the passing of Lynchburg's most eligible bachelor. Sometime, not any time soon I hope, you'll be able to lay a flower on me. I'll be buried in the Tolley plot right next to Uncle Jack.

Lynchburg is halfway between Interstate 65 and Interstate 24, about seventy-five miles south of Nashville, TN.

Tennessee Barbecued Shrimp

Makes 6 servings

Our Tennessee Barbecued Shrimp is a New Orleans-style barbecue shrimp that's not barbecued at all. It's shrimp slathered with a garlicky, buttery, spicy sauce perked up with a little Jack Daniel's. Crusty French bread will be important for sopping. Barbecued shrimp is a great dish when you want folks to lighten up and get to know each other a little better. Serve the shrimp in a big bowl in the middle of the table, pass the bread, and go to town. A little creamy slaw or a spoonful of creamy cheese grits are nice on the side, but resist distractions.

½ cup (1 stick) butter
¼ cup fresh lemon juice
¼ cup Jack Daniel's Tennessee Whiskey
2 tablespoons Worcestershire sauce
2 tablespoons hot pepper sauce, or to taste
4 garlic cloves, minced
Salt and black pepper, to taste
2 pounds large (16 to 20 count) shrimp, shells and tails intact
Crusty bread for dipping

Heat the oven to 500°F. Combine the butter, lemon juice, Jack Daniel's, Worcestershire sauce, hot sauce, garlic, and salt and pepper in a small saucepan. Cook over medium heat until the butter has melted. Blend well. Arrange the shrimp in a single layer on a large rimmed baking sheet. Pour the barbecue sauce over the shrimp. Bake 8 to 10 minutes until the shrimp are pink and the insides are opaque. Pour the shrimp and sauce in a big bowl and serve with crusty bread for dipping.

Chicken and Dressing Skillet Cake

Makes 6 servings

How about this for a weeknight version of Sunday chicken and dressing? The cream-style corn makes the cornbread extra moist, almost like a cake. If you don't have a cast iron skillet, you can bake the mixture in a 9 x 13-inch baking dish. Add a drizzle of oil to the skillet or baking dish and heat it up. A hot pan helps develop the wonderful cornbread crust. Complete your skillet supper with a tangy green salad.

¼ cup (½ stick) butter
1 cup chopped onion
1 cup chopped celery
Vegetable oil
3 cups cooked, diced chicken
1 can (14.75 ounces) cream-style corn
1 ½ cups self-rising cornmeal mix
1 teaspoon rubbed sage or poultry seasoning
Black pepper to taste
1 egg, beaten
½ cup milk

Heat the oven to 400°F. Melt the butter in a 10-inch cast iron or ovenproof skillet. Cook the onion and celery in the butter over medium heat until soft, 5 to 8 minutes. Spoon the cooked vegetables into a large mixing bowl. Add a drizzle of oil to the same skillet and heat it in the oven while you add the chicken, corn, cornmeal mix, sage, pepper, egg, and milk to the vegetables in the mixing bowl. Blend well. Remove the hot skillet from the oven and carefully pour in the batter. Bake about 30 minutes, or until set and golden brown around the edges. Cut into wedges.

Slow-Simmered Marinated Chuck Roast

Makes 8 to 10 servings

If you're a fan of hearty soy marinades such as Dale's, Moore's, and Allegro, you must make this extra-easy hometown chuck roast. It's slow-simmered in our own rich soy marinade flavored with a little Jack Daniel's. I serve this meltingly tender meat over creamy grits to sop up the delicious juices. This little recipe is handy for all kinds of entertaining and makes a fun appetizer or tailgating treat. Pile the meat in halved hot dog buns or mini hamburger buns and top it with a spoonful of Tennessee Sour Onions (page 248). It's our Lynchburg version of the Vietnamese Banh Bao (Big Bun)!

> 1 large onion, cut into thin slivers
> 2 cloves garlic, crushed
> 1 beef chuck roast (3 to 4 pounds)
> ½ cup soy sauce
> ¼ cup Jack Daniel's Tennessee Whiskey
> ¼ cup Worcestershire sauce
> Black pepper, to taste

Scatter the onion and garlic in the bottom of a large slow cooker (at least 4 quarts). Place the chuck roast over the onions and garlic. Add the soy sauce, Jack Daniel's, and Worcestershire sauce. Sprinkle the roast with black pepper. Cover and cook on high 6 to 8 hours or on low 8 to 12 hours. The meat is done when it pulls apart easily with a fork. Remove the roast from the pot. Shred the meat for sandwiches, if desired.

Sauer Mash Smoked Sausage Pot

Makes 4 to 6 servings

You can still make a fine wintery kraut and sausage stew even if a big jar of home-cured kraut is not waiting in your pantry. Refrigerated bags of kraut work just fine. Onion, apple, and carrots tame the kraut's tangy flavor a bit. For even more down-home country flavor, simmer the kraut with a couple of smoked ham hocks until they're fall-apart tender for about an hour. Add the sausage during the last 30 minutes of cooking.

> 1 pound sauerkraut
> 1 medium onion, cut in to thin slivers

1 Golden Delicious apple, cored and chopped

3 large carrots, peeled and cut into 2-inch pieces

1 cup water

¼ cup Jack Daniel's Tennessee Whiskey

2 garlic cloves, minced

1 tablespoon pickling spice

1 pound fully-cooked smoked sausage, cut into 2-inch pieces

Combine the sauerkraut, onion, apple, carrots, water, Jack Daniel's, garlic, and pickling spice in a large Dutch oven. Bring to a boil over medium-high heat. Reduce the heat and simmer, partially covered, about 30 minutes. Add the sausages and continue to simmer about 30 minutes. Serve with boiled potatoes, coarse-grain mustard, and dark crusty bread.

Sausage Cornbread Supper Pudding

Makes 8 to 10 servings

My freezer stash of leftover cornbread ends up not only in dressing but also in this fantastic cornbread supper pudding. This combines the texture of a cornbread dressing with the creaminess of a bread pudding. It's just right for a potluck supper or to enjoy on a cold night. You might even make it for Sunday brunch. Serve with a simple salad, a fruit salad, or even a tangy slaw.

4 cups crumbled cornbread

2 cups cubed white bread

1 pound bulk pork or Italian sausage

1 medium onion, chopped

1 medium bell pepper (any color), chopped

4 eggs

3 cups milk

1 can (14.75 ounces) cream-style corn

1 cup shredded Swiss or sharp Cheddar cheese

Grease a 9 x 13-inch baking dish. Combine the cornbread and white bread in a large mixing bowl. Cook the sausage in a large skillet over medium heat until well browned. Crumble the sausage into uniform pieces as it cooks. Add the sausage to the cornbread mixture, leaving the drippings in the skillet. Cook the onion and bell pepper in the drippings in the skillet (add a little oil if necessary) over medium high heat

until softened and lightly browned. Add the vegetables to the cornbread mixture and blend well. Pour the cornbread mixture into the baking dish. Whisk the eggs in the emptied mixing bowl. Add the milk, corn, and cheese and blend well. Pour the mixture over the cornbread. Cover and refrigerate 1 to 2 hours to allow the cornbread to soften in the milk. Bake at 350°F for 45 to 55 minutes or until the center is set and the top is golden brown.

Country Stuffed Peppers

Makes 6 servings

Peppers of nearly every kind are a common sight in vegetable gardens and farm stands all over Moore County. All through the spring and summer, deep conversations are going on about who's planting what new pepper variety and who prefers what shape, color, and heat level. Peppers are almost as varied tomatoes.

We find a wonderful selection of hot and mild peppers from mid-summer well into the fall at Mr. Farrell's vegetable stand a few miles from the town square. All kinds of vegetables sit on a big table in his front yard, but you won't be handing any money to Mr. Farrell. You might not even see him. Mr. Farrell relies on the honor system. Just leave what you owe in the mayonnaise jar.

Farm fresh peppers make such a difference in this recipe. I imagine old-time country cooks made stuffed peppers when their gardens were overflowing.

6 large bell peppers (any color)

1 medium onion, finely chopped

2 cloves garlic, minced

1 pound ground beef or ½ pound ground beef and ½ pound bulk pork sausage

2 cups cooked rice, cooled

1 can (15 ounces) tomato sauce

1 tablespoon Worcestershire sauce

Salt and black pepper, to taste

1 cup cracker crumbs or breadcrumbs

Heat the oven to 350°F. Cut the tops off the bell peppers. Remove the stem and finely chop the pepper tops to include in the filling. Parboil the pepper cups in a pot of boiling water for 5 minutes. Remove the peppers, drain, and place upright in a shallow baking dish. Cook the onion, pepper tops, and garlic in a large skillet until tender, about 5 minutes. Add the meat and sauté until cooked through. Remove any excessive fat with a spoon, as necessary. Stir in the rice, tomato sauce, and Worcestershire sauce. Season with salt and pepper. Spoon the meat mixture into the pepper cups. Top each with a sprinkling of crumbs. Cover the pan with foil and bake 25 minutes. Remove the foil and continue to bake for 10 minutes.

BARBECUE AND GRILLING

The Jack Daniel's World Championship Invitational Barbecue

Shade Tree Barbecue Basics

Barbecue Gear

Shade Tree Pulled Pork Barbecue
Shade Tree Beef Brisket
Shade Tree Spare or Baby Back Pork Ribs
Shade Tree Smoked Chicken

Old No. 7 Tips for Great Grilling

When Is It Done? Good Grilling Guidelines for Outdoor Cooking

Dry County Dry Rub

Shade Tree Barbecue Competition

Barbecue Sauces

Stillhouse Barbecue Sauce
Simple Cider Vinegar Sauce
Yella Mustard Barbecue Sauce
Dark and Smoky Barbecue Sauce
Lone-Star Barbecue Sauce
Alabama White Barbecue Sauce

Jack's All-Purpose Barbecue Glaze
No Jack Cider Vinegar Mopping Spray
Grandaddy's Pickle Juice Mop Sauce
Jimmy's Jack Marinated Steaks
MoJack Steak Sauce
Grilled and Glazed Salmon
Molasses Whiskey Glaze

Meet Steve May

Tenneessee Whiskey Lynchburgers

Smoky Jack Burgers
Chili Jack Burgers
Honey Jack Onions

Charred Fruit for Jack's Highballs

Jack and Ginger Grilled Peaches
Jack's Sweet Hot Glazed Shrimp
Grilled Potato (and Other Vegetable) Packets
Salt and Peppered Sweet Corn
Crocked Barbecue
Norman Thai Jack Marinade

The Jack Daniel's World Championship Invitational Barbecue

We've been drawing quite a crowd since 1989 when we first held the Jack Daniel's World Championship Invitational Barbecue competition in Wiseman Park just off the Lynchburg Town Square.

A late October Saturday when the leaves begin to turn and the air cools is just right for hosting the ultimate barbecue showdown. In the span of about twenty-four hours our ninety competitive teams from all across the U.S. and from around the world will smoke 3,500 pounds of meat, so just imagine what Lynchburg smells like! We've hosted folks from Ireland, England, Germany, Australia, Canada, Switzerland, and Japan, all competing against each other and the U.S. teams for more than $30,000 in cash and prizes. To qualify for the invitational drawing in September, the teams must have won a "state championship" of at least twenty-five teams, or a competition of more than fifty competitors.

Each entry submitted is judged on a point system for appearance, taste, and tenderness. To become "Grand Champion," a team must earn the most points for its entries in all four meat categories. Individual winners are named in each of the meat categories as well.

And the Jack competition categories are:

Pork Ribs

Pork Shoulder/Butt

Beef Brisket

Chicken

Jack Daniel's Sauce

Cook's Choice (and Home Cookin' from the Homeland for international teams)

Happiest Home in the Hollow—a competition of the team's cook sites

Desserts

It's quite a spectacle for a small country town of 500 to host more than 20,000 visitors on one weekend. We all pitch in and volunteer to direct traffic and park cars, to host a rolling pin toss, or to sweep up on Sunday. Our civic organizations plan all year for their biggest fund-raising event. Around the courthouse square you'll find the Methodist ladies selling delicious baked goods and homemade fried pies. Others sell fried pork skins, funnel cakes, ice cream, and rooster fries.

Besides plenty of barbecue there are lots of fun activities for the whole family. In addition to the rolling pin toss, there's the bung toss, the bag toss, butt bowling (pork butts, that is), a country dog contest, and plenty of musical performances on the square, including our local cloggers.

Shade Tree Barbecue Basics

My Uncle Jack would have been a world-class barbecue champion had such things existed in his day. Making barbecue is a whole lot like making Tennessee whiskey. You use the finest ingredients and follow a tried and true method that you don't fool around with. On top of that, you need an abundance of time and patience. Just like great whiskey, great barbecue cannot be rushed.

So, what is "barbecue," after all? Turns out it's a popular term that means different things to different folks. Around here barbecue is something you eat, not something you do. To us, barbecue is a cut of meat like pork shoulder or beef brisket that is cooked and smoked by a gentle fire for as long as it takes to make that tough cut break down and become fall-apart tender. "Barbecue" is not the act of cooking on a backyard grill or the grill itself. That's just grilling a steak or a burger on a grill.

Slow cooking tough meat over a smoky fire is as old as people, so we ought to be pretty good at it by now. Back in the days before modern refrigeration, smoking preserved all kinds of foods for safe storage, and it made sense not long ago for folks to get together and share in a whole hog barbecue, and I mean from head to toe. Today we do it more for the fun, the friendship, and occasionally, for a prize.

Now here in Tennessee and across the Southeast, we prefer pork barbecue to beef. We'll smoke pork shoulders for pulled pork barbecue and all styles of pork ribs—the long-boned spare ribs, the shorter baby back or loin ribs, and the meaty country style ribs. Go west toward Texas and you're into beef country—brisket and beef ribs. And there's that famous beef tri-tip sirloin in Santa Maria, California.

The good news is that you don't need a competition-sized barbecue rig on wheels to make great barbecue at home. With a modest investment in a good charcoal grill or some easy-to-find smoking equipment and a little time, anyone with a spot to set up a smoker can make delicious barbecue, chicken, and ribs. With a little practice and perseverance, the results get better most every time.

Barbecue doesn't require a recipe as much as it requires following a process. So here it is in a nutshell.

1. A few hours or a day before cooking, season the meat all over with a dry rub seasoning blend.
2. Cook and smoke the meat with a steady, low charcoal or hardwood fire until the connective tissue in the meat melts and it becomes pull-apart tender. Be sure to set up your smoker in a well-ventilated open area away from the house or buildings.
3. While the smoker is doing its thing, go inside and make a good sauce and some nice side dishes and relax.

The key to good barbecue is learning to balance the elements—the meat, the dry rub, the smoke, and the sauce—so that no single flavor or taste hits you over the head when you take a bite. If you've ever had barbecue that tasted only of barbecue sauce or had the flavor of a bitter smoke that reminded you of old chair leg, anything but flavorful seasoned and smoked meat, you know exactly what I'm talking about.

Barbecue is part science, part art, and sometimes a bit of luck, so be patient, keep trying, and enjoy the practice. Serious competitions aside, shade tree barbecue is about fun in the backyard, feeding family and friends, and being neighborly.

Heard around the TABLE

A guest from Canada once said, "The only thing on the table that I recognize is the butter!"

Barbecue Gear

U nless it's your nature to do so, don't go running off in the pickup with the weekly shopper and drag home some big black contraption attached to a set of wheels just to make backyard barbecue. A quick trip to a hardware store, a grill shop, a home improvement center, or a few mouse clicks and a couple days of waiting will get you started. You need a good deep kettle-style charcoal grill with a domed lid or a basic smoker, some charcoal and a way to ignite it, some Jack Daniel's Wood Smoking Chips made from our oak aging barrels, and just a few tools.

The Smoker

Sure you can spend thousands of dollars on a barbecue smoker, and many do. Come to Lynchburg in late October for the Jack Daniel's World Invitational Barbecue Championship and you'll see what I mean. What you really need at home is one of three basic styles.

The Offset or Horizontal Barrel Smoker

Essentially a fancied-up barrel lying on its side (the meat chamber) with a chimney at one end to vent the smoke and a smaller firebox attached at the other for the coals and wood. As the coals slowly burn in the firebox, the heat and smoke travel horizontally into the meat chamber and vent out through the chimney on the far end. Offset smokers start at about $200, require minimal assembly, and can hold three or four shoulders or briskets, three to four racks of ribs, and plenty of chicken.

The Vertical Water or Bullet Smoker

In this cylindrical metal can with a domed lid, the bottom holds the coal fire (or electric heating coil); above that is a pan to hold water for steam to help tenderize the meat (and to protect the meat from a direct blast of heat from below) and a two-level cooking area at the top. Basic water smokers go from around $60 for a bare bones model to about $300. Most include a removable side panel or door to access the coal rack at the bottom.

The Kettle-Style Grill

With careful charcoal placement, this all-purpose charcoal grill makes a great smoker. A modest charcoal fire banked to the sides protects the meat from direct heat and allows the heat and smoke to circulate around the meat before venting out the top. Some folks place a metal pan filled with water in the middle of the coal grate between the charcoal piles to add a little steam.

No matter how much fiddling you do with the air vents on a smoker, always keep the top or cover vent or chimney flue damper open when smoking and grilling. A little smoke goes a long way, and trapping the smoke will only make the meat taste bitter. Take it from a Kansas City Certified Barbecue Judge, "If the meat is bitter, I'm docking you points!" Let the smoke escape.

Also, keep the smoker cover closed unless you're checking the internal temperature of the meat or adding water to the pan. Just like an oven, lifting the cover allows the heat to escape and, even more than an oven, adds considerable time to the already long cooking process.

Open Pit Barbecue

When you're ready to cook a whole pig or are inviting the whole neighborhood over for chicken, ribs, shoulder, and brisket, you might want to get yourself a little more cooking surface. A barbecue pit sounds like a big chore, but it doesn't have to be. Especially if you build it on top of the ground instead of digging a big hole you'll have to fill in after the party.

You can build a three-sided temporary pit on dirt, grass, gravel, or sand. Cinder blocks from the hardware store make a sturdy foundation to support the metal cooking grate and all the meat. Call around to the metal fabricator shops and tell them what you're up to. You'll need about a four-foot by six-foot piece of extruded steel (with that diamond pattern) or a section of heavier mezzanine or catwalk grating. The main difference is that the catwalk grating is sturdy enough to make the long side of the pit the opening for charcoal and wood coal management. A top to hold in the heat can made from a light gauge of plate steel or even a sheet of plywood.

The cooking grate should sit two cinder blocks high to keep plenty of space between the coals and the meat. With an opening at the short end of the pit, it should take about twenty-four cinder blocks below the grate and twelve blocks on top to secure the grate. Make it any size or shape you like, but following the rectangular shape of your steel grate will keep things simple and less expensive.

A secondary fire where your wood or charcoal can be burning into white coals is important for controlling the heat. A thin layer of coals sprinkled with a shovel and refreshed every hour or so will provide plenty of gentle heat and keep the meat from burning before it can tenderize and cook through. Remember that whatever goes on that grate isn't a steak or a hamburger, so it needs only occasional turning.

Fuel and Smoke

Pressed charcoal briquettes are a great source of heat for barbecue. Briquettes burn slowly and evenly even if they are scattered about and not in contact with other briquettes. Natural hardwood or lump charcoal burns hotter and faster than briquettes, and it needs to be in a stack to burn evenly, but it gives off great smoke flavor. We start with a chimney starter full of briquettes and add lump charcoal and oak barrel wood chips throughout the process.

Wood chunks, chips, and smoking pellets are easy smoke generators. Grab a bag of hickory or any fruitwood like cherry, apple, and pecan for milder flavor. The Jack Daniel's Wood Smoking Chips made from our oak aging barrels work with any style of barbecue and give off a lovely hint of Tennessee Whiskey.

Tools

Like a garage workshop or a kitchen, you can shop for tools until the end of time. However, you'll do most of the work with a few sturdy essentials. Gather your grilling tools together and keep them separate from the kitchen gear so they are always at the ready. Use a lightweight bucket or plastic storage container with a good lid to keep everything clean and dry.

Grilling Tongs

Get a couple pairs of good tongs. Spring-loaded, locking tongs from a kitchen and bath shop are preferable to the long, unwieldy sets sold in the grill section. You'll use the nine-inch and twelve-inch tongs the most. When they get to sixteen-inch and seventeen-inch, they are too long and heavy to be of much use.

Thermometer

An instant read thermometer or two is a lifesaver. Get a couple and replace them every year or two. The fancier digital models require a battery which often tends to run out at the wrong time. Either way, there's no need to spend more than $20 on one.

Charcoal Chimney Starter

No need for lighter fluid. This simple metal cylinder easily lights charcoal with a piece of newspaper and a match. When the coals have ashed over, they're ready for use. For barbecue, you'll need a few batches throughout the smoking process, so have another grill going with the starter. You never want to add raw, unburned briquette charcoal once the meat is on (you can add unburned hardwood lump charcoal, however).

Box Fan

If you're near electricity, plug in an inexpensive box fan to run off the flies and mosquitoes and generally add a pleasant breeze to the shade. I've noticed that after a certain point of cooking, good barbecue always attracts the flies. It's a good sign.

Heavy Duty Aluminum Foil

Foil is invaluable for barbecue. It's good practice to put a piece under heavy meats to trap the juices and keep the meat moist and to easily transport the cuts to and from the smoker.

Aluminum Pans

Steam table pans are sturdier than foil and you can get several uses out of a pan. They are a great size for cooking, holding, re-warming, and transporting barbecue. Keep a stack in the pantry.

Kosher Salt

If you've yet to make the switch in the kitchen from regular iodized salt to this gourmet favorite, now's the time. Grab a box in the

seasoning aisle for its clean flavor and use it in brines, rubs, and for seasoning grilled meats and vegetables. A three-pound box looks like it will last forever, but it'll be gone before you know it.

Sharp Knives and a Big Sturdy Cutting Board

These essential tools make the endgame of barbecue easier and more fun. After all that work, you'll want neat slices of brisket and handsomely cut ribs. You'll be pulling pork (and chopping it, if you like) on the board too.

Barbecue Meat Cuts

Pulled pork barbecue is made with a Boston butt, a five-to-eight pound pork shoulder roast that contains plenty of fat, which tenderizes the tough meat as it cooks and also absorbs the smoke. A pork shoulder must reach an internal temperature of 190° to 200°F to be done and easy to pull. The bone, if it comes with one, will lift out with no resistance when the shoulder is fully cooked. Once cooked and drained of excess liquid and bone, the pulled pork you'll have will be about half the weight of the uncooked roast.

Pork ribs come in three different cuts. The short loin ribs or baby backs are very meaty and give you a baker's dozen of ribs from a 2 ½ to 3 pound rack. The longer boned spare ribs, about ten to twelve ribs per rack, come from closer to the shoulder and are usually fattier than baby backs. Spare ribs that have been cut into a neat rectangle (the brisket bone removed) are called St. Louis-style ribs. Country-style ribs are more meat than bone (and sometimes boneless), and when slow cooked they shred nicely like pork shoulder.

Beef brisket is tough and beefy and perfect for the low and slow barbecue method. Like pork shoulder, brisket must cook at a low temperature and reach an internal temperature of 190°F to 200°F before it's really tender. There's no medium rare off a hot grill with a brisket.

A brisket needs a generous layer of fat to succeed. Just like a Boston butt pork shoulder, a fat cap both tenderizes the meat and absorbs the smoke into the beef. A full-size brisket is ten pounds or more, so the half-size flat cut in the supermarket is about four to six pounds. If you can't find a brisket with some fat, the results will be disappointingly dry and chewy. Always slice brisket against the grain (otherwise it's tougher chewing), and keep in mind that cold brisket slices more easily. Brisket is just as delicious when chopped like barbecue.

Shade Tree Pulled Pork Barbecue

1 (5 to 8 pound) Boston butt pork roast
¼ to ½ cup Dry County Dry Rub (page 182)
Barbecue sauce, if you like

1. Generously rub the pork butt with the dry rub. Refrigerate overnight, a few hours, or at least while preparing the fire.

2. Prepare a medium-size fire in your choice of smoker. Because you're adding briquettes or lump charcoal over time, you don't need a raging fire. Allow the coals to ash over before adding the meat to the smoker. Fill the water pan if you're using one.

3. Put the meat on. For easier handling, place the meat on a large piece of heavy duty aluminum foil with the sides lightly folded up around the butt, or in a foil steam table pan. Cover the smoker with the cover vents fully open. You don't want to trap the smoke.

4. Add a handful of smoking wood chips or two to three wood chunks to the fire. That's all you need to generate a light fragrant smoke. When the smoke subsides, add a few more. Do this about once an hour for up to four hours. After that, the meat won't need any more smoke.

5. Some folks like to mop the butt as it cooks to help keep it moist. If you like a crusty exterior, skip this step. Otherwise, every hour baste it with a mop sauce like our No Jack Cider Vinegar Mopping Spray (page 190).

6. Keep a steady, low fire going to finish cooking the meat. If using charcoal briquettes, maintain a second fire in a separate grill or charcoal chimney starter so you can add ashed-over coals, not unburned briquettes, to your smoker. Unburned lump charcoal may be added at any time. Or remove the pork butt from the smoker and place it in a 250° to 300°F oven.

7. The pork butt is ready when it reaches an internal temperature of 190° to 200°F. When it's fully cooked, the bone, if there is one, will lift out easily. The meat will be fork tender and shred easily.

8. Let the meat cool slightly for easier handling, and pull the meat into strands.

9. Now you can pour on some of your favorite sauce or serve it on the side.

10. Congratulations! You've made smoky Tennessee pulled pork barbecue. Serve the barbecue on buns, with cornbread or corncakes, beans, slaw, pickles, or whatever you like.

Shade Tree Beef Brisket

1 (5 to 7 pound) beef brisket
¼ to ½ cup Dry County Dry Rub (page 182)
Barbecue sauce, if you like

1. Generously rub the brisket with dry rub. Refrigerate overnight, a few hours, or at least while preparing the fire.

2. Prepare a medium-size fire in your choice of smoker. Because you're adding briquettes or lump charcoal over time, you don't need a raging fire. Allow the coals to ash over before cooking the meat. Fill the water pan if you're using one.

3. Put the meat on. For easier handling, place the meat on a large piece of heavy duty aluminum foil with the sides lightly folded up around the butt, or in a foil steam table pan. Cover the smoker with the cover vents fully open. You don't want to trap the smoke.

4. Add a handful of smoking wood chips or two to three wood chunks to the fire. That's all you need to generate a light fragrant smoke. When the smoke subsides, add a few more. Do this about once an hour up to four hours. After that, the meat won't need any more smoke.

5. Keep a steady, low fire going to finish cooking the meat. If using charcoal briquettes, maintain a second fire in a separate grill or charcoal chimney starter so you can add ashed-over coals, not unburned briquettes, to your smoker. Unburned lump charcoal may be added at any time. Or, remove the brisket from the smoker and place it in a 250° to 300°F oven.

6. The brisket is ready when it reaches an internal temperature of 190° to 200° F. When it's fully cooked, the meat will feel tender when gently poked with a fork.

7. Let the meat cool slightly for easier handling and slicing. Be sure to slice brisket against the grain for a tender bite. You can also chop the meat into bite-size pieces.

8. Now you can pour on some of your favorite sauce or serve it on the side.

9. Congratulations! You've made barbecued beef brisket. Serve the brisket on buns or crackers, with cornbread or corncakes, beans, slaw, pickles, whatever you like.

Shade Tree Spare or Baby Back Pork Ribs

1 rack baby back loin or pork spare ribs, 2 to 3 pounds
¼ to ½ cup Dry County Dry Rub (page 182)
Barbecue sauce, if you like

1. Look for the thin, chewy membrane on the underside of the ribs so you can remove it before you apply your dry rub (unless it's already been removed). Flip the rack over and look at the bone ends. Use your finger, a spoon handle, or knife tip and carefully lift the membrane away from the meat. The membrane can be a bit slippery, so grip it tightly with a paper towel and pull. If it tears off into a strip, just pry up another piece until most of the membrane is gone. You can also ask your butcher to do this for you.

2. Generously rub the ribs with the dry rub. Refrigerate overnight, a few hours, or at least while preparing the fire.

3. Prepare a medium-size fire in your choice of smoker. Because you're adding briquettes or lump charcoal over time, you don't need a raging fire. Allow the coals to ash over before adding the meat to the smoker. Fill the water pan if you're using one.

4. Put the ribs on. For easier handling, place each rack of ribs on a large piece of heavy duty aluminum foil with the sides lightly folded up. Cover the smoker with the cover vents fully open. You don't want to trap the smoke.

5. Add a handful of smoking wood chips or two to three wood chunks to the fire. That's all you need to generate a light fragrant smoke. When the smoke subsides, add a few more. Do this about once an hour up to four hours. After that, the meat won't need any more smoke.

6. Some folks like to mop the ribs as they cook to help keep them moist. If you like a crusty exterior, skip this step. Otherwise, every hour baste it with a mop sauce like our No Jack Cider Vinegar Mopping Spray (page 190).

Heard around the TABLE

A lady from California asked the hostess whether we have schools in Lynchburg. She must have thought she'd come to the end of the earth. Our hostess asked her if she'd like to live in Lynchburg. The lady responded, "Will I have to talk like you folks?" Absolutely!

7. Keep a steady, low fire going to finish cooking the ribs. If using charcoal briquettes, maintain a second fire in a separate grill or charcoal chimney starter so you can add ashed-over coals, not unburned briquettes, to your smoker. Unburned lump charcoal may be added at any time. Or remove the ribs from the smoker and place them in a 250° to 300°F oven.

8. The ribs are ready when the meat offers little resistance when you pull on a couple of rib bones. Note that if cooked (or reheated) too long, even at a low temperature, rib meat will become so tender that it will fall completely off the bone when you attempt to pick it up. If you're paying for the bone you might as well be able to use it, so check the ribs periodically and test for resistance.

9. To finish the ribs with sauce, you'll need a good medium to medium-high heat from a grill or an oven broiler. Brush the sauce onto the ribs or cut the ribs into 3 to 4 bone sections and submerge them in a saucepan of warmed sauce. Place on the grill and let the sugars caramelize but not burn. A little char is nice, but scorched sugar will ruin all your hard work, so don't leave your post during the finishing stage. With a good sharp sturdy knife or cleaver, cut up the ribs, pile them on a platter, and serve with extra warmed sauce.

Shade Tree Smoked Chicken

Whole, halved, quartered, or cut-up into pieces, it's up to you.

1 chicken, whole, halved, or cut into pieces
¼ to ½ cup Dry County Dry Rub (page 182)
Barbecue sauce, if you like

1. Generously rub the chicken with dry rub. Refrigerate overnight, a few hours, or at least while preparing the fire.

2. Prepare a medium-size fire in your choice of smoker. Because you're adding briquettes or lump charcoal over time, you don't need a raging fire. Allow the coals to ash over before adding the chicken to the smoker. Fill the water pan if you're using one.

3. Put the chicken on. Cover the smoker with the cover vents fully open. You don't want to trap the smoke.

4. Add a handful of smoking wood chips or two to three wood chunks to the fire. That's all you need to generate a light fragrant smoke. When

the smoke subsides, add a few more. Do this about once an hour up to three hours. After that, the meat won't need any more smoke.

5. Keep a steady, low fire going to finish cooking the chicken. If using charcoal briquettes, maintain a second fire in a separate grill or charcoal chimney starter so you can add ashed-over coals, not unburned briquettes, to your smoker. Unburned lump charcoal may be added at any time. Or, remove the chicken from the smoker and place it in a 250° to 300°F oven.

6. The chicken is ready when it reaches an internal temperature of 160°F in the white breast meat and 175° to 180°F in the dark meat legs and thighs. The smoke will turn the meat pinkish, so do not think pink means undercooked. The juices will run clear, and the leg and thigh joint will move and separate easily when the chicken is fully cooked.

7. To finish the chicken with sauce, you'll need a good medium to medium-high heat from a grill or an oven broiler. Brush the sauce onto the chicken, place it on the grill, and let the sugars caramelize, but not burn the chicken. A little char is nice, but scorched sugar will ruin all your hard work, so don't leave your post during the finishing stage. With a good sharp sturdy knife or cleaver, cut up the chicken into serving sizes, pile it on a platter, and serve with extra warmed sauce.

Old No. 7 Tips for Great Grilling

Get ready. Preheat the gas grill for a good 10 minutes or fire up plenty of charcoal and allow 20 to 30 minutes for it to turn a light grey ash. Keep the grill vents open.

Keep it clean. Scrub grill grates with a wire brush, spatula, or a small ball of aluminum foil held by tongs before and after cooking. Oil the grill grates so food doesn't stick.

Season food. Massage meat, poultry, or fish with dry rub before cooking.

No piercing. Use tongs and a spatula to turn food. Piercing with a fork lets out all the precious juices.

No water please. Control flare-ups by moving food away from flames. Close the grill cover to help cut off oxygen supply.

No peeking. Close the grill cover for even cooking and keep it closed. Test doneness with an instant read thermometer.

Baste late. Brush sugary sauces on the food near the end of cooking to prevent burning.

When Is It Done? Good Grilling Guidelines for Outdoor Cooking

This may be the most important question to the backyard cook. Underdone and overdone meats each create their own challenges, so it's best to pay attention and be ready at the right time. Experienced grillers may develop a proper feel for doneness, but a handy instant read thermometer gives everyone an internal temperature reading right away which keeps the guesswork (and the juice-draining meat cutting) to a minimum. Insert the thermometer into the thickest part of the meat without touching any bone and wait a moment. Do not leave the thermometer in meat that is sitting directly on the grill (unless it is specifically designed for that) for longer than it takes to get a quick temperature reading or the glass cover will melt.

Here are the "pull off the grill" temperatures, not final destinations. Remember that all grilled meats (and oven roasted as well) continue cooking at least 5 to 10 minutes after they're removed from the heat.

BEEF		POULTRY	
Rare	125°F	White Meat	160°F
Medium-Rare	135°F	Dark Meat	175°F
Medium	145°F		
Well-Done	170°F		
PORK		**FISH**	
Medium	150°F	Rare	120°F
Well-Done	170°F	Cooked-Through	135°F

Dry County Dry Rub

Makes about 1 cup

No griller or pit master's pantry is complete without a batch of dry rub seasoning. My easy-to-mix, basic batch is nothing more than equal parts Kosher salt, black pepper, and paprika with a little garlic thrown in. Keep the basic rub simple so you can customize a portion to suit what you're cooking. Add things like cumin, cayenne, coriander, oregano, onion powder, chili powder, thyme, dried lemon peel, and even cloves. For pork ribs, we add a little brown sugar.

Around Memorial Day weekend, I remember to make a big batch by at least tripling the recipe, and we're ready for summer grilling and barbecue. The rub keeps forever, but you won't have it that long. Start with a good tight-sealing wide-mouth jar and store it in the pantry.

¼ cup paprika
¼ cup kosher salt
¼ cup black pepper
1 tablespoon garlic powder

Combine the paprika, salt, pepper, and garlic powder in a jar with a tightly fitting lid. Close the lid and shake to blend spices. Rub into beef, poultry, pork, or fish before grilling.

Shade Tree Barbecue Competition

One of the nice things about success is the opportunities it can create. After fifteen or so years of hosting the Jack Daniel's World Championship Invitational Barbecue, it was time to expand. I don't mean more categories or more prizes. I mean more folks making more barbecue.

We realized that we'd done such a good job giving the professional barbecue teams the chance to earn the top prize in competitive barbecue, it was time to include the non-pros, backyard barbecue's weekend warriors. So, we established the Shade Tree Barbecue Competition and set it up right next to the Jack Invitational down in Wiseman Park. Like the Jack, Shade Tree is organized according to the rules of the Kansas City Barbeque Society. The forty or so teams include folks from the distillery here in Lynchburg and others from nearby Fayetteville, Shelbyville, Tullahoma, and Winchester, and from Alabama, Georgia, and Florida as well.

Debbie Christian, who manages the Jack event, takes care of Shade Tree as well. To determine the teams, Debbie pulls little wooden barrel bungs from a barrel. If your lucky number bung is pulled, you're in.

Debbie is a wonderful gal and a fellow Lynchburg native who grew up on her family's beef and bee farm. A few years ago, Debbie was a server here at Miss Mary's before moving onto the Hardware Store and then the Visitor Center. She smiles when she talks about her dad feeding the distillery's used sour mash slop to his beef cattle. "It's true," she says, "we have a lot of happy cows."

Shade Tree is a slightly more relaxed competition and a great opportunity for our local barbecue experts to compete against each other for fun, bragging rights, and a little prize money. Larry Hensley works in the distillery's maintenance department and agrees. "Backyard cookers tend to be a bit more laid back," he says. "Making barbecue is really about eating and sharing and just having a good time. The teams all want to win, of course, but Shade Tree is not as intense as the Jack has gotten these past twenty years. It's pretty serious now," he says.

Phil Whitaker is the supervisor of all the Jack Daniel barrelhouses and has served as a Shade Tree judge for years. "Shade Tree judges know we're not judging the pros, but we still don't give them much slack," he admits. "You don't need to be a professional to cook good meat. Believe me, backyard people can really cook."

With only three meat categories in the event, Shade Tree is a little less work than competing in the Jack. Even so, producing your best chicken, ribs, and pulled pork under a pop-up tent in a baseball field away from your own backyard and kitchen is plenty of hard work.

Scott Cleek of the distillery's maintenance department is a long-time Shade Tree competitor. "Shade Tree started out as a friendly competition among the folks who work together at the distillery," he recalls. "It's a great big festive party with bluegrass playing and lots of camaraderie among the guys and gals."

Scott knows all about the appeal of a shade tree. Years ago when he entered the first Shade Tree competition, he built his smoker underneath a shade tree in his backyard. Scott turned a fuel tank that had been turned into a slop tank into his smoker.

"I teamed up with my distillery buddies Chad Logan and Tracy Harmon, we figured out a uniform, and we called ourselves the Smooth Smokers. We have a blast out there. My sister, Debbie Baxter, is our "presentation specialist." Things have to look just right for the judges when the cover of that Styrofoam clamshell pops open, so we leave that part to Debbie."

Just because Shade Tree prize money can't rival the Jack, don't think it's not competitive. "We all have a big time trying to beat the guys we work with," Scott says. "There's never a cross word, and we all get along just fine until it's time to box up our entries for judging. Then, we stay away from each other."

So, what's the secret to winning? "You have to figure out how to please six judges, and you just can't do it," Cleek admits. "Besides, it's not your fault if the judges don't know what good barbecue is!"

Larry Hensley offers this advice: make your entries look as delicious as possible. "If it doesn't look good, it won't taste good to the judges," he says. "And remember that since everyone's tastes are different and you are trying to please them all, don't submit anything too sweet or too spicy. And be sure to put some TLC into it," he adds. "My wife still can't figure out why I can make great fried chicken and she can't. I just take care of it when I'm cooking it."

Any tips on what not to do? "Don't overdo your ribs," advises Scott Cleek. "The judges don't like them to fall off the bone. We learned that the first year. As for your chicken, do not let it dry out. And make sure you include both dark and white meat with your entry."

Scott says he needs to start the fire by 3 am so the pork butts (which need the most time) can get smoking and cooking. The chicken and ribs go on by 8 am. "We also throw a couple extra pork butts and a big loaf of bologna into the smoker. You always need something to snack on during the competition."

Here's how the Smooth Smokers prepare their loaf of bologna.

1. Hollow out the middle of the loaf. Blend together in a bowl a three cheese mix—Cheddar, Parmesan, and Monterey Jack.
2. Add chopped jalapeño pepper, chili powder, and garlic to the cheese blend.
3. Stuff the mixture into the middle of the loaf and plug the holes with the hollowed out bologna, just like plugging a whiskey barrel with a wooden barrel bung.
4. Place the loaf on the smoker and get it good and hot before cutting and serving.

Master Distiller Jeff Arnett is a big fan of Shade Tree and loves to serve as a judge when he can. His observation from the bench? "No, they're not professional teams. Just don't tell *them* that."

Heard around the TABLE

A gentleman at the table who really enjoyed the food, especially the fried okra and fudge pie, told our hostess that he'd like to have her as his grandmother.

Barbecue Sauces

The big idea behind barbecue sauce is its balance among three primary flavors—sweet, savory, and sour. Sweet means brown sugar, molasses, honey, fruit preserves, or jellies. Savory usually means ketchup or another tomato based ingredient, but it also includes flavorings like Worcestershire sauce, onion, and soy sauce. Sour means any kind of vinegar, lemon juice, mustard, or even pickle brine. Create you own sauces and finishing glazes by varying these primary flavors to suit you and the meat you are cooking.

Travel across the country and you'll find that every region has a particular style of sauce. Here in Lynchburg, we generally prefer something between the thick and sweet style to our West and the thin and sour style to our East. These days, however, barbecue's popularity has led to a real migration of regional sauce preferences resulting in sauce fusions of all kinds. Make what you like and have fun with it.

Remember that any sauce containing sugar will burn if given the chance. To avoid a burnt, bitter sauce just brush it on near the end of cooking so the sugars can caramelize on the meat. A few minutes and a little heat from a grill or a broiler are enough to finish off ribs and chicken.

Stillhouse Barbecue Sauce

Makes about 2 ½ cups

This is what I call a Lynchburg-style barbecue sauce—tangy with a good bit of vinegar, sweet and spicy, but not as ketchupy and sweet as the sauces to our West in Memphis or Kansas City. Brush some Stillhouse on whatever you're grilling near the end of cooking so the sugars will caramelize but not burn. Everybody will want a little more Stillhouse, so have extra already warm on the table.

2 tablespoons oil
½ cup grated onion
1 cup ketchup
1 cup cider vinegar
½ cup Jack Daniel's Tennessee Whiskey

1 cup brown sugar

2 tablespoons Worcestershire sauce

2 tablespoons hot pepper sauce, or to taste

Salt and black pepper to taste

Heat the oil in a medium saucepan over medium heat. Add the onion and cook until softened. Stir in the ketchup, vinegar, Jack Daniel's, brown sugar, Worcestershire sauce, hot sauce, and salt and pepper. Bring to a boil, reduce heat, and simmer about 30 minutes, or until slightly thickened. Store in the refrigerator in a covered container.

Simple Cider Vinegar Sauce

Makes about 2 cups

The vinegary sauce of eastern North Carolina is peppery, slightly sweet, without a hint of tomato. For pulled pork barbecue, it's the best.

1 cup cider vinegar

3 tablespoons brown sugar

2 tablespoons Worcestershire sauce

1 teaspoon coarsely ground black pepper

1 teaspoon paprika

1 teaspoon kosher salt, or to taste

1/2 teaspoon cayenne pepper, or to taste

Combine the vinegar, brown sugar, Worcestershire sauce, black pepper, paprika, salt, and cayenne pepper in a jar with a tight-fitting lid. Shake well. Store in the refrigerator in a covered container.

Yella Mustard Barbecue Sauce

Makes about 2 cups

Farther south into South Carolina and Georgia, tangy yellow mustard is the predominant flavor and color in this more-sour-than-sweet sauce.

2 tablespoons vegetable oil

1 small onion, grated

1 cup prepared yellow mustard

1/4 cup ketchup

1/2 cup brown sugar

½ cup cider vinegar
1 teaspoon coarsely ground black pepper
½ teaspoon ground cayenne pepper, or to taste
1 teaspoon kosher salt, or to taste

Heat the oil in a small saucepan over medium heat. Add the onion and cook until tender, about 5 minutes. Stir in the mustard, ketchup, brown sugar, vinegar, black and cayenne peppers, and salt. Simmer a few minutes until thickened and smooth. Store in the refrigerator in a covered container.

Dark and Smoky Barbecue Sauce

Makes about 2 cups

Here's a darker, redder sauce with sweetness from molasses and a touch of all natural smoke from a bottle.

2 tablespoons vegetable oil
1 small onion, grated
1 cup ketchup
½ cup molasses
¼ cup cider vinegar
2 tablespoons Worcestershire sauce
2 tablespoons liquid smoke
1 teaspoon black pepper
½ teaspoon ground cayenne pepper, to taste
1 teaspoon kosher salt, to taste

Heat the oil in a small saucepan over medium heat. Add the onion and cook until tender, about 5 minutes. Stir in the ketchup, molasses, vinegar, Worcestershire sauce, liquid smoke, black and cayenne peppers, and salt. Simmer a few minutes until thickened and smooth. Store in the refrigerator in a covered container.

Lone-Star Barbecue Sauce

Makes about 2 cups

Texas beef barbecue calls for more tomato and less vinegar. A touch of chili powder balances out the sweetness.

2 tablespoons vegetable oil
1 small onion, grated
1 ½ cups ketchup
2 tablespoons brown sugar
2 tablespoons cider vinegar
2 tablespoons Worcestershire sauce
1 teaspoon black pepper
1 tablespoon chili powder
1 teaspoon kosher salt, or to taste

Heat the oil in a small saucepan over medium heat. Add the onion and cook until tender, about 5 minutes. Stir in the ketchup, brown sugar, vinegar, Worcestershire sauce, pepper, chili powder, and salt. Simmer a few minutes until thickened and smooth. Store in the refrigerator in a covered container.

Alabama White Barbecue Sauce

Makes about 1 ½ cups

This peculiar mayonnaise-based barbecue sauce is native to Northern Alabama just south of Lynchburg. It is particularly suited to marinating and basting grilled chicken. It's also handy on the table to slather on all kinds of barbecue and as a dipping sauce.

1 cup mayonnaise
½ cup cider vinegar
1 tablespoons sugar
1 tablespoon black pepper
1 ½ teaspoons salt

Combine the mayonnaise, vinegar, sugar, pepper, and salt in a small bowl and blend well. Store in the refrigerator in a covered container.

Jack's All-Purpose Barbecue Glaze

Makes about 2 cups

When it comes to barbecue, there are no bigger secrets than recipes for sauces, mops, and marinades. I've tasted concoctions using everything from cherry preserves, to curry powder, to fish sauce. Seems to me the simpler the better. This easy glaze isn't for slow smoked pork barbecue, but it does wonders to perk up grilled

meats, poultry, or fish. Brush it on just minutes before you pull the meat off the fire to caramelize, but not burn, the sugars.

½ cup Jack Daniel's Tennessee Whiskey
½ cup soy sauce
½ cup ketchup
1 cup brown sugar
1 teaspoon garlic powder

Combine the whiskey, soy sauce, ketchup, brown sugar, and garlic powder in a small saucepan. Simmer until slightly thickened, about 5 minutes.

No Jack Cider Vinegar Mopping Spray

I used to add a little Jack Daniel's to this basting mix, but I finally realized it was doing me more good in a glass. I first learned about this method of keeping barbecued meats moist while wandering among the teams on Barbecue Saturday in October. Every so often a cooker door would pop open and a team member with a spray bottle would quickly douse the pork ribs and butts. Winners swear by it. This is the perfect amount for a pork butt or a couple racks of ribs, but if you've got more, just keep this simple formula in mind: 1 part apple cider vinegar to 2 parts apple cider and ¼ part Worcestershire sauce.

1 cup apple cider vinegar
2 cups apple cider
¼ cup Worcestershire sauce

Combine the apple cider vinegar, apple cider, and Worcestershire sauce in a medium bowl and pour the mixture into a clean spray bottle. Spray on barbecue while cooking to keep meats moist as needed.

Grandaddy's Pickle Juice Mop Sauce

Makes about 2 cups

My granddaddy had a commercial barbecue pit during his "retirement" years. This was his special sauce, and I've never seen another like it. Pickle juice is the main acid, and thinly sliced lemons, rind and all, cook down in the sauce. My cousin Jim Dickey, also a fine pit master, uses it all the time as a mop sauce for pork. He omits the sugar and Worcestershire sauce so the sugars won't burn while cooking.

½ cup (1 stick) butter
1 medium onion, grated
1 cup dill pickle juice
¼ cup cider vinegar
½ cup sugar
2 lemons, thinly sliced
2 teaspoons crushed red pepper
2 teaspoons cayenne pepper
2 tablespoons Worcestershire sauce
Salt and black pepper to taste

Melt the butter in a small saucepan over medium heat. Add the onion and cook until softened, 7 to 8 minutes. Stir in the pickle juice, vinegar, sugar, lemons, crushed red and cayenne peppers, Worcestershire sauce, and salt and pepper and simmer about 20 minutes. Use as a barbecue baste or serve warm on the side. Keep the unused portion refrigerated.

Jimmy's Jack Marinated Steaks

Makes about 1 cup of marinade

Our sixth Jack Daniel Master Distiller and my dear friend, the late Jimmy Bedford, lived on the beautiful farm you pass coming into Lynchburg from Tullahoma. When Jimmy wasn't watching over our Tennessee whiskey, raising several hundred head of cattle, or smoking his own country hams, he was probably at home grilling a steak. Jimmy loved steak more than anyone I know and could target the best steakhouses in any town. Use his marinade on all cuts of tender beef. It makes enough for about 2 ½ pounds of steak, such as two thick T-bones or four tenderloin filets.

½ cup Jack Daniel's Tennessee Whiskey
¼ cup brown sugar
¼ cup soy sauce
2 tablespoons Worcestershire sauce
Juice of one lemon
¼ teaspoon garlic powder
2 large steaks of your choice, or 4 tenderloin filets

Combine the whiskey, brown sugar, soy sauce, Worcestershire sauce, lemon juice, and garlic powder in a medium bowl. Place the steaks in a large resealable plastic bag. Pour in the marinade and seal the bag.

Refrigerate at least one hour. Remove the steaks from the marinade and pat dry with a paper towel to get a better crust. Grill the steaks over medium coals 5 to 7 minutes per side for medium-rare.

MoJack Steak Sauce

Makes about 2 ½ cups of marinade and 6 servings of steak

The citrus flavors of the popular Mexican-style mojo marinades taste great with Jack. Use my Tennessee Whiskey mojo with any steak, but especially with flank, hanger, and skirt steaks for fajitas. MoJack really perks up a chicken breast too. Serve these grilled mojo meats with pinto beans and Pepper Jack Rice Bake (page 124).

> ¼ cup vegetable oil
> 4 cloves garlic, crushed
> ½ cup Jack Daniel's Tennessee Whiskey
> ½ cup orange juice
> ½ cup fresh lime juice
> 1 teaspoon ground cumin
> ½ cup soy sauce
> 2 flank steaks about 2 pounds each
> tortillas, salsa, and your choice of toppings such as chopped tomatoes, onions, avocado slices, lettuce, and jalapeño peppers, for serving

Combine the oil, garlic, whiskey, orange juice, lime juice, cumin, and soy sauce in a large resealable plastic bag and blend well. Place the steaks in the bag and seal. Refrigerate for at least 1 hour or overnight. Grill steaks over high heat 5 to 7 minutes per side for medium-rare. Remove the steaks from the heat and let rest about 10 minutes before thinly slicing across the grain (slice with the grain for skirt).

Grilled and Glazed Salmon

Makes 4 to 6 servings

One of the many pleasant surprises I've discovered while visiting great restaurants across the U.S. and around the globe is how well Jack Daniel's marries with sweet/sour Asian flavors like hoisin sauce, ginger, and soy sauce. This very easy barbecue sauce includes a whole orange. It works particularly well on meaty salmon steaks or fillets. Serve with Icy Pink Cucumbers and Onions (page 245), a quick colorful vegetable stir-fry, and steamed rice.

2 tablespoons oil
2 cloves garlic, minced
1 tablespoon grated fresh ginger
½ cup orange juice
¼ cup hoisin sauce
¼ cup Jack Daniel's Tennessee Whiskey
2 tablespoons soy sauce
1 medium orange cut into thin slices, each slice cut in half
4 to 6 salmon steaks or fillets, about 8 ounces each

Heat the oil in a small saucepan over medium heat. Add the garlic and cook until softened, about 2 minutes. Stir in the ginger, orange juice, hoisin sauce, whiskey, soy sauce, and orange slices and bring to a boil. Simmer the sauce about 15 minutes or until slightly thickened. Place the salmon on squares of aluminum foil. Grill over medium-high heat with the cover down about 10 minutes. Brush with the glaze and continue to cook 2 to 3 minutes longer or until the fish is cooked through. Serve the fish with additional warm sauce spooned over each serving.

Molasses Whiskey Glaze

Makes about 1 cup

Quail hunting in Tennessee is really not about the birds; it's about the beautiful bird dogs raised and trained by many of the hunters around here. Those dogs have endless stamina and an almost magical instinct for deep concentration and stillness. Lacquer your grilled game birds with this molasses whiskey glaze. It's also delicious on roast duck, chicken, turkey, and Cornish game hens.

½ cup (1 stick) butter
½ cup orange juice
¼ cup Jack Daniel's Tennessee Whiskey
2 tablespoons sorghum or molasses
1 tablespoon Worcestershire sauce
2 cloves garlic, minced
Salt and black pepper to taste

Combine the butter, orange juice, whiskey, molasses, Worcestershire sauce, garlic, and salt and pepper in a small saucepan. Bring to a boil and simmer until slightly reduced and thickened. Brush the glaze on grilled meats and poultry during the last 5 to 10 minutes of cooking.

Meet Steve May

As the Director of Jack Daniel's Lynchburg Homeplace, Steve May oversees our busy Visitor Center and all the rest of the Jack Daniel events in Lynchburg. Since 2005 Steve is only the third person to hold this coveted job after Roger Brashears, (1969 to 2002) and Joe Rossman (2002 to 2005). With more than 250,000 visitors to the distillery each year, it's a demanding job taking care of all our guests and running a smooth distillery tour program.

Food and hospitality run in Steve's blood. He grew up in Alabama, where for 50 years his family owned and operated the famous Art's Magic Burger in Attalla, Alabama, the first fast food restaurant in the state with a drive-thru window. "I grew up in that restaurant and worked there until I went off to college," Steve recalls. "I swept floors, washed windows, waited windows, cooked burgers, made the fries and the onion rings, I did it all. And I still love to cook."

After all that, can't you imagine he's got a few cooking secrets of his own? Onion rings are one of one of Steve's specialties, and it's a real treat when he gears up to make a batch at home. He won't divulge the family secret to the batter, unfortunately. All he'll say is that the best onion rings start with really cold raw onion rings right out of the refrigerator before they're dipped into room temperature batter and fried in peanut oil. Vidalia onions from Georgia are his onion of choice.

Steve and his wife live just off the town square a few houses down from Miss Mary's. They live in the home of the parents of former Jack Daniel Master Distiller Frank Bobo. Steve loves nothing more than an evening out on his courtyard grilling steaks, roast pork and loin chops, chicken, and all kinds of vegetables on skewers. "We're probably out there making dinner at home four or five nights out of seven," he says. Steve prefers his Old No. 7 with a splash of citrus soda for a fresh, light taste, especially in our hot Lynchburg summers.

Another of Steve's responsibilities is overseeing the Jack Daniel's World Championship Invitational Barbecue in October. Now our competitive teams aren't much for sharing secrets, either, but here are a few tips Steve has picked up from the pros who set up shop in the park each fall.

1. Know your meat source and use the finest you can find.
2. Be vigilant about controlling the temperature throughout the smoking and cooking process.
3. Get your sauce worked out early so you're not fooling with it at the last minute.
4. Presentation cannot be stressed enough. Make your entries look their very best before delivering them to the judges.

Tennessee Whiskey Lynchburgers

Here are two easy variations for whiskey burgers that draw raves in my backyard.

Smoky Jack Burgers

Makes 6 servings

I like to serve the Smoky Jack burgers open-faced with Cheddar cheese and bacon. Instead of the usual soft bun, try a grilled English muffin half.

 3 tablespoons Jack Daniel's Tennessee Whiskey
 3 tablespoons Worcestershire sauce
 2 teaspoons garlic salt
 2 teaspoons liquid smoke
 1 ½ pounds ground beef
 6 slices cheese, optional
 6 strips cooked bacon, optional
 6 buns or English muffins

Combine the Jack Daniel's, Worcestershire sauce, garlic salt, and liquid smoke in a small bowl. Add three tablespoons of the sauce to the ground beef in a large mixing bowl. Blend well with your hands and form into 6 patties. Sear the patties about 5 minutes per side over medium-high heat. Baste both sides with the remaining sauce and grill until the burgers are cooked to your liking. During the last minutes of cooking, top with cheese and bacon, both optional, and lightly toast the buns or English muffins over medium heat.

Chili Jack Burgers

Makes 6 servings

Chili Jack burgers are wonderful with melted Pepper Jack cheese and fresh tomato salsa.

3 tablespoons Jack Daniel's Tennessee Whiskey

3 tablespoons Worcestershire sauce

2 teaspoons garlic salt

2 teaspoons chili powder

1 ½ pounds ground beef

6 slices cheese, optional

6 strips cooked bacon, optional

6 buns

Combine the Jack Daniel's, Worcestershire sauce, garlic salt, and chili powder. Add three tablespoons of the sauce to the ground beef in a large mixing bowl. Blend well with your hands and form into 6 patties. Sear the patties about 5 minutes per side over medium-high heat. Baste both sides with the remaining sauce and grill until the burgers are cooked to your liking. During the last minutes of cooking, top with cheese and bacon, both optional, and lightly toast the buns over medium heat.

Honey Jack Onions

Makes 6 servings

Sweet Vidalia onions from Georgia are one of my favorite springtime arrivals. Some say Vidalias are so sweet you can bite into them like an apple. I've never tried that, but grilled in a foil packet with a little Jack Daniel's Tennessee Honey, melted butter, and sugar they become a classy side dish. Match them with any kind of pork or smoked turkey.

4 medium sweet onions (such as Vidalia)

2 tablespoons Jack Daniel's Tennessee Honey

4 tablespoons melted butter

1 tablespoon sugar

A few fresh sage leaves, optional

Salt and black pepper

Peel the onions and cut in half from the top to the bottom. Combine the Tennessee Honey, butter, and sugar in a small bowl and blend well. Place the onions on a large sheet of heavy duty aluminum foil. Drizzle with the glaze and sprinkle with sage, salt, and pepper. Fold up and seal the foil packet and roast on the grill over medium heat until tender, about 30 minutes.

When a hostess told her table guests that Miss Mary, who was featured in a Jack Daniel's advertisement at the age of 100, was the oldest woman to appear in the pages of Playboy magazine, a teenager at the table asked, "Was she hot?"

Charred Fruit for Jack's Highballs

U ncle Jack and his charred oak barrels inspired me to try this fun trick one day while waiting for the coals to ash over for grilled steaks. Sprinkle a few slices of lemon, orange, or lime with sugar. Grill them quickly over medium heat just until the sugar melts and caramelizes. The fruit should be lightly charred. Don't worry if you burn a few. Just knock them in the coals and start over. Men particularly enjoy this smoky accent in an icy glass of Jack.

Jack and Ginger Grilled Peaches

Makes 4 to 8 servings

For this sumptuous grilled fruit dessert, use freestone peaches if you can find them—the ones that separate easily from the pit. Clingstone peaches taste just as good but might not look as pretty. Serve them warm or grill them early and serve at room temperature. Try grilling other fruits like a pineapple cut into 1-inch rings and banana slices to round out an ice cream sundae.

⅓ cup brown sugar
¼ cup melted butter
¼ cup Jack Daniel's Tennessee Whiskey
4 or 5 ripe but firm peaches, halved and pitted
1 cup gingersnap crumbs
Your favorite vanilla ice cream

Combine the sugar, butter, and Jack Daniel's in a small bowl. Place the peaches cut-side up in an aluminum foil pan big enough to hold the fruit in a single layer. Pour the mixture over the peaches. Heat a grill to medium heat and cook the peaches about 10 minutes until the sauce is bubbly and the peaches are softened. Sprinkle with gingersnap crumbs. Serve with vanilla ice cream.

Jack's Sweet Hot Glazed Shrimp

Makes 6 servings

Shrimp wasn't exactly the commonest thing for dinner in Middle Tennessee back in Uncle Jack's day. In fact, I don't remember having much shrimp while I was growing up fifty years later, either. But I image if my Uncle were alive today, flamboyant party host that he was, spicy fat shrimp would certainly be a feature on his tables. Serve shrimp skewers as the centerpiece of a meal (with Cheese Grits Bake (page 75) on the side) or pass them around to guests as a tasty tidbit with cocktails before the steaks go on the grill. We like them spicy hot with a good dose of pepper sauce.

>   12 bamboo or metal skewers
>   2 pounds jumbo shrimp, peeled with tails on
>   ¼ cup soy sauce
>   ¼ cup hoisin sauce
>   2 tablespoons Jack Daniel's Tennessee Whiskey
>   2 tablespoons brown sugar
>   2 tablespoons hot pepper sauce, or to taste
>   2 tablespoons fresh lemon juice
>   2 cloves garlic, minced

If you're using bamboo skewers, presoak them for at least thirty minutes so they don't burn on the grill. Thread 3 to 4 shrimp onto two parallel bamboo or metal skewers. Continue until you run out of shrimp or skewers. Double skewers make the shrimp more stable and easier to turn while on the grill. Combine the soy sauce, hoisin sauce, Jack Daniel's, brown sugar, hot sauce, lemon juice, and garlic in a small bowl. Brush the shrimp with the glaze and grill over medium-hot heat until the flesh is opaque, about 3 minutes per side.

Grilled Potato (and Other Vegetable) Packets

Makes 4 servings per packet

My mother never let Daddy do the grilling on our patio. "Well, I knew he couldn't cook," she'd say. She'd start the charcoal herself and throw on the steaks. When our friend Conner Motlow and his family came for supper, Mother would always let Conner give her a hand with the steaks. "He'd get the fire so hot and just burnt the fool out of them," she remembers fondly. "They'd be charred all the way around but

still pink inside." They'd always be served with a big slab of butter melting on top, with a baked potato and a fancy congealed salad on the side. These foil-wrapped packet potatoes would have been perfect for Conner's fiery style of grilling.

> Red, white, or Yukon Gold waxy potatoes
> Olive oil
> Salt and black pepper to taste

Cut the potatoes into 2-inch chunks. Place about 3 cups of cut potatoes in a single layer on a generous sheet of heavy duty aluminum foil per packet. Drizzle with olive oil and season with salt and pepper. Fold the foil around the potatoes making a well-sealed packet. Place it on the grill over medium heat and cook 15 minutes. Flip the packet and continue to cook until the potatoes are tender, about 20 minutes. Each packet makes about 4 servings. You can also use this technique with other vegetables like cauliflower, broccoli, Brussels sprouts, carrots, parsnips, and beets.

Salt and Peppered Sweet Corn

Makes 8 servings

Maybe it's because corn is the main ingredient in Jack Daniel's Tennessee Whiskey that makes me love grilled and roasted corn so much. Every October at the Jack Daniel's World Invitational Barbecue Competition, follow your nose to the fabulous and famous roasted corn served by The Mother Shuckers. Most visitors to the barbecue competition find out early on that pulled pork barbecue isn't the only good thing to eat. At least one smoky ear is a necessity during the fall festivities.

    I know it's showy, but I don't see the need to soak and grill corn in the husk. Good sweet grilled corn takes only minutes over a hot fire and is an easy side dish with almost any summer-through-fall meal. On a rainy day, cook the corn under the broiler until charred on all sides. We always grill more corn than we think we'll need, but we rarely have any left over. When we do, I strip it from the cob and add a smoky touch to salads and casseroles.

> 8 ears of fresh corn on the cob
> ½ cup (1 stick) butter, melted
> Salt and black pepper to taste

Remove the husks and silk from corn, but leave the stem intact to use as a handle.

Grill the corn directly over medium-high heat for 8 to 10 minutes, turning frequently and moving the ears around the grate for an evenly browned look. Stay close to the grill—burnt kernels are chewy and tough. Baste with melted butter as the corn cooks. Salt, pepper, and eat.

Crocked Barbecue

Making backyard barbecue the all-day way isn't for everybody. But that doesn't mean you can't make wonderful smoky barbecue at home. All you need to turn your kitchen into a barbecue pit is a slow cooker and some all-natural liquid smoke. Warning: in a few hours the whole house will take on the aroma of your favorite barbecue shack. With the built-in sauce, your Crocked Barbecue is ready to go. Be sure to make one of the cornbreads (pages 81–83), pick a slaw (pages 92–94), and make a batch of Jack in the Beans (page 135).

½ cup cider vinegar
¼ cup Jack Daniel's Tennessee Whiskey
½ cup brown sugar
½ cup ketchup
¼ cup liquid smoke
1 pork butt (about 6 pounds)
1 tablespoon coarse-ground black pepper
1 tablespoon coarse salt
1 tablespoon paprika
1 teaspoon garlic powder

Combine the vinegar, Jack Daniel's, brown sugar, ketchup, and liquid smoke in a large slow cooker (at least 5 quarts). Add the pork butt. Sprinkle the pepper, salt, paprika, and garlic powder over the meat. Cover and cook on high for 5 to 6 hours or on low for 10 to 12 hours, until the meat is pull-apart tender and the internal temperature is at least 190°F.

Using tongs and a slotted spoon, transfer the meat to a large casserole or foil pan. Let the meat rest until it is cool enough to handle. Pull the meat into strands. It should shred easily. Serve with the meat juices.

To serve the barbecue later: Remove the meat from the slow cooker, cool, and refrigerate. Pour the sauce into a separate container and refrigerate. Before reheating the sauce, skim the hard fat layer off the top and discard.

To reheat: Place the meat in a large saucepan moistened with the sauce. Gently heat over medium-low, stirring occasionally. Or place it in a covered casserole with the sauce and heat in a 350°F oven for 20 to 30 minutes.

Norman Thai Jack Marinade

Makes 2 ½ cups

Who would have ever thought that Thai food would catch on in little Lynchburg, Tennessee? We don't have a Thai restaurant (yet), but we bring back great ideas for home cooking every time we travel.

Our Master Taster Jeff Norman loves spicy Thai food and experiments at home with Thai ingredients like curry pastes and fish sauce. He even grows Thai chile peppers in his garden. Jeff uses his special all-purpose Thai-style marinade to spice up any kind of chicken, pork, or beef that he's got a hankering to throw on the grill.

1 cup soy sauce
½ cup Jack Daniel's Tennessee Whiskey
1/3 cup brown sugar
1 cup finely minced onion
1 tablespoon minced garlic
Thai fish sauce to taste
Hot Thai chile peppers or Serrano peppers to taste
2 ½ to 3 pounds chicken breasts, pork tenderloin, or sirloin steak

Combine the soy sauce, Jack Daniel's, brown sugar, onion, garlic, fish sauce, and chiles in a small bowl. Combine the marinade with the meat of your choice (leave out the sugar with beef) in a large resealable plastic bag. Seal the bag and place it in the refrigerator at least 2 hours or overnight. Turn the bag once in a while so all the pieces are evenly coated. Remove the meat from the marinade and grill the meat. Discard the used marinade.

SWEETS

Bananas Fanning
Bobo's Macaroon Pie
Miss Mary Bobo's Sweet Secret Pie
Basic Pie Pastry
Basic Graham Cracker Pie Crust
Classic Caramel Cake
Late Night Oatmeal Cake with Broiled Butter
Pecan Topping

Jack Dessert Sauces

Jack's Famous Quick Caramel Sauce
Jack's Salted Caramel Sauce
Jack's Punchy Peaches
Jack's Happy Cherries
Jack's Marshmallow Peanut Butter Sauce
Jack's Best-Ever Fudge Sauce
Jack's Butter Maple Raisin Sauce
Jack's Brown Sugar Cream
Jack's Sorghum Chocolate Sauce
Jack's Sugar Box Sauce
Jack's Buttermilk Praline Sauce
Miss Mary's Fudge Pie
Jack Daniel's Whipped Cream

Angelo Lucchesi

Jack's Birthday Cake
JD Bread Pudding
Skillet Cobbler with Cinnamon Sugar Dumplings
Old-Fashioned Apple Dumplings
Pumpkin Patch Squares
Southern Biscuit Shortcake
Tennessee Truffles
Town Square Chess Squares
Debbie's Coconut Tennessee Honey Balls
Easy Made Jam Cake
Jack's Fudge Brownie Pudding
Jack's Bottom's Up Fruit Cobbler
Ola's Citrus Cake
Jack and Cola Pudding Cake
Honey Jack Panna Cotta
Classic Chess Pie

Old No. 7 Chess Pie Variations

Jack Daniel's Pecan Pie
Three Milk Punch Cake
Chocolate Chess Squares
Butter Jack Pudding

Bananas Fanning

Makes 6 servings

This Lynchburg variation of Bananas Foster is named in honor of my Uncle Dale's father, Herb Fanning, who lived well into his nineties. Herby liked to tell folks he was so old he never bought green bananas. You'll likely recognize Herby as he appeared in more Jack Daniel's ads than anyone else. Next time you're in town, be sure to visit the bronze life-size statue of Herby sitting at his beloved checkerboard in front of the Lynchburg Hardware and General Store. You can sit down and have your picture made with him.

> ¼ cup (½ stick) butter
> 1 cup pecan halves
> 4 bananas, sliced
> ½ cup brown sugar
> Pinch of nutmeg
> ½ cup Jack Daniel's Tennessee Whiskey
> Vanilla ice cream

Melt the butter in a large skillet. Stir in the pecans and bananas and cook over medium-low heat, about 3 minutes. Stir in the sugar and nutmeg and cook until the sugar is dissolved, about 2 minutes. Stir in the Jack Daniel's and heat it until bubbly. Carefully ignite the edge of the pan with a match. Serve warm spooned over vanilla ice cream.

Bobo's Macaroon Pie

Makes 6 servings

The surprise ingredient in this macaroon pie is cracker crumbs, believe it or not. The crumbs magically disappear while the meringue bakes, creating a pie that is light and crisp and absolutely scrumptious with seasonal fruits. Summer peaches are especially exotic combined with the flavor of almond. In winter, we spoon Lynchburg Cranberry Relish (page 240), usually reserved for biscuits, over this out-of-the-ordinary dessert.

> 3 egg whites
> 1 cup sugar
> 1 teaspoon almond extract

12 saltine crackers, finely crushed
¼ teaspoon baking powder
⅓ cup chopped dates
½ cup chopped pecans or sliced almonds, toasted
Assorted fresh fruit
Whipped cream

Heat the oven to 350°F. Grease a 9-inch pie pan. Beat the egg whites until frothy in a large mixing bowl with an electric mixer. Gradually beat in the sugar until the egg whites are stiff and glossy. Add the almond extract. Fold in the cracker crumbs and baking powder. Fold in the dates and nuts. Spoon the mixture into the pie plate. Bake 25 to 30 minutes. The top will look golden brown and crisp. Cool before serving. Serve with fresh fruit and whipped cream.

Miss Mary Bobo's Sweet Secret Pie

Makes 6 to 8 servings

A successful country cook needs a good imagination, I say. That's what it takes to turn the simple (plain old oatmeal, in this case) into this wonderful pie. Here the oatmeal adds a satisfying heft and body to the pie, and it's impossible to identify. Honestly, you'll think you're eating pecan pie with coconut. We regularly stump our guests with this dessert, and so far no one has put their finger on the secret. Now you know!

2 eggs, beaten
1 cup uncooked oatmeal, quick or old-fashioned
⅔ cup sugar
⅔ cup butter, melted
⅔ cup light corn syrup
⅔ cup coconut
1 tablespoon brown sugar
1 teaspoon vanilla
½ teaspoon salt
1 (8- or 9-inch) Basic Pie Pastry, partially baked, but not brown (recipe on page 206)
Jack Daniel's Whipped Cream (recipe on page 215)

Heat the oven to 325°F. Combine the eggs, oatmeal, sugar, butter, corn syrup, coconut, brown sugar, vanilla, and salt in a medium mixing bowl

and blend well. Pour the mixture into the pie shell. Bake 45 minutes or until the center is set and doesn't jiggle. Cool on a wire rack.

Serve Sweet Secret Pie with Jack Daniel's Whipped Cream.

Basic Pie Pastry

Makes enough for 2 pie crusts

I know you're busy, but anybody can take some time to make a great pie crust and not default to the refrigerated kind. This is the simplest, most wonderful crust, so use it for anything that calls for crust. Of course, we prefer the savory taste and tender texture of crust made with lard.

2 cups all-purpose flour
1 teaspoon salt
$^2/_3$ cup lard or vegetable shortening
$^1/_4$ cup ice cold water

Combine the flour and salt in a medium mixing bowl. Cut in the lard with a pastry blender or two knives until the mixture is crumbly. Sprinkle the cold water over the flour and stir gently with a fork until the dough comes together in a loose ball. Add droplets of additional water if the dough seems too dry. Divide the dough in half and press each piece into a flat ball. Wrap and refrigerate until ready to use. Or place each dough ball on a floured board or pastry cloth. Roll it out in a circle about 1-inch larger than the rim of a 9-inch pie plate. Carefully fit the dough into the pie pan without stretching the dough. Crimp the edges with your fingers. If using a top crust, fold the top rolled pastry edge under the bottom crust edge. Crimp together.

To partially prebake a pastry shell: Often it's a good idea to prebake a pastry that will be filled with a gooey filling. This helps prevent a soggy bottom crust. To do this, prick the bottom of the crust with a fork. Line the crust with foil and place pie weights or loose dried beans in the shell. The weight will help the crust from shrinking. Now just bake the pie until it's set, not browned, in a heated 350°F oven for 10 minutes. Cool. Fill the pie and bake as your recipe directs.

Basic Graham Cracker Pie Crust

A homemade graham cracker crust makes a big difference. And it's so easy.

1 ½ cups graham cracker crumbs (about 20 graham crackers)
¼ cup sugar
⅓ cup butter, softened

Heat the oven to 350°F. Combine the crumbs and sugar in a medium mixing bowl. Stir in the butter until crumbly. Place the crumbs into a 9-inch pie pan. Using the back of a spoon, press the crumbs firmly and evenly against the bottom and up the sides of the pan. Bake 10 minutes. Cool before filling.

Classic Caramel Cake

Makes 16 servings

My uncle Jack was a lively, theatrical man with a big appetite for life, good food, music, and dancing. As Lynchburg's most eligible bachelor and bon vivant, he threw fabulous parties. At his annual Second Sunday in May dinners, hundreds would gather at his house after church and enjoy an all-afternoon feast. The tables would groan with plentiful meats, vegetables, breads, and good gracious, sweets like this traditional caramel cake (my family's favorite).

My nephews John and Conner Tolley absolutely beg my mother for a caramel cake when they're home for a visit. And yes, it's really all about the icing. You must caramelize the sugar in an iron skillet for it to taste right. Don't shy away from trying because once you make it, you'll get plenty of requests and opportunities to practice.

2 cups all-purpose flour
2 teaspoons baking powder
¼ teaspoon salt
¾ cup (1 ½ sticks) butter
1 ¼ cups sugar
6 egg yolks
1 teaspoon vanilla
¾ cup milk
Caramel Icing (recipe follows)

Heat the oven to 375°F. Grease and flour a 9 x 13-inch baking pan. Combine the flour, baking powder, and salt in a medium mixing bowl. Cream the butter and sugar in a large mixing bowl with an electric mixer until light and fluffy. Add the egg yolks, one at a time, and beat until light and creamy. Add the vanilla. Gradually add the flour mixture alternately with the milk mixture. Beat on medium speed until smooth. Scrape down the sides of the bowl as needed. Pour the batter into the greased pan. Bake 25 to 30 minutes or until golden brown and a toothpick inserted in the center comes out clean. Cool and spread with caramel icing.

Caramel Icing

2 ½ cups sugar, divided
1 egg, lightly beaten
½ cup (1 stick) butter
¾ cup evaporated milk
1 teaspoon vanilla

Heat ½ cup of the sugar in an iron skillet over low heat until the sugar has melted and turns light brown. Combine the egg, butter, and the remaining sugar and the milk in a large saucepan. Cook over low heat, stirring constantly, until the butter melts and the mixture comes to a boil. Stir in the browned sugar and cook to the soft ball stage (238°F). Remove from the heat, cool slightly, and stir in the vanilla. Beat the icing until it becomes a spreading consistency. If the icing gets too thick, add a little cream or evaporated milk.

Late Night Oatmeal Cake with Broiled Butter Pecan Topping

Makes 16 servings

In their youth my mother and father ran around with a group of friends that included Daddy's cousins, who were Lem Motlow's three younger sons Robert, Conner, and Hap. "We all knew the Motlows were in the whiskey business, but we really didn't think much anything of it," Mother recalls. "Back in those days it was the commonest thing."

Most families around here have moonshiners and distillers somewhere in the family history. Daddy's family owned the Tolley and Eaton Distillery, and it was

even bigger than Jack Daniel's in the late 1800s. Mother says fun with the Motlow brothers always included plenty of laughing and late-night carrying on around the kitchen table over hot coffee and big slices of this homey cake.

1 cup rolled oats
1 ⅓ cups boiling water
½ cup (1 stick) butter, melted
1 ⅓ cups all-purpose flour
1 teaspoon baking soda
1 cup brown sugar
1 cup sugar
2 eggs
1 teaspoon cinnamon
1 teaspoon vanilla
Broiled Butter Pecan Topping (recipe follows)

Heat the oven to 350°F. Grease a 9 x 13-inch baking pan. Add the oats to a large mixing bowl. Pour the boiling water over the oats and let them soften for about 20 minutes. Stir in the butter, flour, baking soda, sugars, eggs, cinnamon, and vanilla. Pour the mixture into the greased pan. Bake for about 35 minutes or until the sides start to pull away from the pan and the top is golden brown.

While the cake is baking, prepare the Broiled Butter Pecan Topping. Spread the topping over the hot cake and place under the broiler until the topping is bubbly and lightly browned, about 5 minutes.

Broiled Butter Pecan Topping

½ cup (1 stick) butter
2 tablespoons milk
1 cup brown sugar
1 cup sweetened shredded coconut
1 cup chopped pecans

Melt the butter in a small saucepan. Blend in the milk, sugar, coconut, and pecans. Spread over the hot cake.

Jack Dessert Sauces

I can't remember all the times any one of these fabulously decadent sauces has rescued me from a dessert jam. Drizzling a little over ice cream is just the beginning. Imagine slices of toasted pound cake and bananas pooled with caramel sauce, layered parfaits with peaches or cherries, brownie sundaes with marshmallow peanut butter sauce, and any apple dessert or bread pudding with the caramel sauce. Broil the brown sugar cream over sweetened fresh fruit in a little oven-proof gratin dish. And what doesn't improve with a little chocolate? If I'm feeling really fancy, I'll make two sauces and mingle them with a dessert.

Jack's Famous Quick Caramel Sauce

Makes about 2 cups

> 1/2 cup (1 stick) butter
> 1 cup brown sugar
> 1/2 cup heavy cream
> 1/4 cup Jack Daniel's Tennessee Whiskey
> 1 cup chopped pecans, optional

Melt the butter in a saucepan over medium heat. Stir in the sugar and cream. Bring to a boil over medium heat, stirring constantly. Remove from the heat. Whisk in the Jack Daniel's. Stir in the nuts. Serve warm or at room temperature. Cover and keep refrigerated.

Jack's Salted Caramel Sauce

Makes 1 1/2 cups

> 1 cup sugar
> 1/4 cup water
> 1/2 cup heavy cream
> 1/4 cup Jack Daniel's Tennessee Whiskey
> 1/4 cup (1 stick) butter
> Coarse sea salt to taste

Place the sugar and water in a small cast iron skillet or heavy-bottom medium saucepan. Cook over medium heat, stirring frequently, until the mixture turns the color of whiskey, about 15 minutes. Be sure to watch the sugar carefully. Immediately remove from the heat and stir in the cream, Jack Daniel's, and butter. Sprinkle with salt.

Jack's Punchy Peaches

Makes about 2 cups

3 ripe peaches, peeled and sliced or 1 bag (12 ounces) frozen sliced peaches
⅓ cup brown sugar
2 tablespoons butter
2 tablespoons Jack Daniel's Tennessee Whiskey
1 teaspoon cornstarch

Combine the peaches, sugar, and butter in a medium saucepan. Cook over low heat and simmer just until the sugar dissolves. Combine the Jack Daniel's and cornstarch and stir until the cornstarch is dissolved. Pour the mixture into the peaches. Cook until slightly thickened and bubbly. Serve warm or at room temperature. Cover and keep refrigerated.

Jack's Happy Cherries

Makes 3 cups

¼ cup (½ stick) butter
¼ cup slivered almonds
½ cup sugar
¼ cup Jack Daniel's Tennessee Whiskey
1 tablespoon fresh lemon juice
2 cans (about 14.5 ounces each) pitted sweet cherries, drained

Melt the butter in a medium saucepan over medium heat. Stir in the almonds and cook until lightly browned, 1 to 2 minutes. Stir in the sugar, Jack Daniel's, and lemon juice. Cook until bubbly. Gently stir in the cherries. Cook until heated through. Cover and keep refrigerated. Reheat in a small saucepan over medium heat, stirring frequently, or spoon into in a microwavable dish, cover loosely with plastic wrap, and microwave on high for 1 minute. Stir before serving.

SWEETS

Jack's Marshmallow Peanut Butter Sauce

Makes about 1 cup

> 1 jar (7ounces) marshmallow cream
> 1/4 cup creamy or crunchy peanut butter
> 1/4 cup Jack Daniel's Tennessee Whiskey

Combine the marshmallow cream, peanut butter, and Jack Daniel's in a small saucepan. Simmer over medium heat about 3 minutes or until silky smooth, stirring constantly. Serve warm. Cover and keep refrigerated. Reheat in a small saucepan over medium heat, stirring frequently, or spoon into in a microwavable dish, cover loosely with plastic wrap, and microwave on high for 1 minute. Stir before serving.

Jack's Best-Ever Fudge Sauce

Makes about 2 cups

> 1 cup heavy cream
> 1/4 cup Jack Daniel's Tennessee Whiskey
> 8 ounces good quality semi-sweet chocolate, cut into small chunks

Bring the cream and Jack Daniel's to a boil in a medium saucepan over medium heat. Remove from the heat. Stir in the chocolate until smooth and melted. Serve the sauce warm or at room temperature. Cover and keep refrigerated. Reheat in a small saucepan over medium heat, stirring frequently, or spoon into in a microwavable dish, cover loosely with plastic wrap, and microwave on high for 1 minute. Stir before serving.

Jack's Butter Maple Raisin Sauce

Makes about 1 cup

> 3/4 cup real maple syrup
> 1/4 cup Jack Daniel's Tennessee Whiskey
> 2 tablespoon butter
> 1/2 cup raisins
> 1 tablespoon fresh orange or lemon zest, optional
> Toasted pecans or walnuts, optional

Combine the maple syrup, Jack Daniel's, butter, raisins, and zest in a small saucepan. Bring to a boil and simmer until slightly thickened, about 5 minutes. Stir in a small handful of toasted pecans or walnuts if you like. Cover and keep refrigerated. Reheat in a small saucepan over medium heat, stirring frequently, or spoon it into a microwavable dish, cover loosely with plastic wrap, and microwave on high for 1 minute. Stir before serving.

Jack's Brown Sugar Cream

Makes about 1 cup

1 cup sour cream
¼ cup brown sugar
2 tablespoons Jack Daniel's Tennessee Whiskey
Assorted fresh fruit, for serving

Combine the sour cream, brown sugar, and Jack Daniel's in a small bowl and blend well. Cover and keep refrigerated. Serve with fresh fruit such as berries, pineapple chunks, seedless grapes, sliced bananas, and peach slices.

Jack's Sorghum Chocolate Sauce

Makes 1 cup

6 ounces semi-sweet chocolate, coarsely chopped
½ cup sorghum or mild flavored molasses
2 tablespoons butter
2 tablespoons Jack Daniel's Tennessee Whiskey
Pinch of salt

Combine the chocolate and sorghum in a small saucepan. Melt the chocolate over medium-low heat. Stir in the butter and Jack Daniel's. Add a pinch of salt to taste. Serve warm over ice cream. Cover and keep refrigerated. Reheat in a small saucepan over medium heat, stirring frequently, or spoon it into a microwavable dish, cover loosely with plastic wrap, and microwave on high for 1 minute. Stir before serving.

Jack's Sugar Box Sauce

Makes about 2 ¾ cups

1 box (1 pound) dark brown sugar
1 ½ cups Jack Daniel's Tennessee Whiskey
½ teaspoon salt
1 stick (½ cup) butter, optional

Combine the sugar, Jack Daniel's, and salt in a small saucepan. Cook over medium heat just until the mixture boils and the sugar has completely dissolved. Remove from the heat and stir in the butter, if using, until it has melted. Cool and store in a jar with a tight fitting lid in the refrigerator. Reheat in a small saucepan over medium heat, stirring frequently, or spoon it into a microwavable dish, cover loosely with plastic wrap, and microwave on high for 1 minute. Stir before serving.

Jack's Buttermilk Praline Sauce

Makes about 3 cups

1 cup sugar
½ cup buttermilk
½ cup (1 stick) butter
2 tablespoons corn syrup
2 tablespoons Jack Daniel's Tennessee Whiskey
1 cup chopped pecans

Combine the sugar, buttermilk, butter, and corn syrup in a small saucepan. Cook over medium heat, stirring constantly, until the mixture is smooth and turns a light golden brown. Stir in the Jack Daniel's and nuts. Serve warm or at room temperature. Cover and keep refrigerated. Reheat in a small saucepan over medium heat, stirring frequently, or spoon it into a microwavable dish, cover loosely with plastic wrap, and microwave on high for one minute. Stir before serving.

Miss Mary's Fudge Pie

Makes 8 servings

Here it is! Our most requested pie recipe at Miss Mary's. A good fudge pie surely satisfies every chocoholic's cravings and proves, once and for all, that an old-fashioned recipe can top a trendy flourless chocolate torte any day of the week. And it's surprisingly easy to make. Fudge pie certainly deserves a big dollop of whipped cream kissed with a little Jack. Notice how this fudge pie is similar to the Chocolate Chess variation (page 233), but it's a little creamier because of the evaporated milk, and we always prepare it in a graham cracker crust. Be sure to not overcook this pie. The filling will still be a bit jiggly after baking and will firm up as it cools.

ꟷꟷ ¼ cup (½ stick) butter
ꟷꟷ 1 ½ cups sugar
ꟷꟷ 3 tablespoons cocoa powder
ꟷꟷ 2 eggs, beaten
ꟷꟷ ½ cup evaporated milk
ꟷꟷ 1 tablespoon Jack Daniel's Tennessee Whiskey
ꟷꟷ 1 (9-inch) Basic Graham Cracker Pie Crust (page 207)
ꟷꟷ Jack Daniel's Whipped Cream (recipe follows)

Heat the oven to 350°F. Melt the butter in a saucepan over medium heat. Stir in the sugar and cocoa powder. Stir in the eggs, evaporated milk, and Jack Daniel's. Pour the mixture into the prepared piecrust and bake for 30 to 35 minutes. Cool completely. Serve slices with a dollop of whipped cream sweetened with sugar and a little Jack Daniel's. Sprinkle the cream with a dusting of cocoa powder.

Jack Daniel's Whipped Cream

Makes 2 cups whipped cream

ꟷꟷ 1 cup heavy cream
ꟷꟷ 2 tablespoons to ¼ cup powdered sugar
ꟷꟷ 1 tablespoon Jack Daniel's Tennessee Whiskey

Whip the cream in a chilled bowl with an electric mixer or a whisk until soft peaks form. Add the powdered sugar and whip until well blended. Fold in the Jack Daniel's. Cover and refrigerate.

215

SWEETS

Angelo Lucchesi

Angelo Lucchesi may be the one person who has as many friends as Uncle Jack had.

In 1945, when Angelo was in his twenties, he became friends with the four Motlow brothers, and in 1953 he became the very the first salesman for the Jack Daniel Distillery. He is among our dearest friends. Angelo's sunny disposition and welcoming smile have helped make many friends for Jack Daniel's Tennessee Whiskey too.

Among his noted achievements, Angelo became life-long friends with none other than Frank Sinatra. Angelo recalls the time when Sinatra was to perform at The Copacabana Club and because of whiskey rationing at the time, the club had no Jack Daniel's for its No. 1 fan. When Angelo received word of the problem, he made sure the whiskey was delivered in time.

Shortly thereafter, Angelo's phone rang, and he knew instantly with whom he was speaking. "How'd you know it was me?" Sinatra asked. "Well, no one sounds like you, Mr. Sinatra," Angelo replied. Sinatra shared his personal phone numbers with Angelo with the caveat that he keep them close to his heart. "When Frank died I burned them," Angelo recalls. "He said to me once, 'Angelo, we are friends until the end of my life, and the end of your life.' And we were. If it were not for Jack Daniel's, I would never have met him."

When your next distillery tour guide invites you to watch our movie, look above the entrance and see "The Angelo Lucchesi Theater" named for our No. 1 promoter. If you run into him at the Jack barbecue, have a pen ready as Angelo is one of only four people in the world authorized to sign the products of the Jack Daniel Distillery.

Jack's Birthday Cake

Makes 16 servings

We made more than a few of this handy cake years ago to serve at Jack's 150th birthday celebrations all around the country. You can make it in a tube or Bundt pan for looks, but I prefer a good old 9 x 13-inch baking pan. A sheet cake is easier to tote around and nicely cuts into neat squares.

2 ¼ cups all-purpose flour
2 teaspoons baking powder
½ teaspoon salt
1 cup (2 sticks) butter
2 cups firmly packed brown sugar
4 eggs
½ cup Jack Daniel's Tennessee Whiskey
1 cup chopped pecans
1 package (6 ounces) semi-sweet chocolate chips
Hot Buttered Whiskey Glaze (recipe follows)

Heat the oven to 325°F. Grease a 9 x 13-inch baking pan. Combine the flour, baking powder, and salt in a medium mixing bowl and set aside. Melt the butter in a large saucepan over low heat. Remove from the heat; stir in the brown sugar, eggs, flour mixture, and Jack Daniel's, stirring well after each addition. Pour the batter into the greased pan. Sprinkle evenly with pecans and chocolate chips. Bake 45 to 50 minutes or until the center of the cake is firm and the edges begin to pull away from the sides of the pan. Cool on a wire rack and drizzle with glaze.

Hot Buttered Whiskey Glaze

¼ cup melted butter
2 cups powdered sugar
3 tablespoons Jack Daniel's Tennessee Whiskey
1 teaspoon vanilla

Combine the butter, sugar, Jack Daniel's, and vanilla in a small bowl. Blend well with a wooden spoon. Drizzle over the cake.

Note: The cake may be baked in a greased 10-inch tube or Bundt pan.

Our favorite Miss Mary Bobo's guest of all time is long-time Jack Daniel's friend Angelo Lucchesi of Memphis, Tennessee. In 1953, he was the first salesman ever hired for Jack Daniel's. All our hostesses want him to sit at their tables.

Increase baking time to 1 hour. Cool in the pan 10 minutes; turn out onto a wire rack, and cool completely. Drizzle with the glaze.

JD Bread Pudding

Makes 12 servings

A great bread pudding recipe spirited with a little Jack Daniel's is essential to the well-rounded Southern kitchen. Few things can top whiskey-soaked raisins, and I'm especially fond of the zing from the fresh orange zest. Be sure to always use good quality white bread. Years ago Miss Mary's boarder Ruth Hall, a former Moore County extension agent and Miss Mary's table hostess, made her bread pudding with leftover homemade biscuits!

1 cup raisins
1 tablespoon fresh orange zest
⅓ cup Jack Daniel's Tennessee Whiskey
7 cups cubed white bread, lightly toasted
4 eggs
1 cup sugar
3 cups milk
1 teaspoon vanilla
¼ cup butter
Nutmeg to taste

Combine the raisins, zest, and Jack Daniel's in a small bowl. Let it soak about 20 minutes. Butter a 9 x 13-inch baking dish. Place the bread cubes in the prepared dish. Whisk together the eggs and sugar in a large mixing bowl. Stir in the milk and vanilla. Fold the raisin mixture into the bread cubes. Pour the egg mixture over the bread and let stand about 15 minutes.

Heat the oven to 375°F. Dot the top of the bread mixture with butter and sprinkle with nutmeg. Bake until golden brown and set in the center, about 35 to 40 minutes. Serve warm. Drizzle each serving with heavy cream, if desired.

Skillet Cobbler with Cinnamon Sugar Dumplings

Makes 8 to 10 servings

I love fruit cobblers made with delicate crisp pastry strips, but sometimes you can't beat the ease of quick-stir biscuit dough made with melted butter. If you don't yet own an iron or ovenproof skillet, pour the warm fruit into a buttered 2-quart baking dish before topping with the dumplings and baking. I especially like a combination of blackberries and peaches, or cranberries with apples or pears in the fall. Mix and match your favorite seasonal fruits—it's all delicious. And don't forget last summer's peaches and berries in the freezer. They'll work well too.

Cobbler

4 tablespoons butter

¾ cup sugar

¼ cup Jack Daniel's Tennessee Whiskey

2 tablespoons all-purpose flour

7 to 8 cups sliced, peeled fresh peaches, peeled and thinly sliced apples or pears, berries, or cranberries in any combination

Dumplings

1 ½ cups self-rising flour

¼ cup plus 1 tablespoon sugar

1 teaspoon cinnamon

½ cup milk

4 tablespoons butter, melted

1 teaspoon vanilla

To prepare the cobbler: Heat the oven to 425°F. Melt the butter in a 9-inch cast iron skillet. Stir in the sugar, Jack Daniel's, and flour; blend well. Bring to a boil and cook the mixture about 2 minutes. Stir in the fruit; reduce the heat to medium-low, and simmer while preparing the dumplings.

To make the dumplings: Combine the flour, ¼ cup sugar, and the cinnamon in a medium mixing bowl. Add the milk, butter, and vanilla. Stir with a fork just until a soft dough forms. Drop by tablespoonfuls over the hot fruit. Sprinkle the dumplings with the remaining 1 tablespoon of sugar. Bake 20 minutes or until the dumplings are golden brown. Serve warm or at room temperature with ice cream, whipped cream, or drizzled with heavy cream.

Old-Fashioned Apple Dumplings

Makes 6 servings

It doesn't take much dinner-table polling to learn that our guests don't have the opportunity to enjoy much homemade pastry anymore (or nearly any at all, sadly). When we serve these apple dumplings completely encased in delicious homemade pastry, you wouldn't believe the gasps of delight around the table. Pastry is especially easy to make when you use a pastry cloth. It's just a big square of canvas to roll out your pie crust, cookie dough, and biscuit dough on. The flour-coated canvas prevents the dough from sticking, making it very easy to roll out. Even better, the kitchen counter stays clean (well, relatively clean!). I keep my floury pastry cloth folded up in a plastic bag in the freezer. That way it stays fresh and ready.

Dumplings

1 recipe Basic Pie Pastry (page 206)
6 medium Golden Delicious or Granny Smith apples
½ cup sugar
1 teaspoon cinnamon
3 tablespoons butter, softened

Sugar Syrup

1 ¼ cups water
1 tablespoon lemon juice
¼ cup Jack Daniel's Tennessee Whiskey
¾ cup sugar
3 tablespoons butter
1 teaspoon cinnamon

To make the dumplings: Heat the oven to 375°F. Grease a 9 x 13-inch baking dish. Divide the pie pastry into 6 equal portions. Roll each ball out into a 7-inch square. Peel and core the apples. Place each apple on a square of pastry. Combine the sugar, cinnamon, and butter in a small bowl. Mix well with a fork. Fill each apple cavity with the sugar mixture. Moisten the edges of the pastry with water. Bring the four corners of the dough up over each apple and seal by pinching and pressing the edges together. Place the apples in the greased baking dish without touching. Bake 15 minutes while you make the sugar syrup.

To make the syrup: Combine the water, lemon juice, Jack Daniel's, sugar, butter, and cinnamon in a small saucepan. Bring to a boil and simmer about 5 minutes. Pour the hot syrup over and around the dumplings and continue to bake 30 minutes or until the apples are tender. Spoon some of the syrup over the apples again near the end of baking. Serve with ice cream or whipped cream.

Pumpkin Patch Squares

Makes 16 servings

After a taste of this cake, pumpkin pie won't be the only dessert on the Thanksgiving sideboard next year. In fact, you might be fielding calls for pumpkin birthday cake as well. Reliable canned pumpkin puree makes this cake exceptionally moist and tender. I often find that many pumpkin pies and cakes overdo the spices to the point of bitterness. This one is refreshingly pure and perfect with just a hint of Jack Daniel's and cinnamon. Canned pumpkin is a wonderful product to use. Just be sure you're buying pure pumpkin puree and not pumpkin pie filling that's already seasoned.

> 2 cups self-rising flour
> 2 cups sugar
> 2 teaspoons cinnamon
> 4 eggs, beaten
> 1 cup vegetable oil
> 2 cups pumpkin puree
> 2 tablespoons Jack Daniel's Tennessee Whiskey
> 2 teaspoons vanilla
> Cinnamon Cream Cheese Frosting (recipe follows)

Heat the oven to 350°F. Grease a 9 x 13-inch baking dish. Combine the flour, sugar, and cinnamon in a large mixing bowl. Stir in the eggs, oil, pumpkin, Jack Daniel's, and vanilla until smooth. Pour the batter into the greased baking dish. Bake 30 to 35 minutes or until lightly browned and a toothpick inserted in the center comes out clean. Cool and spread with Cinnamon Cream Cheese Frosting.

Heard around the TABLE

A lady told a hostess after dinner that she was sure she'd died and gone to heaven. She'd never had Southern country cooking before.

Cinnamon Cream Cheese Frosting

Makes 3 cups

1 package (8 ounces) cream cheese, softened
¼ cup (½ stick) butter
1 tablespoon Jack Daniel's Tennessee Whiskey
2 teaspoons vanilla
½ teaspoon cinnamon
1 box (16 ounces) powdered sugar

Cream the cream cheese and butter in a large mixing bowl with an electric mixer until light and fluffy. Add the Jack Daniel's, vanilla, and cinnamon. Gradually blend in the sugar until thick and creamy. Spread on the cooled cake.

Southern Biscuit Shortcake

Makes 10 shortcakes

We serve a rich biscuit shortcake at Miss Mary's in the late spring and summer when fresh peaches and berries are abundant. You can make shortcake with any biscuit, but here the recipe calls for butter instead of lard or shortening, and a touch of sugar. Serve the fruit blended with enough sugar to combat the tartness and let the mixture sit at room temperature for the flavors and juices to develop before serving. Of course, you can splash in a tablespoon or two of Jack Daniel's.

2 cups self-rising flour
3 tablespoons sugar
½ cup (1 stick) butter, cut into small pieces
About ⅔ to ¾ cup milk
Butter for spreading on the shortcakes
6 cups sweetened fresh berries or peeled and sliced peaches
Whipped cream

Heat the oven to 450°F. Combine the flour and sugar in a medium mixing bowl. Cut in the butter with a pastry blender or two knives until the mixture resembles coarse crumbs. Add the milk and stir just until a soft dough forms. Knead the dough on a lightly floured surface just until smooth, about 10 times. Roll out the dough to ½ thickness. Cut it with a

floured cutter or into squares with a knife. Place on a baking sheet about 1 inch apart and bake about 10 minutes or until golden brown. Split and butter the shortcakes. Fill and top with sweetened fruit and whipped cream.

Pastry Shortcake: Prepare the pastry (page 206). Roll out the dough to about ⅛-inch thick. Cut into 3-inch squares or circles. Arrange the pieces on a large baking sheet. Bake at 425°F for about 10 minutes. Cool. Layer sweetened fruit and whipped cream between two pieces of pastry. Top with additional fruit and cream.

Tennessee Truffles

Makes 25 to 30 servings

A quick glance at these pages might suggest that Lynchburg folks share a community sweet tooth. It's true, we love a good homemade dessert. Take fancy chocolate truffles. Here is one of those deceptively easy treats that appears far too exotic to prepare in a home kitchen. Nothing could be further from the truth.

The only real key to truffles is the chocolate—use the best you can find. To impress guests after dinner, I like to offer a pretty little plate scattered with truffles and big, beautiful toasted pecan halves along with snifters of Jack Daniel's Single Barrel or icy cold shots of Jack Daniel's Tennessee Honey.

½ cup heavy cream
8 ounces good quality semi-sweet chocolate, coarsely chopped

2 tablespoons Jack Daniel's Tennessee Whiskey
Unsweetened cocoa powder

Bring the cream to a boil in a saucepan over medium heat. Combine the hot cream and the chocolate in a medium bowl, stirring until the chocolate has melted. Add the Jack Daniel's and stir until smooth. Cover and refrigerate until slightly firm. Form into bite-size balls and roll each in cocoa powder. Store the truffles in an airtight container in the refrigerator. Before serving, let them sit at room temperature about 30 minutes to soften.

Town Square Chess Squares

Makes 16 servings

Lynchburg's courthouse square anchors our beautiful town and serves as the county seat of little Moore County. Everyday life revolves around the square and the quaint shops and local businesses that serve our needs and welcome the tens of thousands of folks who visit us each year. Take a stroll around and you'll feel right at home.

These rich chess squares are often at the center of Miss Mary's dessert of the day. Let's just say they're utterly rich and sugary, and if that's not enough, we top them with Jack's Whiskey Buttermilk Butterscotch Sauce. Trust me, one square and you'll need to take another stroll.

1 cup butter
2 cups brown sugar
½ cup sugar
4 eggs
1 teaspoon vanilla
2 cups self-rising flour
1 cup chopped pecans
Jack's Whiskey Buttermilk Butterscotch Sauce (recipe follows)

Heat the oven to 350°F. Grease a 9 x 13-inch baking pan. Cream the butter and sugars in a large mixing bowl with a mixer until fluffy. Add the eggs and vanilla, beating until smooth. Blend in the flour. Stir in the pecans. Pour into the greased pan. Bake for 20 to 25 minutes or until just set. Cool. Cut into squares and serve with a spoonful of Jack's Whiskey Buttermilk Butterscotch Sauce.

Jack's Whiskey Buttermilk Butterscotch Sauce

Makes about 2 cups

1 cup sugar
½ cup buttermilk
½ cup (1 stick) butter
2 tablespoons corn syrup
2 tablespoons Jack Daniel's Tennessee Whiskey

Combine the sugar, buttermilk, butter, and corn syrup in a small sauce-pan. Bring to a boil, stirring constantly. Simmer until the sugar has melted and the mixture is smooth. Stir in the Jack Daniel's. Serve warm or at room temperature. Cover and keep refrigerated.

Debbie's Coconut Tennessee Honey Balls

Makes about 40 balls

Every experienced home cook, and Lynchburg is full of them, develops a reliable stable of dishes and desserts that, after a while, are prepared with ease and no thought of a recipe. Debbie Baxter is one such home cook. Here the inventive Debbie takes full advantage of our Tennessee Honey by including it in her famous holiday season coconut whiskey balls. Debbie recommends that even if you put off your holiday shopping to the bitter end, get a jump on your holiday treats preparation and make these in early December. That way they'll have time to mellow in the refrigerator and be perfectly aged by Christmas Eve.

3 ½ cups (about 12 ounces) crushed vanilla wafer cookies
1 ½ cups sweetened flaked coconut
1 cup finely chopped pecans
1 can (14 ounces) sweetened condensed milk
¼ cup Jack Daniel's Tennessee Honey
Powdered sugar

Combine the cookie crumbs, coconut, and pecans in a large mixing bowl. Stir in the condensed milk and Jack Daniel's Tennessee Honey and blend well. Chill the dough until firm, about 4 hours. Pour a cup or two of powdered sugar in a shallow bowl. Shape the dough into 1-inch balls and roll them in the powdered sugar. Cover and store in the refrigerator.

*A lady guest had just
won a golf tournament.
Her big prize was a day
in Lynchburg and dinner
at Miss Mary Bobo's.*

Easy Made Jam Cake

Makes 16 servings

*Home-canned jam has long been a convenient staple for Tennessee homemakers
to flavor and sweeten a dessert out of season. Traditional Tennessee jam cake is
usually made with blackberry jam that gives it an unusual purplish hue. The original old-fashioned cake is a towering, and tiring, three layer all-day extravaganza.*

*This handy 9 x 13-inch version retains the cake's traditional flavor (and funny
color) but simplifies the cake batter. I've even streamlined the icing with a luscious
brown sugar whiskey icing instead of traditional caramel (page 208). Either way,
it's really "easy made," as Mother likes to say.*

3 eggs
1 ½ cups brown sugar
1 cup vegetable oil
1 cup seedless blackberry jam
½ cup buttermilk
2 ½ cups self-rising flour
1 teaspoon cinnamon
½ teaspoon cloves
½ teaspoon nutmeg
1 cup chopped pecans, black walnuts, or walnuts
Brown Sugar Whiskey Icing (recipe follows)

Heat the oven to 350°F. Beat the eggs in a large mixing bowl. Stir in the
brown sugar, vegetable oil, jam, and buttermilk. Blend well. Stir in the
flour, cinnamon, cloves, and nutmeg, beating until smooth. Fold in the
nuts. Pour into the greased baking pan. Bake 30 to 35 minutes or until
the sides begin to pull away from the pan and the top is firm and lightly
browned. Let cool and frost with Brown Sugar Whiskey Icing.

Brown Sugar Whiskey Icing

Makes 2 cups

½ cup (1 stick) butter
½ cup brown sugar
¼ cup milk
2 tablespoons Jack Daniel's Tennessee Whiskey

1 teaspoon vanilla

2 cups powdered sugar

Melt the butter in a medium saucepan over medium heat. Stir in the brown sugar, milk, and Jack Daniel's and bring to a boil. Cook and stir the mixture until thick and bubbly, about 2 minutes. Remove the pan from the heat. Stir in the vanilla and sugar. Beat with a wooden spoon until smooth and spreadable. Spread over the cooled jam cake.

Jack's Fudge Brownie Pudding

Makes 10 servings

Remember back in the 1980s when flourless chocolate cakes were the rage? Seems that just about every restaurant I visited in my travels offered one. Following that obsession came the new "power chocolate dessert," the molten chocolate cake with a liquid center. All the while every bakery was selling ultra rich candy-like brownies. Honestly, I believe all these are variations of one recipe. Now that homey comfort desserts are back in style (having never departed Lynchburg), here's that same gooey chocolate cake batter with a splash of Jack baked in a casserole. I call it Jack's Fudge Brownie Pudding. Using a simple casserole let's you just scoop and bake. The rich creamy texture and delicate crispy top are to die for. Don't be alarmed if the cake sinks a bit while cooling. That's perfectly normal.

    Serve slices with a big spoonful of Jack's Happy Cherries on top (page 211). Or go the simpler route with generous dollops of Jack Daniel's Whipped Cream (page 215).

1 cup (2 sticks) butter

8 ounces semi-sweet chocolate, coarsely chopped

5 eggs

¼ cup Jack Daniel's Tennessee Whiskey

1 ½ cups sugar

¼ cup all-purpose flour

¼ teaspoon salt

Heat the oven to 325°F. Grease a shallow 2-quart casserole or dish. Melt the butter in a small saucepan over medium-low heat. Remove the pan from the heat and add the chocolate. Let sit until the chocolate has melted. Whisk the eggs in a medium mixing bowl until frothy. Add the Jack Daniel's, sugar, flour, and salt and whisk until smooth. Stir in the

melted chocolate mixture. Pour the batter into the prepared pan. Bake 40 to 45 minutes or until the top is puffy and crusty, but the center still seems soft and under baked. Cool slightly and serve with ice cream. Keep refrigerated, but bring it to room temperature before serving.

Jack's Bottom's Up Fruit Cobbler

Makes 12 servings

The only challenge to this cobbler is resisting the natural inclination to stir! Don't do it! It is truly magical to see how a simple batter in the bottom of a baking pan can bake around a mixture of sweetened fruit. This little dessert could not be easier or a better use of fresh summer fruit. I often use fresh berries and sometimes a combination of berries and peaches. On the sugar, I suggest ½ cup to sweeten the fruit, but feel free to adjust that amount to suit your sweetness preference.

½ cup (1 stick) butter
6 cups ripe fruit such as sliced peeled peaches, nectarines, apples, unpeeled plums or berries
1 cup sugar, divided
¼ teaspoon almond extract
1 ½ cups self-rising flour
1 ¼ cups milk
1 teaspoon vanilla
½ cup sliced almonds

Heat the oven to 350° F. Melt the butter in a 9 x 13-inch baking pan in the oven while it heats. Combine the fruit with ½ cup of the sugar and the almond extract in a medium bowl and set aside. Combine the flour, remaining ½ cup sugar, milk, and vanilla in another medium mixing bowl. Blend well. Pour the batter over the melted butter in the baking pan. Don't stir! Spoon the peaches and juices over the batter. Again, don't stir! Sprinkle with the almonds. Bake 45 to 50 minutes or until the top is golden brown and crusty.

Ola's Citrus Cake

Makes about 12 servings

*It's funny how all manner of skills and talents can find their way through genera-
tions of families. Good home cooking and baking fortunately rank high on the list
of family traits for the Cleeks. Debbie Baxter's mother, Ola Cleek, makes this no-
nonsense, delicious lemon cake that benefits from the presence of citrus cola soda.*

*One visit to Lynchburg and you'll quickly learn that citrus soda is a local favor-
ite. Ola and Debbie love how it punches up the lemon flavor in this simple cake.
And, as most things taste better with a little Jack, citrus soda as a mixer is no exception, so remember to bring some home with you. During our hot Tennessee summer
months, Debbie serves Ola's cake topped with a generous serving of her homemade
vanilla ice cream. Her husband, Goose, is a lucky man indeed.*

> 1 box (18.5 ounces) lemon cake mix
> 1 small box (3.4 ounces) lemon instant pudding
> 1 can (12 ounces) citrus soda
> ¾ cup vegetable oil
> 3 eggs
> 1 cup powdered sugar
> 2 or 3 tablespoons lemon juice, citrus soda, or water

Heat the oven to 350°F. Grease and flour a Bundt pan. Combine the cake
mix, pudding mix, soda, oil, and eggs in a large mixing bowl. Blend with
an electric hand mixer on low speed until moistened. Beat at medium
speed about 2 minutes until the batter is smooth and creamy. Pour
the batter into the prepared pan. Bake 38 to 43 minutes or until golden
brown. Cool slightly. Invert onto a cake plate. Blend the powdered sugar
and lemon juice or water together in a small bowl. Drizzle the glaze over
the warm cake.

Jack and Cola Pudding Cake

Makes 8 servings

*I'd be willing to wager that if you were dropped off just about anywhere in the civi-
lized world you could ask for a Jack and Cola and get one. Without exaggeration,
Jack and Cola is one of the world's most popular cocktails, if not the most popular.
So why not have a little fun in the kitchen and push this blessed wedding a step*

further? This Jack and Cola Pudding Cake lets you have your cocktail and a handful of peanuts all at once. No ice required.

    1 cup self-rising flour
    ³⁄₄ cup sugar
    ¹⁄₂ cup chopped salted peanuts
    ¹⁄₂ cup milk
    ¹⁄₄ cup butter
    1 teaspoon vanilla
    1 cup Cola
    ¹⁄₄ cup Jack Daniel's Tennessee Whiskey
    1 cup brown sugar
    2 tablespoons cocoa powder

Heat the oven to 350°F. Combine the flour, sugar, and peanuts in a medium mixing bowl. Stir in the milk, butter, and vanilla. Beat with a wooden spoon until smooth. Pour the batter into an ungreased 8- or 9-inch glass baking dish and set aside.

Heat the Cola until almost boiling. Combine the hot Cola, Jack Daniel's, sugar, and cocoa powder in a small mixing bowl. Whisk until smooth. Pour the mixture over the batter in the baking dish. Do not stir. Bake 35 to 40 minutes or until the cake is golden brown and set in the middle. The pudding will be bubbling up from the bottom around the edges of the cake. Remove the cake from the oven and let stand on a wire rack about 15 minutes. Serve warm in small bowls with a scoop of vanilla ice cream or a generous dollop of whipped cream, spooning the warm pudding over the top.

Honey Jack Panna Cotta

Makes 4 to 6 servings

Panna Cotta is a simple Italian dessert that I would call cream gelatin. In Lynchburg, we have a long history of liking just about anything congealed. Panna cotta is easy, elegant, and offers lots of possibility—just as whipped cream does. This one is delicately flavored with Jack Daniel's Tennessee Honey. When you serve this in rustic, homey, pint-size mason jars, your guests will know you've done something really special. Fill the jars ⅓ to ½ full, leaving plenty of room for seasonal fruits like fresh peaches, strawberries, blackberries, stewed rhubarb, or even cranberries in the wintertime. A few chopped pecans sure are a nice touch as well.

¼ cup Jack Daniel's Tennessee Honey
1 envelope powdered gelatin
2 ½ cups half and half
¼ cup sugar

Pour the Jack Daniel's Tennessee Honey in a small bowl. Sprinkle the gelatin over the whiskey and let it soften while you continue with the recipe, about 2 minutes.

Combine the half and half and sugar in a small saucepan over medium heat. Stir to dissolve the sugar and bring just to a boil. Remove from the heat and pour the softened gelatin and whiskey into the cream mixture. Stir until the gelatin is completely dissolved, about a minute. Pour the warm cream into a pitcher or large measuring cup with a spout. Pour the mixture evenly into custard cups or small canning jars. Chill until set, 2 to 4 hours.

Classic Chess Pie

Makes 8 servings

Miss Mary's guests who've never had Chess Pie think we're saying "chest" pie. In fact, as the saying goes, chess pie got its name by folks misunderstanding "just pie." The humble chess pie is another great example of how country folks have always made the best use of pantry regulars. It's just a sweet egg pie with a little cornmeal added for texture. Pay close attention to the Old No. 7 fancy chess variations below and expand your repertoire.

1 unbaked 9-inch Basic Pie Pastry shell (recipe on page 206)
1 ½ cups sugar
1 tablespoons self-rising cornmeal mix (or plain, finely ground white cornmeal)
¼ teaspoon salt
¼ cup butter (½ stick), melted
3 eggs, beaten
¼ cup milk
1 tablespoon vinegar
1 teaspoon vanilla

Heat the oven to 350°F. Prebake the pie shell for 10 minutes until set but not browned, so the filling won't make the bottom crust soggy. Combine the sugar, cornmeal, salt, butter, eggs, milk, vinegar, and vanilla in a medium mixing bowl. Whisk until well blended. Pour the filling into the warm pie crust. Bake 40 to 45 minutes until the filling is just set.

Old No. 7 Chess Pie Variations

1. Lemon Chess: Add the grated zest of one lemon to the filling and substitute fresh squeezed lemon juice for the milk. Omit the vinegar.
2. Brown Sugar Whiskey Pecan Chess: Substitute brown sugar for the white sugar and Jack Daniel's Tennessee Whiskey for the milk. Top with ½ cup chopped pecans before baking.
3. Buttermilk Chess: Substitute ½ cup buttermilk for the ¼ cup of milk. Omit the vinegar.
4. Orange Coconut Chess: Substitute thawed orange juice concentrate for the milk and add ⅓ cup flaked coconut to the filling.
5. Coconut Chess: Add ½ cup flaked coconut to the filling.
6. Chocolate Chess: Stir ¼ cup cocoa powder into the dry ingredients of the filling. Omit the vinegar.
7. Pumpkin Chess: Omit the vinegar and use half-and-half instead of milk. Add 1 cup of pumpkin puree. Add a ½ teaspoon cinnamon and ¼ teaspoon each of cloves, nutmeg, and ginger. Or you can add a teaspoon of pumpkin pie spice instead of the seasonings.

Jack Daniel's Pecan Pie

Makes 8 servings

Fresh pecans are the key to a delicious Southern pecan pie. Buy them in the fall and keep them in the freezer to use all year long. Sometimes I like to add a handful of chocolate chips to the recipe. I always like to add a little Jack Daniel's. If you leave the Jack Daniel's out of the pie, be sure to add a little to your whipping cream.

3 eggs
1 cup sugar
1 cup corn syrup
¼ cup butter, melted
2 tablespoons Jack Daniel's Tennessee Whiskey, optional
1 teaspoon vanilla
¼ teaspoon salt
1 ½ cups pecan halves
½ cup chocolate chips, optional
1 unbaked 9-inch pie pastry

Heat the oven to 350 F. Combine the eggs, sugar, corn syrup, butter, Jack Daniel's, and vanilla in a large mixing bowl. Stir in the pecans and chocolate chips. Pour the filling into the pie pastry. Bake 45 to 50 minutes, or until the center is just set and no longer jiggles. Cool completely on a wire rack. The pie will continue to set while cooling.

Three Milk Punch Cake

Makes 16 servings

If you add a splash of Jack Daniel's to the creamy milk sauce on the wildly popular Hispanic Tres Leches cake, it's remarkably like the classic Southern brunch cocktail Honey Milk Punch (page 21). Our Tennessee-style Tres Leches variation makes perfect sense. Whip up a few egg whites and make an easy sponge cake that amazingly absorbs the Milk Punch Sauce. Be forewarned—this is one heavy cake, so make the servings small.

Sponge Cake

> 6 eggs, separated
> ½ cup sugar, divided
> 1 cup self-rising flour

Milk Punch Sauce

> 1 can (12 ounces) evaporated milk
> 1 can (14 ounces) sweetened condensed milk
> ½ cup half-and-half cream
> ¼ cup Jack Daniel's Tennessee Whiskey
> Nutmeg to taste

Cream Topping

> 1 cup heavy cream
> 2 tablespoons powdered sugar
> 1 tablespoon Jack Daniel's Tennessee Whiskey

Heat the oven to 350°F. Grease a 9 x 13-inch baking dish.

To make the cake: Whip the egg whites with an electric mixer until frothy. Add ¼ cup sugar and whip until soft peaks form. Set aside. In another bowl whip the egg yolks and the remaining ¼ cup of sugar until light and lemon colored. Spoon the egg yolks over the egg whites. Sprinkle the flour over the egg whites. Gently fold the mixture together until well blended. Pour the batter into the baking dish. Bake 20 to 25 minutes until the top is nicely browned and the top springs back when gently pressed with your finger. Let cool slightly while you make the milk punch sauce.

To make the milk punch sauce: Combine the evaporated milk,

A former hostess liked to tell her table there is not enough Jack Daniel's in the food to help you and not enough to hurt you either!

235

SWEETS

condensed milk, half-and-half, Jack Daniel's, and nutmeg in a medium bowl. Whisk until well blended.

Poke holes over the surface of the cake. Slowly pour the sauce over the cake. Spoon the sauce over areas of the cake that need more sauce. Cover with plastic wrap and refrigerate a few hours or overnight.

To make the cream topping: Before serving, whip the cream until soft peaks form. Add the powdered sugar and Jack Daniel's. Whip to incorporate the ingredients. Spread the cream over the chilled cake. Cut into squares. Serve plain or with fresh fruit such as sliced peaches, strawberries, or blackberries.

Chocolate Chess Squares

Makes 12 servings

We don't make brownies, we just add chocolate to yet another chess variation. Maybe we should rename this Sweets chapter the "Chess" chapter. When might you want to make these? When you don't feel like making pie crust, when you want a little something chocolatey, when you need a dessert to take to a potluck supper, or when you need a quick dessert to serve at home. Pretty much anytime, I'd say. This surely is a crowd pleaser at Miss Mary's.

3/4 cup (1 1/2 sticks) butter
3 squares unsweetened chocolate
1 1/2 cups sugar
1/2 cup flour
3 eggs, beaten
1 cup chopped pecans
1 teaspoon vanilla extract

Heat the oven to 350°F. Grease a 9 x 13-inch baking pan. Combine the butter and chocolate in a medium saucepan. Melt over low heat, stirring constantly. Remove from the heat and stir in the sugar, flour, eggs, pecans, and vanilla. Blend well with a wooden spoon. Pour the batter into the prepared pan. Bake 20 to 25 minutes until set. Cool. Cut into squares and serve with and a dollop of Jack Daniel's Whipped Cream (page 215).

Butter Jack Pudding

Makes about 8 servings

Butter Jack Pudding is our spirited version of homey butterscotch pudding. All you do is cook it up in a saucepan on the stovetop thanks to the thickening power of cornstarch. Of course, the pudding's fine flavor is courtesy of Lynchburg's own great corn product. Pour the thick creamy pudding into serving dishes and chill for later. Instead of the usual custard dishes, try fancy teacups, wine goblets, mason jars, or martini glasses. Top the pudding with whipped cream, toasted pecans, shaved bittersweet chocolate, or sweetened fresh fruits. Or cover banana slices and vanilla wafers with the pudding and chill for a really fine banana pudding.

1 cup dark brown sugar
¼ cup cornstarch
¼ teaspoon salt
3 cups whole milk
3 egg yolks
¼ cup Jack Daniel's Tennessee Whiskey
¼ cup (½ stick) butter
1 teaspoon vanilla

Blend the sugar, cornstarch, and salt in a large saucepan. Whisk together the milk, egg yolks, and Jack Daniel's in a medium mixing bowl. Stir the milk mixture into the sugar mixture in the saucepan. Cook over medium-low heat, stirring constantly, 5 to 7 minutes until thickened and boiling. Boil about one minute to cook the starchy taste from the pudding. If the pudding appears lumpy, whisk until smooth. Remove from the heat and stir in the butter and vanilla. Ladle the pudding into dessert dishes. Cool slightly and refrigerate.

Heard around the TABLE

A group of Japanese guests offered a hostess a special treat from their homeland. She had a hard time choking down that rice cake wrapped with seaweed, especially on a full stomach. It just seemed to grow larger as she chewed! Now she's a little more sympathetic with those who think okra is weird.

RELISHES AND LITTLE EXTRAS

Lynchburg Cranberry Relish
Everyday Sweet Red Pepper Relish
Holiday Ambrosia
Jack's Red Dipping Sauce
Cave Spring Cabbage Relish
Mango Pineapple Jack Salsa
Sweet and Sour Orange Cherry Sauce
Tangy Tomato Onion Relish
Icy Pink Cucumbers and Onions
Cranberry Jack Chutney
Squash Bread and Butter Quick Pickles
Texas Hot Relish
Tennessee Sour Onions
Tennessee Honey Peaches

Old Timey Sorghum Molasses by Randy "Goose" Baxter

Jack Daniel's Molasses Butter
Black and Blue Cheese Butter

Honey Jack Jars

Tennessee Honey Onion Marmalade
Bobo Brittle—Pork Rind Brittle and Corn Nut Brittle

Lynchburg Cranberry Relish

Makes about 5 cups

Lynchburg Cranberry Relish is the most unfussy accent to our holiday dinner menu, and it's on the table every day in December. Delicious as it is, cranberry relish is also a solid starting point for your own creative additions. Consider chunks of fresh pineapple, chopped toasted pecans or walnuts, chopped fresh apples and pears, and a sprinkling of cinnamon. I've seen it with horseradish, pistachio nuts, onion, and chopped dried figs. Be sure to chill the relish overnight for the flavors to really meld.

> 4 cups fresh cranberries
> 1 whole orange quartered, seeds removed
> 2 cups sugar
> ¼ cup Jack Daniel's Tennessee Whiskey

Chop the cranberries and the orange in a food processor. Add the sugar and process the mixture just to combine. Place in a covered container and chill overnight. Add Jack Daniel's just before serving.

Everyday Sweet Red Pepper Relish

Makes 8 cups

Not a day passes at Miss Mary's that a guest doesn't ask for the recipe for our sweet pepper relish. Whenever beans are on the menu (which is most days), our diners generously spoon this crimson sweet-savory relish atop their speckled butter beans, pintos, white beans, crowder peas, and black-eyed peas. Use a food processor for the quickest route to uniformly chopped peppers and onions.

> 2 cups cider vinegar
> 2 cups sugar
> 2 tablespoons tomato paste
> 6 large red bell peppers, cored, seeded and finely chopped
> 2 medium onions, finely chopped
> 2 teaspoons salt
> 2 teaspoons whole mustard seed
> 1 teaspoon whole celery seed
> A pinch of crushed red pepper

Combine the vinegar, sugar, and tomato paste in a large saucepan. Bring to a boil. Add the peppers, onions, salt, mustard seed, celery seed, and crushed red pepper. Simmer about 30 minutes. Cool, cover tightly, and refrigerate. If you're a canner, seal in ½ pint or pint jars.

Holiday Ambrosia

Makes 10 servings

I confess to being a purist about many Southern recipes, but not ambrosia. I say the sky is the limit. In addition to the required sweet oranges and grated coconut, add pineapple, grapes, grapefruit, or even kiwi. I'm especially fond of the sparkle that pomegranate seeds bring. Of course, you can add a little Jack Daniel's Tennessee Honey. This colorful sweet fruit served in a gleaming cut crystal bowl is an absolute holiday requirement. Adjust the sugar to your liking.

8 large navel oranges
¾ cup sugar
1 ½ cups grated coconut
Additional fresh fruits such as pineapple chunks, grapes or kiwi slices, pomegranate seeds, optional

Peel the oranges and carefully remove the orange sections, cutting away all the white membrane. If you're in a hurry, just slice the peeled oranges into rounds, then in half. Toss with sugar and coconut in a large bowl. Add additional fruit as you like. Chill before serving.

Jack's Red Dipping Sauce

Makes about 2 cups

At Miss Mary's we dip our delicious fried catfish into this versatile sauce. Add a spoon-ful of fresh horseradish and serve it with chilled shrimp or cocktail catfish nuggets. And absolutely everyone loves to dunk cocktail wieners into the warmed sauce.

1 ½ cups ketchup
2 tablespoons brown sugar
2 tablespoons Worcestershire sauce
1 teaspoon dry mustard
⅓ cup Jack Daniel's Tennessee Whiskey
A few drops of hot pepper sauce or a spoonful of prepared horseradish to taste

Combine the ketchup, brown sugar, Worcestershire sauce, and dry mustard in a small saucepan. Bring to a boil, stirring occasionally. Stir in the Jack Daniel's and simmer for 5 minutes. Refrigerate until serving time. Stir in the hot pepper sauce or horseradish. Serve with fried catfish nuggets or cocktail wieners.

Cave Spring Cabbage Relish

Makes about 5 cups

Cabbage is abundant and inexpensive, and no one knew that better than Miss Mary. In her day, when times were tight, cabbage appeared in dish after dish, from casseroles to slaws to relishes. Recalling her days in Miss Mary's kitchen, long time cook Dee Dismukes always laughed about the many times when Miss Mary's phone would ring with pleas from the distillery to add a few extra table settings for hungry guests.

"We'd just about throw a fit, scared we'd run out of food," Dee recalls. "Miss Mary would strut into the kitchen like a mother hen with her hands up under her arms and holler, 'Just stretch it!' One more cabbage dish often saved dinner, even if slaw, kraut and wieners, and boiled cabbage were already on the table!"

4 cups finely chopped cabbage (about ½ a head, or 1 bag of prepared chopped cabbage for slaw)
1 medium green bell pepper, chopped
1 cup chopped celery
1 jar (4 ounces) chopped pimiento
¼ cup brown sugar
¼ cup cider vinegar
1 teaspoon salt
½ teaspoon celery seed
½ teaspoon whole mustard seed

Combine the cabbage, bell pepper, celery, and pimientos in a large bowl. Combine the sugar, vinegar, salt, celery seed, and mustard seed in a small bowl and pour over the cabbage mixture. Blend well. Refrigerate before serving.

Heard around the TABLE

Quite often our hostesses answer the same questions:

Are you Miss Bobo? Where do I apply for your job? I thought all the table hostesses were old.

Mango Pineapple Jack Salsa

Makes 3 cups

This sure isn't a traditional Tennessee recipe, but it reminds me of how much my own cooking has been influenced by cooks, ingredients, and cooking styles from around the world. Beyond our own everyday pecans and peaches, Jack Daniel's complements spicy and fruity flavors in foods I'd never even heard of as a child, like this exotic salsa.

Make it whenever soft ripe mangos are available and you're in the mood for grilled salmon or shrimp. It's a wonderful accompaniment to the Grilled and Glazed Salmon on (page 192) and Jack's Sweet Hot Glazed Shrimp (page 199).

2 ripe mangos, peeled and diced
1 cup chopped fresh pineapple or one cup canned pineapple tidbits, drained
¼ cup chopped red or green onion
¼ cup chopped cilantro
2 jalapeño peppers, seeded and minced
2 tablespoons Jack Daniel's Tennessee Whiskey
1 tablespoon sugar
1 tablespoon fresh lime juice
¼ teaspoon salt

Combine the mangos, pineapple, onion, cilantro, peppers, whiskey, sugar, lime juice, and salt in a medium bowl. Blend well. Chill before serving.

Sweet and Sour Orange Cherry Sauce

Makes about 1 cup

I often serve this easy sauce with pan-fried thin scallops of pounded pork tenderloin dredged in flour. Stir the sauce into the skillet with the pan drippings and drizzle over the meat on a platter. When grilling, make a batch in a small saucepan to brush over pork, chicken, or duck. Our Lynchburg duck hunters love this sauce, so unless you hunt or know a generous hunter with a full freezer, hunt down a duck in your supermarket.

½ cup orange marmalade
2 tablespoons soy sauce
¼ cup Jack Daniel's Tennessee Whiskey
¼ teaspoon dry mustard

243

¼ tea spoon garlic powder
2 tablespoons chopped dried cherries

Combine the orange marmalade, soy sauce, Jack Daniel's, dry mustard, garlic powder, and dried cherries in a small saucepan or skillet. Bring to a boil over medium heat. Cook and stir until slightly thickened. Add a little water if it becomes too thick.

Tangy Tomato Onion Relish

Makes about 2 ½ cups

Raisins in a tomato onion relish might surprise you, but plumped up with a little Jack Daniel's, they're just right. Grilled pork tenderloin really benefits from a touch of this relish, especially when the tenderloin is thinly sliced and served on soft rolls for tailgating and cocktail parties. Be sure to cook the onions long and slow to develop their sweet flavor.

> ¼ cup golden raisins
> ¼ cup Jack Daniel's Tennessee Whiskey
> 3 large sweet onions (such as Vidalia), coarsely chopped (about 6 cups)
> 2 tablespoons oil
> 1 tablespoon brown sugar
> 1 can (14.5 ounces) diced tomatoes, drained
> Pinch of thyme
> Salt and black pepper to taste

Combine the raisins and Jack Daniel's in small bowl; set aside to soak. Cook the onions in oil in a large skillet over medium-low heat until tender and golden brown, about 15 minutes, stirring occasionally. Stir in the brown sugar and continue to cook 5 minutes. Stir in the tomatoes and the raisin and Jack Daniel's mixture. Increase the heat and bring to a boil. Reduce heat and simmer 10 minutes or until thickened. Season with thyme, salt, and pepper. Cool, cover, and refrigerate. Serve chilled or at room temperature.

Icy Pink Cucumbers and Onions

Makes 6 cups

Warm grilled meats beg for the crisp tangy bite of these cold pickled onions and cucumbers. The vinegar turns red onions a pastel pink. The cool cucumbers and the creeping heat of jalapeños add a bright crunch to a picnic table filled with traditional creamy summer salads. Adjust the sugar level to your liking. An inexpensive plastic mandoline or V-slicer makes perfect paper-thin cucumber slices in seconds. Serve this in a clear glass bowl to show off the spectacular colors and shapes.

  1 large red onion, cut into quarters, then into very thin wedges
  2 large or three medium cucumbers, peeled and thinly sliced
  3 jalapeño peppers, seeded and thinly sliced
  2 cups distilled vinegar
  2 to 4 tablespoons sugar to taste
  1 tablespoon salt

Combine the onion, cucumbers, peppers, vinegar, sugar, and salt in a medium bowl. Blend well. Cover with plastic wrap pressing the vegetables into the brine. Refrigerate overnight. Serve cold.

Cranberry Jack Chutney

Makes 4 cups

Couldn't we all use a little extra color during the darker winter season? I stock the freezer in December with holiday cranberries so I can serve this bright, tangy, spicy chutney with pork loin all winter long.

1 cup cider vinegar
½ cup Jack Daniel's Tennessee Whiskey
1 cup brown sugar
1 medium onion, finely chopped
1 ½ cups chopped mixed dried fruits such as raisins, apricots, apples, prunes, figs
1 teaspoon cinnamon
1 teaspoon ground cloves
1 bag (12 ounces) fresh or frozen cranberries
Pinch of salt

Combine the vinegar, Jack Daniel's, brown sugar, onion, dried fruits, cinnamon, and cloves in a medium saucepan. Bring the mixture to a boil over medium-high heat. Simmer about 5 minutes or until the sugar has dissolved and the fruits begin to soften. Add the cranberries and continue to simmer until the cranberries begin to pop and become tender. Add a pinch of salt. Transfer to a bowl and cool. Cover and keep refrigerated.

Squash Bread and Butter Quick Pickles

Makes 1 quart

Quick refrigerator pickles are the way to go if, like me, you just want a jar every so often rather than making a case of jars at one time. We love these squash pickles in ultra-thin slices that only a mandoline slicer can provide. It's funny how shape can affect taste. Sloppy thick cuts just aren't as refined in looks or flavor.

1 ½ pounds (about 4 to 5 medium) yellow squash
1 large onion
1 tablespoon kosher or pickling salt (not iodized salt)
1 ¼ cups cider vinegar
1 ¼ cups sugar
1 medium clove garlic, peeled and smashed
1 teaspoon pickling spice blend

1 teaspoon mustard seed

½ teaspoon turmeric, optional

Slice the squash into paper-thin discs and slice the onion very thin as well. Use a mandoline for very even slices and quick, easy work. Place the vegetables in a colander in the sink and sprinkle with the salt. Let the vegetables stand about 1 hour to draw out the moisture. Drain. Press the water out with your hands. Place the squash and onion in a sterile quart jar or two pint jars.

Combine the vinegar, sugar, garlic, pickling spice blend, mustard seed, and turmeric in a medium saucepan. Bring to a boil. Pour the hot liquid over the vegetables until covered. Cool. Cover and refrigerate. They'll be ready to eat in a few days. Keep them refrigerated and eat within two months.

Texas Hot Relish

Makes about 3 cups

We serve some kind of bean every day at Miss Mary's. They might be pintos, white beans, black-eyed peas, green beans, crowder peas, or my favorite, speckled butter beans. No matter the bean, during the summer months they all benefit from our fresh tomato relish. You may recognize this as our Tennessee variation of what folks now call salsa or pico de gallo. In fact, one day I overheard one of our hostesses tell the guests at the table that her mother once said, "Why I've been making tomato relish forever, but I sure didn't know I was making salsa!" Fresh summer tomatoes are a must whenever available.

4 ripe tomatoes, chopped

1 small onion, chopped

1 green bell pepper, chopped

1 cayenne or jalapeño pepper, finely minced

2 tablespoons white vinegar

1 tablespoon water

1 teaspoon sugar

Salt and black pepper to taste

Combine the tomatoes, onion, bell pepper, jalapeño pepper, vinegar, water, sugar, salt, and pepper in a medium bowl. Cover and chill until serving time.

247

Tennessee Sour Onions

Makes 1 ½ cups

Sour onions offer a nice balance to the richness of pulled pork and chuck roast. Put these to work on little appetizer sandwiches made with leftover Shade Tree Pulled Pork Barbecue (page 175). Cut hot dog buns in half, pile on the warm meat, and top with tangy sour onions. These onions offer quite a pucker compared to our Icy Pink Cucumbers and Onions (page 245).

> 1 medium onion, peeled and very thinly sliced
> 1 to 2 jalapeño peppers, thinly sliced
> 1 medium carrot, peeled and thinly sliced
> 1 cup white vinegar
> 1 teaspoons salt
> 1 teaspoon sugar

Combine the onion, jalapeño, carrot, vinegar, salt, and sugar in a small bowl. Cover and chill until serving.

Tennessee Honey Peaches

Makes 4 to 5 12-ounce jars

Southern summer peaches are as wonderful a gift to us as Tennessee summer tomatoes. To prolong the experience into the cooler season, combine fresh peaches with a little Jack Daniel's Tennessee Honey and store them in mason jars. If you go that extra canning step, a jar of these makes a lovely holiday gift.

> 3 cups water
> 2 cups sugar
> 3 cinnamon sticks
> 12 medium ripe, but firm, peaches
> 1 cup Jack Daniel's Tennessee Honey

Combine the water, sugar, and cinnamon sticks in a medium saucepan and bring to a boil to dissolve the sugar. Set aside. Bring a large pot of water to a boil. Make an ice water bath in a large bowl in the sink. To loosen the skin on the peaches, boil the peaches for 1 minute in two batches. Greener peaches may take a little longer than riper ones. Place the boiled peaches in the ice water bath to cool slightly. Repeat with the remaining peaches. Cut the peaches in half and remove the skin and pit. Remove any tough spots of skin with a paring knife. Cut the halves into medium-size wedges. Add the peaches and the Tennessee Honey to the sugar syrup and simmer until the peaches are tender, but still hold their shape, about 5 minutes.

Divide the peaches evenly among 4 or 5 12-ounce sterilized jars using a slotted spoon. Pour the syrup evenly over the peaches to ½ inch of the top of the jar. Add a half of a cinnamon stick to each jar, if desired. Wipe the rims clean and seal the jars. Refrigerate and use within one month or process the peaches in a water bath for 25 minutes for longer storage. (For high altitude cooking, consult your favorite canning manual for the correct processing time.)

Heard around the TABLE

A school teacher shared this story: A student wasn't doing well and was not turning in his work. She told him, "I must give you a zero on your paper." He replied, "Well, that's better than nothing."

Old Timey Sorghum Molasses by Randy "Goose" Baxter

Randy "Goose" Baxter is our top dog distillery tour guide and the husband of my assistant manager, Debbie. Every October Debbie, Goose, Goose's father, and a group of their friends press the sugar cane stalks grown by Debbie and Goose and cook down the juice into sweet sorghum syrup (also called molasses). One hundred years ago, Americans made twenty million gallons of sorghum each year, but now we make less than a million. It's just too much work! Here's how Debbie and Goose got themselves into this little annual event.

About thirty years ago Goose and his daddy came across an abandoned Chattanooga sugar cane mill once used by the folks in the community where Goose's mother is from. Everybody would get together at harvest time and help each other press the sugar cane with the Chattanooga mill.

After careful inspection and some pondering, the two agreed that the old mill was in reasonable enough condition to take the next step. They dug it up, hauled it home, took it completely apart, and cleaned every piece. The brass bearings for the rollers that crush the sugar cane were shot, but everything else looked good. "So, I reached out to a fella, "friends in low places" as I like to say, and told him what we needed," Goose recalls. In a few weeks Goose and his daddy found themselves in possession of a set of brand new bearings. "And that's what's in it today," Goose says proudly. The Chattanooga mill was good to go.

But how will it go? They didn't have a mule. And Goose wasn't volunteering (though his Daddy did offer that suggestion). "So, Daddy comes up with an idea," Goose recalls. "Tells me, 'I got us a mule. It's a red one. It's called Honda!'" After a hearty laugh, the red four-wheeler was hired.

And why bother with a stubborn live creature, anyway? "Old Honda's faster, and you don't have to feed it," Goose laughs. "It's as smooth as can be, and it don't back-talk you!"

Goose insists on sowing the cane seeds no later than the tenth of June, so the cane is full-sized before the first frost when he cuts them down. "You've got to get them by the second week of October," he says. "Otherwise, the juice sours."

To make the sorghum ordeal worth the work, Goose plants about a half an acre of cane. He says his friends and neighbors love to come over to his place for the once-a-year fall sorghum production. "It's a real a community thing," Goose tells. "The old-timers really want to see it still being made, just like the old days when everybody grew some cane. It's a dying art these days, and we just don't want that to happen. We need to keep these traditions going into the future," he believes.

Goose knows the process well. "First we strip the leaves off the cane and let it be for two or three days. This speeds up the ripening time. Then, we cut the heads off the cane and cut the cane down with big old corn knives and load it all onto the hay wagon. Off to the cane mill at the house it goes. We'll start by grinding the cane stalks in the mill pulled by Old Honda. It'll take about 15 to 18 gallons of cane juice to make one gallon of sorghum. That's a lot of cooking.

"My cooking pan is four- by eight-feet wide, and it's divided into three compartments. You start cooking the pressed juice in the first compartment, and as it cooks, you have got to skim the top constantly. Otherwise, the sorghum will be bitter, and then all that work will be for nothing."

"We don't go by time, we go by eye-ball. You just keep on cooking and skimming. After a while we'll move that first batch of juice into the second compartment to keep cooking it so we can add the new juice to the first pan. To speed up the cooking time, we'll divide the middle pan in two pans. Just keep moving it along and keep cooking, cooking, cooking. And skimming."

"Now, when a batch reaches the third pan, you have got to really watch it. As the sorghum cooks down, it gets heavy, and so we use wooden paddles to keep it moving and keep from scorching it. To test it we lift the paddle out, turn it upside down and back again, and we watch the sorghum drip off the paddle. When it starts to hang off the paddle in a string, that's when Daddy and I get to arguing about how much longer. I say, 'Five more minutes, Daddy,' and he says, 'I don't know, Son.' It goes on like that, you know, back and forth."

When they finally both agree it's ready to come out, Goose grabs a handful of old cane stalks and tosses them onto the fire to lower the heat for a few minutes which helps prevent the sorghum from scorching. Controlling a wood fire at that critical last step in the cooking process takes practice. "We tried firing the pans with gas once, thought that might be easier, but we decided that wood was the only way to go," Goose recalls. "Daddy agreed. He said, 'You're right, Son, let's stick with wood. Besides, a wood fire is the old-timey way.' So, now we only use wood."

Goose holds the hot, finished syrup in large aluminum cans for several days before storing it in mason jars. "A mason jar is the handiest thing in the world," says Goose. "That way the sorghum is ready for Debbie to add it to her baked beans. Me, I like it on a good hot biscuit in the morning. And Debbie's brother, Scott, puts it in his Shade Tree Barbecue Competition Sauce."

Jack Daniel's Molasses Butter

Makes 1 ¼ cups

A dollop of this molasses butter on every kind of baked winter squash, baked sweet potato, and plain old carrots and parsnips will reenergize your winter interest in root vegetables. For breakfast applications, just leave out the Worcestershire sauce and salt, and spread it on a hot biscuit. This might be my favorite use, especially if it's made with Debbie and Goose's homemade Tennessee sorghum molasses (page 250). A tablespoon of fresh orange zest adds a nice citrus touch.

> 1 cup butter, softened
> ¼ to ½ cup molasses or sorghum molasses
> 2 tablespoons Jack Daniel's Tennessee Whiskey
> Dash of Worcestershire sauce
> Salt to taste

Blend the butter, molasses, Jack Daniel's, and Worcestershire sauce together until smooth. Add the salt. Serve a dollop on cooked winter squash or baked sweet potatoes. Cover and keep refrigerated.

Black and Blue Cheese Butter

Makes about ¾ cup

Black and Blue Cheese Butter melting over a juicy grilled steak is a blessed culinary union, but that's not the only happy marriage of flavors. You might be surprised by how easily this compound butter can make a sophisticated side dish out of a simple baked sweet potato. Instead of the usual brown sugar and marshmallows, the contrasting flavors of creamy, savory blue cheese only makes sweet potatoes sweeter. Try this once and you'll repeat it often.

½ cup (1 stick) butter, softened
¼ cup (2 ounces) crumbled blue cheese
1 tablespoon Jack Daniel's Tennessee Whiskey
1 tablespoon finely chopped parsley, optional
1 tablespoon finely chopped chives, optional
1 small clove garlic, chopped and mashed into a paste

Combine the butter, blue cheese, Jack Daniel's, parsley, chives, and garlic in a small bowl. Blend well with a wooden spoon. Roll the mixture into a 1 ½-inch diameter cylinder in a piece of waxed paper. Seal the ends and refrigerate until firm. Slice and place a pat of the butter over a grilled steak or serve with baked sweet potatoes.

Honey Jack Jars

Honey Jack Jars are fruits swimming in Jack Daniel's Tennessee Whiskey or Jack's Tennessee Honey. They're easy to make and don't require canning. Just fill your jars, give them a few days in the refrigerator, and see what happens. I'll use any of these over ice cream or pound cake, and I keep the Jack Cherries handy by the bar.

Here's What You Need

Canning jars (pint and quart size are the most useful sizes)
Jack Daniel's Tennessee Whiskey, Jack Daniel's Tennessee Honey, or Gentleman Jack Rare Tennessee Whiskey
Your choice of dried, fresh, or canned fruit

Try Some of My Favorites

Tennessee Honey Apricots—Canned apricots are quite tasty in this application if you can't find fresh. Pack a canning jar with the fruit and pour in the Tennessee Honey.

Cinnamon Prunes in Gentleman Jack—Add a cinnamon stick to the jar. I like to use those bite-size prunes for easy serving. Cover with Gentleman Jack.

Jack Cherries—A small jar of maraschino cherries macerating in Jack makes a great gift for any classic cocktail lover. Canned cherries, dried, or fresh cherries soaked in Jack are delicious as well.

Honey Raisins—Pack a jar with golden raisins and cover with Tennessee Honey.

Honey Figs—Pack a jar with canned, dried, or fresh figs and cover with Tennessee Honey. Serve these on a fancy cheese tray.

Tennessee Honey Onion Marmalade

Makes about 1 ½ cups

You'll wonder how you lived without this savory sweet marmalade after you try it. I like it with pork, on a ham biscuit, on a cheeseburger, and even blended with cream cheese for a quick appetizer. The important thing to remember when making onion marmalade is that, like whiskey making, you cannot rush the process. Cook the onions in the bacon drippings low and slow. You can keep it in the refrigerator for a couple of weeks or go ahead and freeze it.

> 4 large onions, cut into thin slivers (about 5 cups)
> ¼ cup bacon drippings
> ½ cup sugar
> ¼ cup Jack Daniel's Tennessee Honey
> ¼ cup cider vinegar
> About ½ teaspoon of salt
> Black pepper to taste

Cook the onions in the bacon drippings in a large heavy pot with a lid over medium-low heat for 30 minutes, stirring frequently. Keep the pot partially covered while the onions cook slowly. Gently melt the onions and do not allow them to brown quickly (or burn). Remove the lid and stir in the sugar, Tennessee Honey, and vinegar. Cook over medium to medium-low heat, maintaining a gentle simmer until the juices have thickened and the onions are very soft and a rich amber color, about 20 minutes. Season with salt and pepper. Keep refrigerated, but serve at room temperature.

Bobo Brittle—Pork Rind Brittle and Corn Nut Brittle

Makes about 25 pieces

Who decreed the peanut to be the only crunchy ingredient permitted in a batch of brittle? Here's a brittle breakthrough for you—try making brittle with two of our other favorite salty Southern snacks—pork rinds and corn nuts. I also love a brittle made with a combination of pork rinds and peanuts. Just add a cup of raw peanuts to the recipe. These unusual brittles dress down for tailgates and crash fancy cocktail parties with the best of them. No matter the crowd or the occasion, pork rind and corn nut brittles will have them at "hello."

2 cups sugar

½ cup corn syrup

½ cup water

2 tablespoons butter

½ teaspoon salt

½ teaspoon baking soda

3 cups coarsely crushed pork rinds (regular, or hot and spicy) or 2 generous cups corn nuts

Line a rimmed baking sheet with foil and lightly coat the foil with cooking spray. Combine the sugar, corn syrup, and water in a medium saucepan. Bring to a boil. Boil on medium-high heat without stirring until the mixture turns a golden brown, about 15 minutes. Remove from the heat and quickly stir in the butter, salt, and baking soda. Stir rapidly to blend well. Stir in the pork rinds or corn nuts. Quickly pour the mixture onto the foiled baking sheet and spread it evenly with a greased spatula. Cool completely. Break the brittle into pieces. Store in an airtight container at room temperature.

We Offer Our Thanks . . .

To Margaret Tolley and Leola Dismukes who taught Lynne how to cook;

To Debbie Baxter, Lynne's right hand, who keeps Miss Mary's running so smoothly;

To Tom Brown who keeps Lynne happy;

To R. B. Quinn who kept things organized and us laughing;

To Steve May of Jack Daniel Distillery and Dave Stang of Brown Forman who encouraged and supported this book;

To the Thomas Nelson team: Joel Miller, Heather Skelton, Julie Allen, Lori Lynch, Brenda Smotherman, Stephanie Tresner, and Chad Cannon;

To the cooks, hostesses, and servers who for generations have fed so many at Miss Mary Bobo's Boarding House; and

To all our guests.

Index

A

Apples
  Apple Crisp Coffeecake, 73
  Baked Lynchburg Candied
    Apples, 120
  Old-Fashioned Apple Dumplings,
    220
  Skillet Lynchburg Candied
    Apples, 121
Apricots
  Apricot Dinner Casserole, 133
  Tennessee Honey Apricots, 254
Arnett, Jeff, Master Distiller, 19
artichoke dip, 51

B

Bacon
  Crisp Bacon Strips
  Foolproof Oven Bacon, 86
Bananas Fanning, 204
Barbecue
  Dry County Dry Rub, 182
  barbecue gear, 170
  barbecue meat cuts, 174
  Jack Daniel's World Championship
    Invitational Barbecue, 166
  Crocked Barbecue, 201
  Shade Tree barbecue basics, 168
  Shade Tree Barbecue
    Competitition, 183
  Shade Tree Beef Brisket, 176
  Shade Tree Pulled Pork Barbecue, 175
  Shade Tree Smoked Chicken, 178
  Shade Tree Spare or Baby Back
    Pork Ribs, 177
Baxter, Randy "Goose," 250
Beans
  Jack in the Beans, 135
  Low and Slow Baked Beans, 135
  Green Butter Bean Dip, 55
  Tennessee Tomato White Bean
    Cornbread Salad, 106
  Creole Red and Green Beans, 116
  Succotash Salad with Lemon
    Dressing, 94

Beef
  Chili Jack Burgers, 196
  Jimmy's Jack Marinated Steaks, 191
  Kitchen Beef Brisket, 146
  Miss Mary's Famous Meatloaf, 152
  Shade Tree Beef Brisket, 176
  Skillet Steaks with Lynchburg Pan
    Sauce, 144
  Slow-Simmered Marinated Chuck
    Roast, 160
  Smoky Jack Burgers, 196
  Tennessee Whiskey Lynchburgers,
    196
  Tolley Town Pot Roast, 145
  Sweet, Hot, and Sour Mash
    Meatballs, 44
beets, 98
Beverages. *See Cocktails*
Blueberry Buckle Skillet Cake, 88
Bobo Hotel, history of, 62
Breads and Muffins (*see also Cornbread
  & Cornmeal; Coffee Cakes; French Toast*)
  Biscuit Dumpling Variation, 148
  Butter Pecan Coffee Cake
    Muffins, 87
  Corn Light Bread, 82
  Fish Fry Hushpuppies, 79
  Game Day Sweet Potato Muffins, 85
  Homemade Buttermilk Biscuits, 76
  Miss Mary's Mayo Rolls, 72
  Muffin Cup Ham Biscuits, 73
  Southern Spoon Rolls, 74
Butters
  Black and Blue Cheese Butter, 253
  Jack Daniel's Molasses Butter, 252

C

Cabbage
  Cave Spring Cabbage Relish, 242
  Crispy Kraut Salad, 104
  Dry County Cabbage Casserole, 132
  Easy Cabbage Casserole Additions,
    132
  Sauer Mash Smoked Sausage
    Pot, 160

Cakes
    Blueberry Buckle Skillet Cake, 88
    Classic Caramel Cake, 207
    Easy Made Jam Cake, 226
    Jack and Cola Pudding Cake, 229
    Jack's Birthday Cake, 217
    Pumpkin Patch Squares, 221
    Late Night Oatmeal Cake with
        Broiled Butter
        Pecan Topping, 208
    Ola's Citrus Cake, 229
    Three Milk Punch Cake, 235
Candies
    Bobo Brittle—Pork Rind Brittle and
        Corn Nut Brittle, 255
    Debbie's Coconut Tennessee Honey
        Balls, 225
    Tennessee Truffles, 223
Carrots
    Bobo's Carrot Raisin Salad, 105
    Carrot Ambrosia Gelatin
        Salad, 109
Cheese
    Honey Blue Cheese Spread, 56
    Honey Jezebel Cheddar Spread, 56
    Hot Artichoke Pimiento Cheese
        Dip, 51
    Hot Pimiento Cheese Dip, 52
    Look No Further Pimiento
        Cheese, 39
    Pimiento Cheese Barrel Bungs, 50
    Pimiento Cheese . . . Let Us Count
        the Ways, 38
    Pineapple Cheddar Dinner
        Casserole, 134
Cherries
    Jack Cherries, 254
    Jack's Happy Cherries, 211
Chicken
    Chicken and Dressing Skillet
        Cake, 159
    Crispy Oven-Fried Chicken with
        Pork Rind Crust, 154
    How to make perfect Southern
        fried chicken, 138
    Jack Hot Wings, 36
    Miss Margaret's Best Southern
        Fried Chicken, 139
    Miss Mary's Chicken with Pastry or
        Biscuit Dumplings, 147

Pan-Fried Tennessee Whiskey
    Chicken Breasts, 143
Shade Tree Smoked Chicken, 178
Three keys for fried chicken
    success, 138
Cocktails
    Almond Jack Frost, 32
    ApriJack Nectar, 24
    Bold Custard 31
    Classic Jack Manhattan, 9
    Classic Jack Mint, 14
    Classic Tennessee Whiskey Sour, 23
    Coconut Orange Jack, 25
    Cool Jack Apple Mint Tea, 21
    Finishing touches to a well-served
        cocktail, 9
    Garnishes for, 7
    Gentleman's Sour Apple
        Manhattan, 11
    Ginger Jack, 15
    Hot Buttered Tennessee Honey, 30
    Hot Tennessee Toddy, 28
    Hot Tomato Jack, 28
    Honey and Cream, 32
    Honey Milk Punch, 21
    Hound Dog Hot Bouillon, 29
    Hula Jack, 24
    Iced Tennessee Honey Tea, 26
    Jack Black Cow, 17
    Jack and Citrus Soda, 17
    Jack and Cola, 17
    Jack and Cola Float, 17
    Jack Daniel's Citrus Cider, 22
    Jack Daniel's Old Fashioned, 11
    Jack Daniel's Warm Pear Nectar
        Sipper, 29
    Jack Jajito Sour, 23
    Jack's Pomegranate Lemonade, 26
    Licorice Manhattan, 9
    Lynchburg Lemonade, 25
    Madras Jacket, 25
    Mulled in Moore County, 29
    Orange Jack, 16
    Orange Manhattan, 10
    Perfect Gentleman Jack
        Manhattan, 9
    Pineapple Jack Julep, 14
    Pineapple Jack Sour, 23
    Setting up the bar, 6
    Shoo Fly Punch, 22

Spiced Jack, 16
Tennessee Chocolate Almond
    Manhattan, 10
Tennessee Chocolate Mint
    Manhattan, 10
Tennessee Cider, 12
Tennessee Cranberry Smash
    Manhattan, 11
Tennessee Honey Bellini, 12
Tennessee Honey Coffee Melt, 32
Tennessee Honey Hot Tea, 30
Tennessee Honey Julep, 14
Tennessee Honey Royale, 12
Tolley Town Celebration Punch, 21
coffeecake, 73
cooking tips, 66
Corn
    Creamy Shoepeg Corn Salad, 101
    Mother's Best Fried Corn, 122
    Salt and Peppered Sweet Corn, 200
    Succotash Salad with Lemon
        Dressing, 94
Cornbread and Cornmeal
    Barbecue Barrel Bungs, 51
    Cast Iron Cornbread, 81
    Chicken and Dressing Skillet
        Cake, 159
    Cornbread Crepes, 71
    Corn Light Bread, 82
    Dressing with a twist, 115
    Fully Loaded Cornbread, 83
    Okra Barrel Bungs, 50
    Pepper Jack Barrel Bungs, 49
    Pimiento Cheese Barrel Bungs, 50
    Real Southern Cornbread
        Dressing, 114
    Sausage Cornbread Supper
        Pudding, 161
    Self-Rising Cornmeal Mix, 81
    Squash Casserole with Cheddar
        Cornbread Crumbs, 130
    Tennessee Tomato White Bean
        Cornbread Salad, 106
Cranberries
    Cranberry Fruit Fluff, 103
    Cranberry Jack Chutney, 246
    Lynchburg Cranberry Relish, 240
Cucumbers
    Icy Pink Cucumbers and Onions,
        245

Squash Bread and Butter Quick
    Pickles, 246

D
Daniel, Jack (Jasper Newton): "Uncle
    Jack the Man," 53
Debbie's Tips on Making Naturally
    Fermented Kraut in Canning Jars, 104
Desserts
    Bananas Fanning, 204
    Chocolate Chess Squares, 236
    Holiday Ambrosia, 241
    Honey Jack Panna Cotta, 231
    Jack's Bottom's Up Fruit Cobbler, 228
    Old-Fashioned Apple Dumplings, 220
    Skillet Cobbler with Cinnamon
        Sugar Dumplings, 219
    Southern Biscuit Shortcake, 222
    Town Square Chess Squares, 224
Dips
    Green Butter Bean Dip, 55
    Hot Artichoke Pimiento Cheese
        Dip, 51
    Hot Pimiento Cheese Dip, 52
    Peaches and Cream Country Ham
        Dip, 55
dinner menu planning guidelines, 112
Dressing & Stuffing
    Chicken and Dressing Skillet
        Cake, 159
    Dressing with a twist, 115
    Real Southern Cornbread
        Dressing, 114
Dumplings
    Biscuit Dumpling Variation, 148
    Miss Mary's Chicken with Pastry or
        Biscuit Dumplings, 147
    Old-Fashioned Apple Dumplings, 220
    Skillet Cobbler with Cinnamon
        Sugar Dumplings, 219

E
Eggs
    Cornbread Crepes, 71
    Hominy Brunch Scramble, 71
    Really Good Deviled Eggs, 40

F
Fish and Seafood
    Crispy Fried Catfish or Crappie, 152

Grilled and Glazed Salmon, 192
Hot Catfish Cocktail Sandwiches, 35
Jack's Sweet Hot Glazed Shrimp, 199
Pantry Salmon Croquettes with
    Creole Mustard Sauce, 150
Pickled Okra Party Shrimp, 54
Tennessee Barbecued Shrimp, 158
Tennessee Smoked Trout Spread, 45
French toast, 84
Frosting
    Brown Sugar Whiskey Icing, 226
    Caramel Icing, 208
    Cinnamon Cream Cheese
        Frosting, 222
Fruit
    Charred Fruit for Jack's
        Highballs, 198
    Cinnamon Prunes in Gentleman
        Jack, 254
    Country Citrus Fruit Salad, 99
    Cranberry Fruit Fluff, 103
    Fruit Salad, 100
    Holiday Ambrosia, 241
    Honey Figs, 254
    Honey Jack Jars, 252
    Jack's Bottom's Up Fruit Cobbler,
        228
    Pineapple Cheddar Dinner
        Casserole, 134
    Skillet Cobbler with Cinnamon
        Sugar Dumplings, 220
frying tips, 68

G
Gravy
    Giblet, 115
    Pan Drippings, 77
    Redeye, 77
grilling
    guidelines for outdoor cooking, 181
    tips for great, 180
Grits
    Cheese Grits Bake, 75
    Easy way to make, 75

H
Ham
    Baked Ham and Cheese French
        Toast, 84
    How to bake a Tennessee country

ham in a bag or on a rack in a
    roaster, 142
    Muffin Cup Ham Biscuits, 83
Helpful Hints for Cooking with Jack, 43
Hominy
    Creamy Hominy Spinach Casserole,
        118
    Hominy Brunch Scramble, 71
hostess tips and tricks, 97

I
iron skillet seasoning, 68

J
Jack Daniel Distillery Tour, 156

L
Lucchesi, Angelo, Marketing-Public
    Relations Consultant, Jack Daniel
    Distillery, 216

M
May, Steve, Director, Jack Daniel's
    Lynchburg Homeplace, 194
meatloaf, 153
meatballs, 44
menu planning guidelines (dinner), 112
Miss Mary Bobo's Boarding House,
    planning your visit, 80
Miss Mary Bobo's Dinner Menu
    Planning Guidelines, 112
molasses butter, 252

N
Norman, Jeff, Master Taster, 27

O
Okra
    Everyday Southern Fried Okra, 127
    Okra Barrel Bungs, 50
    Oven Roasted Okra, 126
    Oven Roasted Okra, Tomatoes and
        Onions, 126
    Pickled Okra Party Shrimp, 54
    Roasted Okra, 34
Old Timey Sorghum Molasses by Randy
    "Goose" Baxter, 250
Onions
    Honey Jack Onions, 197
    Icy Pink Cucumbers and Onions, 245

Tangy Tomato Onion Relish, 244
Tennessee Honey Onion
    Marmalade, 255
Tennessee Sour Onions, 248

P

Pasta & Noodles
    Boarding House Baked Macaroni
        and Cheese, 113
    Pepper Jack Mac Salad, 107
Peaches
    Jack and Ginger Grilled Peaches, 198
    Jack's Punchy Peaches, 211
    Tennessee Honey Peaches, 248
pea, English, 101
Peppers
    Country Stuffed Peppers, 162
    Everyday Sweet Red Pepper
        Relish, 240
Pies
    Basic Graham Cracker Pie Crust, 207
    Basic Pie Pastry, 206
    Bobo's Macaroon Pie, 204
    Classic Chess Pie, 232
    Jack Daniel's Pecan Pie, 234
    Miss Mary Bobo's Sweet Secret
        Pie, 205
    Miss Mary's Fudge Pie, 215
    Old No. 7 Chess Pie Variations, 233
Pork
    Bobo's Pork Roast, 149
    cooking with cured pork, 66
    Crocked Barbecue, 201
    Oven Barbecue Tennessee Pork
        Tenderloin, 147
    Shade Tree Pulled Pork
        Barbecue, 175
    Shade Tree Spare or Baby Back
        Pork Ribs, 177
Potatoes
    Grilled Potato (and Other Vegetable)
        Packets, 199
    Hash Brown Potato Bake, 78
    Mashed Potatoes Au Gratin, 121
    Oven fried potatoes, 34
    Pudding
    Butter Jack Pudding, 237
    Jack's Fudge Brownie Pudding, 227
    JD Bread Pudding, 218
Pumpkin Patch Squares, 221

R

Raisins
    Bobo's Carrot Raisin Salad, 105
    Honey Raisins, 254
Relishes
    Cave Spring Cabbage Relish, 242
    Cranberry Jack Chutney, 246
    Everyday Sweet Red Pepper
        Relish, 240
    Lynchburg Cranberry Relish, 240
    Tangy Tomato Onion Relish, 244
    Tennessee Sour Onions, 248
    Texas Hot Relish, 247
rice, 124

S

Salads
    Bobo's Carrot Raisin Salad, 105
    Carrot Ambrosia Gelatin Salad, 109
    Country Citrus Fruit Salad, 99
    Cranberry Fruit Fluff, 103
    Creamy English Pea Salad, 101
    Creamy Shoepeg Corn Salad, 101
    Crispy Kraut Salad, 104
    Early Spring Greens with Warm
        Bacon Dripping Dressing, 102
    Fruit Salad, 100
    Lynchburg Lemonade Congealed
        Salad, 108
    Pepper Jack Mac Salad, 107
    Succotash Salad with Lemon
        Dressing, 95
    Tangy Sweet Summer Garden
        Salad, 107
    Tennessee Tomato White Bean
        Cornbread Salad, 106
salsa, 243
Sandwiches
    Hot Catfish Cocktail Sandwiches, 35
    Tomato sandwiches, 34
Sauces, Barbecue
    Alabama White Barbecue Sauce, 189
    Dark and Smoky Barbecue Sauce, 188
    Grandaddy's Pickle Juice Mop
        Sauce, 190
    Jack's All-Purpose Barbecue Glaze,
        189
    Lone-Star Barbecue Sauce, 188
    No Jack Cider Vinegar Mopping
        Spray, 190

Norman Thai Jack Marinade, 202
Simple Cider Vinegar Sauce, 187
Stillhouse Barbecue Sauce, 186
Yella Mustard Barbecue Sauce, 187
Cranberry Jack Chutney, 246
Creole Mustard Sauce (for Salmon
    Croquettes), 151
Sauces, Dessert
Jack Daniel's Whipped Cream, 215
Jack's Best-Ever Fudge Sauce, 212
Jack's Brown Sugar Cream, 213
Jack's Butter Maple Raisin
    Sauce, 212
Jack's Buttermilk Praline Sauce
Jack's Famous Quick Caramel
    Sauce, 210
Jack's Happy Cherries, 211
Jack's Marshmallow Peanut Butter
    Sauce, 212
Jack's Punchy Peaches, 211
Jack's Salted Caramel Sauce, 210
Jack's Sorghum Chocolate Sauce, 213
Jack's Sugar Box Sauce, 214
Jack's Whiskey Buttermilk
    Butterscotch Sauce, 225
Sauces, Dipping
Hot Mustard Jack Dipping Sauce, 47
Jack's Red Dipping Sauce, 241
Peppery Jack Blue Cheese Dipping
    Sauce, 47
Tennessee/Louisiana Border
    Dipping Sauce, 48
Sauces, Dipping
Hot Buttered Whiskey Glaze, 217
Jack's Whiskey Buttermilk
    Butterscotch Sauce, 225
Jimmy Bedford's Country Ham
    Glaze, 141
MoJack Steak Sauce, 192
Molasses Whiskey Glaze, 193
sauce for Jack's Hot Wings, 37
Sweet and Sour Orange Cherry
    Sauce, 243
Sausage
Sauer Mash Smoked Sausage
    Pot, 160
Sausage Cornbread Supper
    Pudding, 161
Smoked sausage slices and
    mustard, 34

Sweet, Hot, and Sour Mash
    Meatballs, 44
Setting up the bar, 6
Sippers (shot-glass "soups")
Jack Aphrodisiac Slurps, 42
Jackgrita Sippers, 41
Peachy Jack Sippers, 41
Tennessee Honey Lemon Drop
    Sippers, 42
Smoked sausage slices and mustard, 34
smoked trout, 45
Smoky Warm Potato Chips, 34
Snacks
Bacon Grease Bruschetta, 59
Barbecue Barrel Bungs, 51
Barbecue Peanuts, 57
Crispy bacon strips, 34
Crispy Pecan Cheese Wafers, 36
Grilled pimiento cheese
    sandwiches, 34
Honey Blue Cheese Spread, 56
Honey Jezebel Cheddar Spread, 56
Hot Catfish Cocktail
    Sandwiches, 35
Jack Hot Wings, 36
Jack's Sweet Hot Party Pecans, 57
Look No Further Pimiento
    Cheese, 39
Muffaletta baguette, 34
Okra Barrel Bungs, 50
Oven fried potatoes, 34
Pepper Jack Barrel Bungs, 49
Pickled Okra Party Shrimp, 54
Pimiento Cheese Barrel Bungs, 50
Pimiento cheese bruschetta, 34
Pimiento Cheese . . . Let Us Count
    the Ways, 38
Pumpkin Pie Honey Spiced
    Almonds, 58
Quick cocktail snacks for the busy
    hostess, 34
Really Good Deviled Eggs, 40
Roasted okra, 34
Sweet, Hot, and Sour Mash
    Meatballs, 44
Spinach
Baby Spinach and Beets with Hog
    Jowl Dressing, 98
Creamy Hominy Spinach
    Casserole, 118

Spreads
    Honey Blue Cheese Spread, 56
    Honey Jezebel Cheddar Spread, 56
    Tennessee Smoked Trout Spread, 45
Squash
    Squash Casserole with Cheddar
        Cornbread Crumbs, 130
    Tennessee Butternut Squash, 129
Sweet Potatoes
    Game Day Sweet Potato Muffins, 85
    Sour Mash Sweet Potatoes, 130

T
Tennessee Walking Horse National
    Celebration, 143
Things Taste Better with Jack, 123
Tips
    cooking, 66
    for great grilling, 180
    hostess, 97
    on making naturally fermented
        kraut in canning jars, 104

for using Jack to enhance savory
    flavor, 123
for using Jack to enhance sweet
    flavor, 124
Tomatoes
    Oven Roasted Okra, Tomatoes, and
        Onions, 126
    Sweet Tomato Supper Pudding, 128
    Tangy Tomato Onion Relish, 244
    Tennessee Tomato White Bean
        Cornbread Salad, 106

V
Vegetables
    Easy Country Greens, 116
    Grilled Potato (and Other Vegetable)
        Packets, 199
    Oven Roasted Okra, Tomatoes, and
        Onions, 126